Archaeological Field Survey in Britain and Abroad

Edited by Sarah Macready and F. H. Thompson

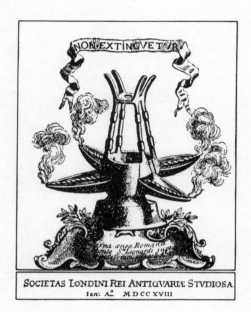

Occasional Paper (New Series) VI

THE SOCIETY OF ANTIQUARIES
OF LONDON

Burlington House, Piccadilly, London W1V 0HS
1985

Distributed by Thames and Hudson Ltd

© 1985 The Society of Antiquaries of London
ISBN 0 500 99041 7

TYPESET AND PRINTED IN GREAT BRITAIN
AT THE BATH PRESS, AVON

Contents

iv

Editorial Note

The fifth in the series of one-day seminars organized by the Society of Antiquaries took place on Friday 13th May 1983, and the theme explored was the principles of archaeological field survey and their application in Britain and the Mediterranean countries. Professor Barri Jones, F.S.A., took the chair, and ten speakers contributed papers on their work in Britain, France, Spain, Yugoslavia, Greece and Libya. All these are published here, and in addition it has been possible to include shorter contributions from other fieldworkers who did not speak at the seminar, which enabled survey work in Italy to be brought into the discussion. These papers, by Mr. Brian Simmons, F.S.A., Messrs. Vince Gaffney and Martin Tingle, Dr. Grenville Astill and Dr. Wendy Davies, Mr. Peter Hayes, Professor Alastair Small, F.S.A. *et al.*, and Dr. Joseph Carter, F.S.A., with Sig. Cesare D'Annibale, have been interspersed among the appropriate regional headings. We are most grateful to Professor Jones for presiding and for contributing both an introduction and a concluding comment to this collection of papers, to Mr. Rick Jones, who originally suggested the theme, and to all who took part.

November 1984   S.M.
                                                                                    F.H.T.

Illustrations

Introduction

Barri Jones, F.S.A., *Chairman*

FIELD SURVEY TODAY

'Like earnest mastodons petrified in the forests of their own apparatus archaeologists come and go . . . diligently working upon the refuse heaps of some township for a number of years they erect on the basis of a few sherds or piece of dramatic drainage a sickly and enfeebled portrait of a way of life. How true it is, we cannot say; but if an eskimo were asked to describe our way of life deducing all his evidence from a search of a contemporary refuse dump, his picture might lack certain formidable essentials.'

These words written by Laurence Durrell, while ensconced in his beloved White House at Corfu, typify an all too pervasive view that regards archaeology as synonymous with excavation. Indeed, in many countries, especially the Near East and North Africa, excavation is archaeology.

Archaeology can, however, only be the worse in any intellectual sense if another dimension, namely evidence on the ground, is excluded from the record. Intellectually, of course, and indeed practically, it is difficult to separate evidence from above and below the ground. The seminar papers that form the core of this book concentrate on a variety of approaches derived from studies in surface topography and comprise an approach to archaeology from non-excavational evidence. I am sure that all those who participated in the seminar on which this publication is based are indebted to the Society of Antiquaries, particularly through its General Secretary and its Editors, for spotlighting the role of field archaeology (*sensu stricto*) in the present spectrum of practical archaeology and at the same time providing a platform for many of the important contributions by British fieldwork to archaeological research abroad.

Field archaeology is the essential tool in first identifying, then analysing, the man-made contribution to the evolution of the landscape. Increasingly, specialists in other disciplines, such as geomorphologists and climatologists, have important elements to contribute, but in this subject area the archaeologist's peculiar role is that of overall synthesizer. His synthesis can involve anything from handfuls of lithic or ceramic material to single or multiple and multi-period 'sites' (and, as you will see, in these pages that term is one that requires careful consideration), or to entire relict landscapes or regions.

As such, at whatever scale, surface archaeology represents a study of the relationships between past human behaviour and evidence potentially detectable at surface level in a variety of different ways.

Much follows conceptually from this, and I can hardly do better than quote three sentences written by the present Secretary of the Royal Commission: 'clearly this sort of approach involves recognition of a continuum both conceptually and practically . . . In this context . . . period specialization is conceptually the antithesis of topographical archaeology, although, of course, it may be necessary for practical reasons in any given instance. Equally a narrow view of what is proper for archaeology to be doing would find the general argument here anathema, particularly when the argument is taken to its next step which is that this sort of archaeological approach fundamentally involves the use and understanding of a considerable range of non-archaeological evidence, notably from documents and the environmental sciences' (Fowler 1977).

Hence the invention of the phrase 'total archaeology', the use of all available evidence regardless of form in the study of the interaction of man with the landscape, an art, or should I say science, that is almost wholly non-destructive and has the merit of being repeatable.

Implicit in this is the underlying assumption that we are dealing with a body of knowledge that can still be expanded even in the most well-trodden areas. The trend is still with us and growing. Part of this approach is perhaps a quintessentially British one, with its strong tradition of amateur contributions emphasized by Mercer. But there are stronger reasons for its continuation and growth. First, and probably foremost, is simply the existence since the early years of this century of the Royal Commissions, the role of which was, from 1908, in England, to record the remains considered 'illustrative of the contemporary culture to 1714', and, since 1963, later, a description that therefore includes not only field remains but also standing buildings. The second and third factors relate more particularly to the latter half of this century. Since the Second World War there has been a steady growth of arable cultivation in this country, notably through the government-subsidized encouragement of the development of marginal land. This in turn has triggered not only increased fieldwalking at a variety of levels, but above all perhaps the development of aerial photography, albeit patchily and at times inefficiently applied. The broadening application of this third factor is perhaps the single most significant technical development in topographical archaeology, and its conceptual impact can hardly be underestimated as the prime mover in the development of fieldwork towards 'total archaeology'.

In assessing the development of multi-period survey methodologies one must admit, along with Mercer, that for much of this century the academic level of survey has remained approximately the same, encapsulated perhaps best of all in the writings of O. G. S. Crawford in the 1930s and later. Now, however, there have been fundamental changes in archaeologists' approach to survey, whether under the promptings of university-based intensive fieldwork, often abroad, or through the pressures of the formation of sites and monuments records for county and other units in this country.

What, then, is the current perception of surface archaeology? It is the relationship between past human behaviour and archaeology represented potentially at surface level in different ways at different times. The old concept of sites separated by blank areas, beloved of those creating distribution maps, has been modified to a considerable extent, as Foley has perhaps best described (1981), by the idea of 'off site' archaeology, but no less by the massive quantitative revolution of low-level air photography. Foley's ideas were prompted by the study of hunter-gatherers and pastoralists whose mobility and behaviour patterns have meant that they left 'contour maps' of finds relating to different activities, thus creating different densities of sites in different locations. For instance, hunter-gatherers would return each year to a general location like a lake basin and leave archaeological material all round it, unless a cave was used to funnel activities into one particular location. Indeed, agricultural society, despite having villages, hamlets and farms, can also leave the same sort of contour maps of archaeological relics. So, as a result, many of today's survey projects are experimenting with techniques of totally or partially recording contour maps of the recoverable surface archaeology. One hastens to say that this is being done on varying budgets over varying areas, and those with an eye for finance may judge, for instance, between the work of Snodgrass and Bintliff in Boeotia and the much less well-endowed Megalopolis survey. Experimental surveys of this kind can be conducted by a variety of bodies, of course, but the role of our universities abroad (sometimes operating a collaborative venture, like the Sheffield–Siena project at Montarrenti) is an impressive one. If much of the best work is being done abroad, that similar results can be produced in this country is becoming clear, notably through work on major concentrations of flint scatters in the Peak District by Beswick, Barker, Hodges and others. This school of work is exemplified in these papers by Mills's surveys in the Auvergne, and by others in central Italy. Likewise, Shennan's deliberate decision to sample areas of Hampshire chosen on a geological basis follows the same pattern. A similar approach will also be found in these papers exemplified by the work on the Roman villa project at Maddle, which concentrates as much on the periphery as on the centre of the site, albeit within a limited geographical scale.

Amid the current methodologies of landscape studies there is now general agreement on the need, if total survey is not possible, to sample the landscape by examining a percentage of each major natural unit, e.g. plain edge, hillslope, upper slope or valley bottom. This represents a move away from the concept of looking at the presumed richer areas and instead gives each element of the landscape, whether selected on geological or other grounds, an equal chance of revealing its archaeology, if it has any. Again the Maddle project comes to mind in this context. So today various grids, transects and proportions of natural units are being sampled by a variety of methods. While avoiding the pitfalls of geographical determinism, scholars have increasingly realized that appreciation of the geomorphology of an area is an essential ingredient to their surveys. This is all the more so in understanding apparent blank areas where, for instance, sites like many in central or southern Italy have been buried by later colluvium or alluvium, or alternatively destroyed by river or other forms of erosion.

In changing the nature of surface archaeology one essential component of the move from the old concept of 'sites found equal a survey map' on the lines of the Ordnance Survey classics of the past is the growing recognition that surface archaeology can change dramatically from year to year. One reason for this can simply be the action of man's destructive agencies. For instance, much of the work of the Southern Etruria survey by the British School at Rome would be unrepeatable in its present context and produce extremely limited results after twenty years of constant agricultural and residential development of the Roman *campagna*. This is an extreme case of destruction perhaps, but otherwise the work of Lloyd and Barker in the Molise has catalogued the way in which scatters of classical building material are more or less apparent, from one year to the next, in areas that were deliberately re-surveyed as the land use, vegetation or plough conditions altered. The Megalopolis survey has also encountered this difficulty and attempted to monitor the disappearance of sites in scrub conditions. Likewise, the Sheffield–Siena project at Montarrenti mentioned above has been investigating the Val di Rosia with this particular problem in mind. Individual site nucleii are sherded year by year on 5-m. grids to compare changing densities and distributions in order to quantify the fragmentation of tile and pottery, the amount of downslope movement and other such phenomena. This is an attempt to produce a quantitative data base for the kind of processes involved; it is hoped that these developments will see the more general introduction of survey forms which record the daylight conditions, the state of the ploughsoil, the percentage of vegetation, the degree of visibility, and so on.

These improvements in techniques adumbrated above are playing their part in an improved recognition of the relationship between buried structures and their ground-level remains, clearly a very complex question with no simple answers. With classical-period structures, for example, like those located by Mills in the Luni survey, major Roman buildings have appeared beneath very small spreads of surface debris.

If one wants to document the reverse process, then at Mount Pleasant in the Peak District very little in the way of features was found in relation to major flint scatters and the presumption must be that the original settlement, if any, probably comprised seasonal huts or tents. These examples represent opposite extremes. On the other hand there is a growing recognition (particularly in Italy and Spain) of places where deep ploughing has completely destroyed a major site; yet the layout of the site remains visible as surface material for an indefinite period. For classical remains, such as the great villas identified by Agache's survey on the *limon* soils of the Somme, such a process is unlikely to destroy recoverable remains completely, yet for some, perhaps many, prehistoric sites we may have to accept that there is no subsoil archaeology and that the recognizable archaeology can only be found in the ploughsoil.

So there is general agreement today for the need to sample systematically, although arguments remain over the merits of the many systems proposed. There is now also a far greater general realization of the complexity of surface archaeology. It is no longer seen as a way simply of putting a dot on a map. The need for experiment and for quantification of the processes involved is now well recognized, but the problem still remains as to whether this kind of exploratory work is best conducted by large-budget projects or through relatively small-scale funding of projects, often university-based and executed abroad using the greatest archaeological asset the universities can offer, namely the participation of students in a problem-orientated project across a number of years. The problem of conflicting methodologies is, of course, likely to remain with us for a long time. The varying scale of survey work may perhaps ultimately come to be seen as the criterion on which the methodology should be based. After all, the surveys described in this book vary from a few square kilometres, through 100, 200 or 300 square kilometres, to the enormous territories being tackled by the UNESCO Libyan Valleys Survey. At the same time, the budgets available are also critically important to the methodologies adopted, and the methodologies have all sorts of implications for the compilation of sites and monuments records, whether in this country or abroad, where the Assendelft Project in Holland leads the way in financial terms and demonstrates an ideal of integrated field survey and sample excavation.

In the previous paragraphs most of the examples are drawn from outside Britain, where survey work, as one can see from these papers, is constrained to be more vigorously problem-orientated through the pressures of finance, manpower availability and other factors. In contrast, the vagaries of modern county or local boundaries, or the role and functioning of an archaeological agency within a local or regional bureaucratic administration, sometimes tend to blunt the efficacy of problem-orientated approaches in this country.

To oversimplify, it is not altogether unfair to suggest that there are effectively three types of survey in practice: the problem-orientated, the administration-orientated and the exploratory, or even random. On all counts, save the social, the first is the most successful, remembering, of course, that the value of the project reflects the value of the problem tackled. On the other hand it must probably be admitted that, on the strictest criteria, the majority of survey projects currently in hand in this country are orientated to the perceived needs of the administration. Normally this means that the field-survey work of a Unit in recording, assessing sites and reacting to rescue pressures is undertaken by persons, or indeed sometimes a Field Officer, maintained by the Manpower Services Commission. Obviously, so much of this delicate equation depends on the academic and related experience of the staff taken into employment. Inherent in this is a series of problems adumbrated by Mercer and particularly Fowler (1981). In assessing the lessons of the *Survey of Surveys* (RCHM 1978), the latter questioned the financial or academic value of most 'identification' surveys familiar from the 1970s, which were normally believed to be the basis for establishing excavation requirements in a particular area. If highly selective programmes are to be forthcoming, then such pleas to acquire greater conceptual and methodological rigour are well in order, rather than the implicit assumption, often encountered, that more staff equals better results. As mentioned by Mercer, one particular related problem within the methodology remains that of classification by type. In the context of group project work the dangers of subjectivity should be acknowledged as perhaps greater than appreciated; and, if computerization is involved, moves to record by positive attribute only should be encouraged so that computerized search for particular sets of site attributes relates to positive features relevant to the subject both now and, it is hoped, in the future. It is hoped, too, that this kind of consistent approach will foster an improvement in our response to rescue threats, which often remains academically random and represents a balancing of practical, rather than archaeological, considerations. In this respect, partly from their work in Dorset, Groube and Bowden (1982) have published a suggested basis on which sites and monuments records can perhaps be used to reach rational decisions about the academic usefulness of a given project. The development of this subject area in the future is essential in bringing greater clarity to the objectives of field survey.

Part of the recent adverse comment on the methodological status of field survey has focused on its evident failure to develop generally beyond the standards of O. G. S. Crawford fifty years ago. In this context, however, there is one area of analytical skill where by general agreement considerable methodological progress has been forthcoming. The exception comprises the field of artifact scatter collection and analysis as set out in various papers by Cherry, Gamble and Shennan in particular. If one looks for reasons for progress in this, rather than any other field, then surely they lie in developments in sampling and related techniques that have been introduced into current excavational practice. Yet there is another area where progress in analytical skills could be achieved relatively easily, namely in the application of aerial photography and its results. One point that emerges strongly from these papers is that, whereas work abroad has access to little or no air-photographic cover, field projects in Britain often have the enormous benefit of substantial cover, e.g. that of Bodmin Moor. But that cover is often widely variable in quantity (let alone quality) between areas and not readily assimilable either regionally or nationally.

The enormous amount of new evidence that aerial photography has created in this country is slow to be assimilated into the archaeological record. It is only in the last few years, for instance, that after half a century of flying the objectives and end products of air photography are being more analytically categorized. Despite the great increase in knowledge there still exists a case in this country for continued, primarily locational, work in areas such as Devon that have been starved of funds; and, secondly, for the study of classes of individual monuments such as henges; but it is in the third category, namely territorial analysis, that there has come the realization that, special cases apart, single site recognition and examination is no longer academically acceptable—that the single dot on a map is only the most elementary step forward in our understanding. Yet this line of thinking was at once accelerated and in a sense exacerbated by the weather conditions of 1975 and 1976, and indeed 1984, when the sheer volume of new locational evidence in many ways served to bring the conceptual problem to a head and leave practitioners of aerial photography with a series of fundamental questions that have to be resolved and passed into the main data-collecting systems available.

Clearly outstanding amongst those questions was the vexed problem of how effectively to map and interpret the enormous backlog of evidence recorded from the air and available in one way or another. Behind this, of course, lies the second point, and there is still considerable disagreement 'not only about the best methods for recording and representing the information derived from air photographs but also, and more worryingly, about the essential purpose and objective of such work. For too long efforts have been focused in two essential but narrow directions, to the continuing acquisition of information from the air and the rapid transfer of that data to maps for the purposes of either general planning control or of highly specific single site ground investigation. Only recently . . . has it become apparent that these initial objectives can, and must, be supplemented by a third intermediate level of investigation devoted to intensive analysis, comparison and classification of the total sample of evidence in terms of its surrounding archaeological landscape. Such studies have the ability to provide an essential middle route between the necessarily coarse interpretation that may be achieved from simple sketch plottings and the meticulous but rarely available detail of extensive excavation' (Whimpster 1982).

In evolving an agreed set of objectives and methodologies for air photography and kindred studies, equally important is the development of a mutually understood and accepted framework of cartographic, terminological and classificatory conventions, a consistent and coherent language and grammar that will allow direct comparison of work carried out in different areas. I believe that lead should come from the Commissions who are making such a contribution to the subject, particularly in Scotland through the work of Maxwell and his team. But this is a plea to create a standard dictionary when the language in question is in danger of becoming a rare species, save on the lips of a few enthusiasts. I say this because the picture of actual air photography being carried out in Britain overall is still unrealistically weighted to areas of traditionally fertile results. There still remain many areas, particularly in the North and West, where lack of funds has prevented the formation of a basic air-photographic archive. In this respect, I believe that the funding of air photography as a whole should depend on a more critical analysis of results from the better-provided areas. Ironically in some ways, it is in the upland zones (and one thinks of the marvellous information being analysed on Bodmin Moor) that the creation of archives is more easily effected. Abroad, Dr. David Kennedy of the University of Sheffield has systematically built up an archive of large portions of Jordan using vertical cover. At the same time, I believe that many of our recording systems are expensive and inefficient; and that we must develop low-cost, low-level recording techniques that will enable us through photogrammetry to move to direct plotting of upland sites such as those in the South-West and the Pennines.

It is hoped that these aims will be achieved in the not too distant future; meanwhile the papers in this volume demonstrate the impressive results of field survey currently being carried out both in this country and abroad.*

* My thanks are due to Dr. G. W. W. Barker, Dr. N. J. Higham and Mr. J. Walker for their help and discussion in the writing of this introduction.

BIBLIOGRAPHY

Foley, R. 1981. *Off Site Archaeology and Human Adaptation in Eastern Kenya*, Cambridge Monographs in African Archaeology 3, BAR S97, Oxford.
Fowler, P. J. 1977. *Approaches to Archaeology*, London.
— 1981. 'The Royal Commission on Historical Monuments (England)', *Antiquity*, lv, pp. 106–14.
Groube, L. R. and Bowden, M. C. B. 1982. *The Archaeology of Rural Dorset, Past, Present and Future*, Dorset Nat. Hist. and Arch. Soc. Monograph 4.
Whimpster, R. 1982. Draft programme, CBA Air Photographic Committee.

I. GREAT BRITAIN
A View of British Archaeological Field Survey

Roger Mercer, F.S.A.

The need for increased sophistication and speed in data recording, and the increased resources to facilitate this, has been a *leitmotif* of comment on the subject of British archaeological field survey for at least a decade (Fowler 1972, 1981; Mercer 1982). Fowler, writing in 1981, reflected the conclusions of the *Survey of Surveys* report undertaken by the RCHM England (RCHM 1978) in his frank denial of the value ('academic', or 'for money') of much of the 'identification' type of survey undertaken during the 1970s as a means of establishing the 'excavation requirement' in any particular region. The haziness of its objectives formed one target for Fowler's strictures, but the general lack of any 'advance, conceptually or methodologically, on the standards enshrined in Crawford's *Archaeology in the Field*', also felt the weight of his criticism. The present writer, looking at the problem from a rather different standpoint in 1982, stressed the urgent need for the development of the skills of analytical field survey, using its results to construct the models of local archaeological development which could then be tested by highly selective and accurately directed excavation programmes. Such development will inevitably require the conceptual and methodological rigour demanded by Fowler.

Such fundamental criticism may indeed strike the reader as harsh, or at best anti-climactic, coming, as it does, after 400 years of the distinguished and massive achievement of British field archaeology. To read the invaluable account by Crawford (1953, pp. 43–9) of the development of this study since 1900 is to witness a 'saga-like' recitation of name and deed that is, in itself, positively intimidating. But, saga-like again, much of the action has taken the form of 'single-combat'—the lone fieldworker ploughing his own furrow (or grinding his own axe)—producing idiosyncratic unevenness in coverage, in perception and in record, and effectively denying to field survey the corporate accumulation of experience that has been so much a feature of the development of excavation technique in Britain since the 1920s.

8

With the major exception of artifact scatter collection and notation (papers in Cherry, Gamble and Shennan 1978; Crowther 1983), in essence the methodology of field survey has changed little since the 1930s. This single exception is in any case to be explained, the writer believes, by the receptivity of this particular problem to techniques of sampling, location and recording used in the development of excavational procedures.

The lack of any development of a methodology for analytical field survey is perhaps a cause for surprise after a decade when methodological considerations, generally speaking, have figured very prominently on our 'bill of fare'. This is to be explained, the writer believes, by the lone nature of the task (which has at once discouraged contemplation of matters regarded as the proper sphere of individual experience and denied the time for such contemplation). Furthermore the issue has, to some extent, been concealed by three closely related matters that have received prominent attention. The first of these is the *inventory of monument-types*—'what you will encounter in the field and how you identify it'—best exemplified by the excellent Ordnance Survey handbook, *Field Archaeology in Britain* (HMSO 1973). The second is the manual of surveying practice—'how you plan, and plot a field monument on to the map, once you have located it'—starting long ago with Sir Norman Lockyer's treatise (1909) (with its admittedly rather specialist bias) and culminating in Hogg's splendid compendium (1980). Thirdly, there has been very considerable attention paid, particularly in the last decade, to the problem of how to deal with the quintessential product of field survey—the spatial distribution of artifacts as plotted (ultimately) by archaeological field surveyors (Hodder and Orton 1976; Clarke 1977; Groube 1981). Considerable statistical sophistication has been brought to bear on this problem, and it is perhaps ironic that such a high level of procedural rigour should have been developed to deal with data the observational basis of which has never been closely defined.

We are, of course, peculiarly fortunate that three Royal Commissions, appointed to make 'an inventory of the Ancient and Historical Monuments and Constructions connected with or illustrative of the contemporary culture, civilization and conditions of life of the people of this country from the earliest times', have existed here for nearly 75 years. Their work has been prodigious, but understandably still only covers much less than a quarter of the country, with much of this cover being executed prior to the Second World War. Their objective is the nearest approximation that we have to a work of total record, only now coming to terms with the fact that time is its major enemy and only that which remains *can* be totally recorded. Agriculture, industrial development and simple erosion may well get there first.

But archaeological field survey is not only an act of record, although this of course must remain one of its principal bases of discipline. It is, at once, the product and the generator of ideas, perceptions and questions leading to research design, and such ideas very often move even faster than ploughs and bulldozers. Field survey, as well as serving as an act of record, is also an act of reassessment in the unending procedure of the enhanced understanding of the processes that have created our present landscape. We have perhaps become accustomed to viewing excavation as the principal investigating technique for the explanation of these processes. Andrew Fleming on Dartmoor, George Jobey in the Borders of Scotland, among many others, have, however, been showing us for many years that field survey is not only an explanatory process in its own right but that it creates the vital preliminary plinth upon which excavational activity can be based. Both at intra- and inter-site level the expensive commitment of resources and personnel that characterizes excavation must be accurately directed (see Mercer 1982).

To some extent our notions of archaeological field survey have been dominated by the terms 'site' and 'monument', and it is probably fitting that we should attempt to define these concepts. The word 'site' is a term used in two quite distinct ways in British archaeology. To the writer it would appear to signify: (a) the location where archaeological work, usually excavation, is taking place; and (b) the location where a monument has stood, but owing to destruction or some other circumstance has ceased to be visible on the surface today—as in the Ordnance Survey's use of the words 'Roman Villa (site of)'. In both usages the term can be seen to have an essentially pragmatic significance and to carry no chronological or morphological implication. A site may occasionally include many more than one monument—it may, sadly, on occasion include none.

A monument is an artifact of a specific kind, essentially characterized by its immobility. Only by this quality can it clearly be differentiated from stone, ceramic or other mobile artifacts that may be scattered within or around it. Its immobility, however, does not, of course, imply its immutability or the immobility of the landscape within which it is set. Its immobility does, however, ensure that movement and mutation which do take place both within and around the monument, in almost every instance, lead to the establishment of demonstrable relationships both in time and space between successive and contemporary activities in the landscape of which the monument is a part. The permanence of a monument secures and establishes diachronic relationships where mobile artifacts, by and large, establish only synchronic ones.

Herein lies the great complexity concealed by the term 'monument'. In essence there are four kinds of monument in the sense that a monument is an artifact of single conception and manufacture by man: (1) monument *simpliciter*—e.g. a clearance cairn; (2) a *monument complex*—a cairnfield, a clearance cairn with a hut circle built abutting it. These two classes can be expressed in their chronological dimension by the terms synchronic or diachronic. Of course, excavation is the only final (if fallible) arbiter of the precise nature of these relationships, but field survey may frequently indicate the likelihood of diachronic complexity and may thus enable description as a diachronic, or synchronic, monument or monument complex to be applied.

Now this four-fold subdivision is perhaps a non-starter from the point of view of everyday usage. It is unlikely that hillforts will be referred to as 'probably diachronic monument complexes', although in all likelihood this is what they are, and it is from this standpoint that any survey and description of them should be undertaken and that use of this data, once formulated, should proceed. The existence of whole areas of our landscape that can themselves be termed 'a diachronic monument complex' does, however, give point to the phrase and avoids use of the thoroughly misleading term 'prehistoric landscape'—a concept that physically cannot now exist.

But the use of the word 'hillfort' leads us inexorably to the other major area of difficulty which has become inseparable from our concept of the term monument. Since the days of Stukely we have developed a typological infrastructure within the monument concept which enables us, on the basis of surface morphology, to refer to different types of monument by generic terms, e.g. causewayed enclosure, henge, barrow, hillfort, as well as specific terms, e.g. saucer-barrow, disc-barrow. This 'typological' approach, while admittedly difficult to evade, ignores the essential diachronic and contextual complexity of the immobile artifact over and above that of the mobile artifact to which the technique is perhaps more aptly applied. There will not be, it is to be imagined, many field archaeologists who will not have felt that terms like 'causewayed-camp', 'broch', 'henge' and 'hut-circle' have acted as severe constraints and distorting influences upon the development of our ideas as to the role that individual monuments or monument-complexes have played, both in their local and broader context. These terms have imparted a deceptive simplicity which, at the expense of the dimension of variety, chronological and morphological, has facilitated the construction of facile and incoherent models of monument development and distribution. This hegemony of monument typology requires careful examination and disassembly. It then requires the development of a descriptive rather than attributive vocabulary, inevitably perhaps clumsier, which will, in turn, enable the development of more rigorous and sophisticated comparative procedures which will allow the incorporation into our understanding of the immense chronological, morphological and functional variety that lies at present so thoroughly concealed. Such attributive definition will have to include elements that describe the raw material, the mode of construction, the morphology and the preservational constraints applying to any given monument or monument complex (see Mercer forthcoming).

To this end we require an approach to field survey that is not dominated itself by the very hegemony of chrono-functional terminology that persists at present. Inspection of any area of ground chosen must be *total* in order to avoid the perpetuation of monument-concentrations already recognized. It may well be that total inspection will only 'prove' these concentrations by negative result, a major advance in itself, but frequently altogether more complex patterns will emerge. Alongside the total coverage advocated an unbiased approach to the monuments encountered should be adopted. Detailed description and planning has, frequently, in the past been adopted only for those monuments, those immobile artifacts, that comply readily with the typological components of the established system. 'Hut-circles' will be planned, but what of the 'horrid blurs', enclosures of distressingly irregular form, that crop up with increasing frequency as one widens and deepens the degree of coverage of any area? Only the discipline of detailed planning offers the prospect of any understanding of these crucial monuments that represent the penumbra of variety from which our eyes to some extent have remained averted. Furthermore, *all* man-made alterations of the landscape of whatever date, down to a recent threshold, must be recorded at an equal level of detail, as the nature of the immobile artifact dictates that its diachronic dimension receives equal attention to its morphological equivalent. Thus the distribution and morphology of later monuments within one environment will reflect intimately upon the known distribution and morphology of earlier examples (and *vice versa*), as well as providing a template against which the absence or presence of these earlier or later equivalents can be assessed.

My advocacy so far has been a simple one, a very great deal more work for any given area—total ground inspection followed by the detailed planning of all monuments, with total coverage of all artifacts of every period up to the very recent past and, moving on to the final point in this polemic, as near total and rapid publication as can be attained.

Field survey *is* a response to ideas and questions; it is not simply a matter of record. Ideas and questions do develop and change with astonishing rapidity, and the need to fuel this process demands the rapid and wide dissemination of our results. For this reason we have to develop cheap, effective means of publication and we have to produce field survey results as rapidly as possible—whether it be for the pragmatic reason that sites may well be destroyed unless their presence is widely advertised, or whether it be that the lonely fieldworker needs the reassurance as well as the stimulation of other investigators' problems to guide, beckon and excite him.

It is against this background of thought that this lonely fieldworker has been at work. How can we maintain any kind of pressure of activity in terms of the area covered, and thereby the sample obtained, if we impose upon the fieldworker the massive burden of extra labour that the polemic requires? There can only be one answer to this, and that is the creation of large fieldwork teams involving larger bodies of personnel (and expenditure) in order to expedite the level of recording and coverage that has been advocated. In the fieldworker this immediately, and understandably, provokes the response that once this occurs, once multiple involvement is admitted, then standards of interpretation and drawn representation begin to vary to an extent that is unacceptable. The excavator has, of course, lived with this problem, without vocal complaint, since Lt.-General Pitt-Rivers began the whole business of large-scale investigation. Hundreds of volunteers are likely to be involved in a major excavation, all of them with differing qualities of observation, ability and experience. Yet the basis of the site recording system will depend entirely upon them. In terms of drawn recording, frequently ten or fifteen different 'fists' will be apparent in the archive of an excavation—often many more—all solemnly expressed in one drawn style in the eventual excavation report, the only truly unifying factor being the directorial eye that oversaw every production. With the advent of large-scale excavation as the only method by which an adequate sample could be obtained of the material under consideration, this procedure became a *sine qua non* and, therefore, unquestioned. It is my proposition that archaeological field survey has now reached in Britain a similar *impasse*. In order to record the variety and volume of data that is necessary to create the basis for greater conceptual rigour, we are going to have to adopt collective methods. In doing so we shall encounter the problem, knowingly, that excavators have accepted without (published) question for over half a century. Such collective methods, however, will in turn require a sound methodological basis and a 'grammar' of accepted terminology, facilitating objective monument description and representation in order to minimize observational variation.

The briefing for this symposium required contributors to make especial reference to organizational aspects of the field survey activity in which they have been involved. These, of course, do have specific relevance to large-scale surveying activity where, because of dispersal of personnel and the very wide variety of problems and activities encountered, managerial problems can be acute. While a detailed description of the survey method employed by the writer is available elsewhere (Mercer 1980, 1981), a number of salient points can be briefly enumerated.

Management

1. *Safety*. Many of those areas that present the most attractive prospect for the archaeological field surveyor lie in relatively remote areas of the Highland Zone. All such landscapes have their hazards, but naturally some are more hazardous than others. In Britain, particularly in the highland zone, the 'open season' for field surveying is seriously constrained by prevailing circumstances of climate and vegetation. Generals Janvier and Février (and Décembre and Novembre) stand upon one flank, when weather is simply too unreliable, and potentially too hostile, to allow work to take place at all. By late May into June, gorse, bracken and heather (and, a little later, midges) come into full bloom, obscuring much information and rendering access difficult. In effect March, April and May are the optimum—some would say the only—months for working, another pressure leading us towards the employment of large teams in intensive survey. Even in these months, however, particularly in March, conditions can be absolutely foul. This liability to bad weather, combined with early darkness, emphasizes the need for safety precautions that can be quickly dealt with under six headings.

a. Prior notification of standing safety agencies in the area of the survey team's presence (Police, Mountain Rescue, etc.).
b. Personnel always in pairs, properly equipped, adequately clothed in bright and, if possible, idiosyncratic colours and carrying unobtrusive safety equipment—whistles, compasses, bivvy bags, iron rations.
c. Detailed briefing as to routes and areas to be covered and absolutely strict adherence to these.
d. Absolutely strict adherence to timings at meeting-places and fall-back meeting-places.
e. As close an attempt at constant vigilance as is humanly possible to forestall any accident.
f. Swift and totally committed reaction to the merest possibility of difficulty.

Safety must be fundamental to the organization of such exercises, not a 'hidden extra'.

2. *Briefing*. Before the team leave their home-base they are issued with a 'child's guide' to drawing conventions, descriptive keywords and instructions for the completion of the Monument Record Forms (MRFs) used in the field. They also receive instructions in the use of the equipment encountered on the exercise. During the survey thorough briefing daily of each team as to the exact nature of routes, areas, tasks to be completed and equipment to be carried takes place on the evening before the day in question. Equipment is checked in the morning and the supervisor visits each team at least once during the day. These 'tours of visitation' by the survey supervisor are carefully routed to provide an opportunity for him to visit all recognized monuments in the area and to check a sample of the terrain.

3. *Checking*. Every evening each team completes the drawing up and inking in of all the work accomplished during the day. This is then checked and filed along with the MRF in numerical order. Each drawing is numbered on a check-list to facilitate rapid assessment of the 'state of play' at any point. Finally, all drawings are checked in the field by an experienced surveyor and all MRFs checked for accuracy and completeness. 'Task maps' with coded symbols for each task on each site are compiled and then each symbol removed as each task is completed. By these means the quality and completion of each task is checked—absolutely necessary in a complex area containing, say, 300 monuments spread over an area of 40 or 50 sq. km.

4. *Equipment*. It is absolutely essential that for a team of twelve to fifteen surveyors the scale of equipment should be sufficient to ensure efficient operation at all times. At least two vehicles are necessary, with at least two drivers insured to drive each vehicle. Depending on the area, a vehicle of 4-wheel drive capacity may be desirable, but only very seldom in Britain has it been found to be essential. Eight to ten theodolites, twenty-five to thirty 30-m. tapes, ten to fifteen portable drawing-boards, illustrate the scale of equipment that is desirable. Second-hand theodolites, provided that they are purchased from a reputable supplier, are adequate, relatively inexpensive (£750), and easily come by. The high number is a product of the need for 'spares', as instruments dry out from use in foul weather. Unlike during excavation, drawing and surveying tasks cannot be spaced out to ease pressure on equipment, and equipment must adjust to the pressure.

5. *Accommodation*. In Britain the writer would hold to the view that surveying teams working in the optimum months in the highland zone must be given accommodation with plenty of hot food, lashings of hot water, work-space for the evening and warm and dry bedding. Camping is therefore not a possibility, and hostel or hotel accommodation is a *sine qua non*. In these months favourable rates can usually be negotiated and the additional cost, experience shows, repays itself amply in enhanced efficiency.

Method

The survey method used falls naturally into five processes.

1. *Walking*. Teams of two, equipped with MRFs, clip-boards and brightly painted wands, cover pre-designated numbered areas which, depending on terrain, are usually of the order of 1–2 sq. km. per day. Each team will walk the area in strips of 100 m., the pair walking roughly 50 m. apart. Monuments encountered will be allotted a number consecutively from 1, an MRF completed, a wand stuck into the monument to assist relocation and the wand labelled with the number. The position of each monument is marked 'by eye' on 1:10,000 extracts for each area. Fair copies of MRFs are made and the task maps composed.

2. *Photography*. This is handled as one centralized exercise over two or three days. Multiple-'fist' drawing is not a serious problem given proper supervision—multiple-'fist' photography *is*, as the prospect of the site is far more subjectively selected and is very difficult to govern, and it is generally best controlled by execution by one person only.

3. *Plotting.* Teams of two or three, equipped with theodolite, staff, tripod and booking sheets and carrying with them the MRFs and hand-plotted 6-in. extracts for each area, move on to the area to plot the precise position of each monument. This phase may be preceded by the setting out of survey baselines across areas where few mapped landmarks are available. Where these latter do exist, however, they will be used as control points. One of the team of two or three will be a member of the original fieldwalking team—the others will, as a matter of policy, not be. Usually, during this phase, more monuments are recognized, numbered (consecutively to the area numbers) and MRFs completed. Thus task maps have to be kept up to date.

4. *Monument planning.* All monuments 'where planning is felt to be useful' will be planned at scales 1:50 or 1:100. This is inevitably a subjective judgement—its quality best exemplified by the decision-making process which quite definitely requires justification of 'why a monument should *not* be planned' rather than 'why it should be planned'. In essence, the vast majority of unitary monuments other than field walls will be planned at 1:50/1:100 scale. Theodolite teams will also be separately detailed to record extended monument-complexes (field systems, cairnfields, etc.) at scales 1:500/1:1,000. Where possible, dispersal of groups will be minimized at this juncture to maximize the possibilities of supervision and consultation.

5. *Checking.* As segments of the task map are cleared of their debris of symbols, so one or two experienced surveyors will take all plans and MRFs in to the area to check them on the ground, correct errors and, in any instance necessary, mark the monument up for replanning. With this possibility, and the possibility of last-minute recognition of monuments, in view, the survey programme should always be planned with one day free at the end. It never is free.

On return to base fair copy MRFs and inked-in drawings and map plots should already be available. The MRFs will already be attached to copy information relating to the monument in question, e.g. OS Card copies which will have been obtained and correlated before the survey commences.

From this base, preparation of the final survey report commences. This will comprise a gazetteer of all monuments now assigned final 'survey numbers' from 1, map extracts of the area surveyed with monuments located and numbered and final production drawings produced from the working drawing of each monument at large scale. Attached to this data will be an analytical account commenting upon variate morphology, construction and location of monuments and, where possible, upon their possible chronological arrangement. This analytical account will attempt to focus upon the development of research themes within the area for the future, to be pursued either by further survey or by excavational approaches. The research worker is thus furnished with a register of likely start-points within the area in question and the 'cultural resource manager' is provided with an enhanced, fully descriptive list of known material and, furthermore, a template of 'research viability' against which to test sites facing the threat of destruction.

It now remains for the writer to illustrate the kind of result that such analytical survey can produce. He has chosen to use, as an example, work completed in 1982 that, among many other aspects of data retrieved in the survey of a large area south-west of the present-day town of Thurso in Caithness, recorded five long cairns of probably Neolithic date. All of these monuments were known before, although one (Mon. No. FOR 373) has been recognized as a monument of this type for the first time. The monuments are all recorded in the RCAHMS *Inventory* for Caithness (RCAHMS 1911) and they are all described in detail in Miss Henshall's magisterial survey of Scottish stone-built chambered tombs (Henshall 1963 and 1972). The writer has chosen quite deliberately to illustrate the value of such survey in an instance where previous recording of high quality has taken place on each site, judging that if valuable new insights can be gained in these circumstances then the value of such work in examples where no, or only poor, recording has taken place in the past is self-evident.

It should be noted that the five monuments described here have now been joined by five others encountered and similarly recorded in survey conducted in 1983, and the whole recorded group comprises over 75 per cent of such monuments known in Caithness. Within this group of ten monuments (most of them of considerable physical stature) are two that have not been previously recognized. Serious recent and otherwise unrecorded damage has been recorded on three of the sites.

The group falls within the category set out by Henshall in 1972 and described by her under the broad heading of 'long cairns'. She clearly recognized these monuments as 'diachronic monument complexes' and set out a 'provisional classification' of them (Henshall 1972, p. 223). On the basis of the work of both 1982 and 1983 in Caithness, it is likely that a fairly major reworking of this problem will be possible (see Mercer forthcoming), but on the basis of the 1982 material some changing perspectives can clearly be indicated.

Firstly, we may pass the material in review, each monument numbered according to its final 1982 monument number (Mercer forthcoming) and according to Henshall's inventory (CAT. no.).

CAT. 41 Na Tri Shean (Mon. No. FOR 92) (fig. 1). This monument was one which Miss Henshall selected as her type-site for this group of cumulative long cairns in 1963. In 1972 the greater refinement of her classification allowed her to claim the monument as of her Class 3A—a long cairn containing two circular mounds. On this site the proximal mound is fairly clearly flattened on its SE face, suggesting, in association with the horns present at this point, that this represents a heel-shaped cairn in, it has to be said, an uncertain relationship with its long 'tail'. The cairn stands to a height of 3 m., an altogether more substantial cairn than that which formed the proximal heel-shaped cairn excavated at Tulach an t' Sionnaich, Caithness (Corcoran 1966) (1·8 m. high). In its summit, apparent howking has revealed two upright stones that Miss Henshall has adjudged as slipped lintels of a concealed chamber, and this, together with the height of the cairn, might suggest a secondary phase of proximal mound construction. To the writer the monument is, however, of particular interest on account of the long cairn itself, with the shallow 'bow' of its concave flanks, which set it apart from any other cairn of this cumulative construction group and place it close to the kind of 'non-cumulative' cladding structure that we encounter at South Yarrows (South) and Camster (Long). Yet the cumulative nature of this monument is plain to the field surveyor's eye. The proximal cairn, with its horns, is offset by

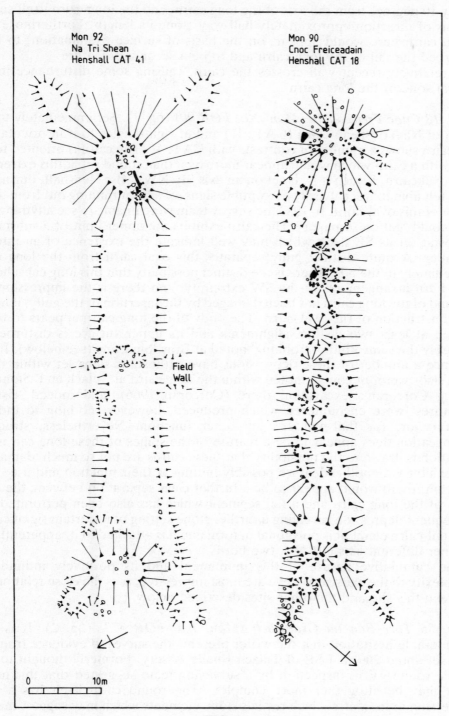

Mon 92
Na Tri Shean
Henshall CAT 41

Mon 90
Cnoc Freiceadain
Henshall CAT 18

Field
Wall

0   10m

FIG. 1

nearly 10 degrees from the axis of the long cairn, and the long cairn itself suffers a crisis of direction approximately half-way along its length. Furthermore, the round cairn here would appear, on the basis of surface examination, to have disturbed the tail of the long cairn and to be a secondary feature.

A relatively recent wall crosses the cairn, causing some disturbance in the central zone of the long cairn.

CAT. 18 Cnoc Freiceadain (Mon. No. FOR 90) (fig. 1). Set immediately to the north of Na Tri Shean cairn (CAT. 41) and at right-angles to it in orientation, this cairn shows a number of contrasts with CAT. 41. The cairn is oriented to the SW, with a cairn which would appear more oval than round set at this extremity. This oval cairn, if such it is, is set on an axis SE–NW. Miss Henshall, during her visit, felt able to trace 'hardly perceptible signs' of a horn running out from the S. sector of this oval cairn. In 1982 the survey team were unable to see anything that they could 'get on to paper'. The cairn exhibits the upper limit of a substantial orthostat on its SE flank which may well indicate the existence of an internal chamber. A quite distinct gully separates this oval cairn from the long cairn immediately to the NE. There is the distinct possibility that this long cairn had its own horn arrangements at the SW extremity, and there is the impression that this end of the long cairn has been damaged by the insertion of the gully, if not by the construction of the oval cairn. The body of the long cairn appears to be set out on at least two distinct alignments and its upper surface is disturbed by precisely the same kind of 'robbing' noted at Brawlbin Long (see below). In this instance a number of these depressions have orthostatic slabs set within them. Such slabs were, of course, noted within the long cairn at Tulach an t' Sionnaich during Corcoran's excavation there (Corcoran 1966), and indeed 'cist-like structures' were encountered which produced, however, nothing to indicate funerary or, for that matter, any other function. Nevertheless, structural complication does appear to be a feature of the spines of these long cairns and attention is drawn to the possibility that these cairns are not so much 'damaged', but exhibit yet another feature possibly hinting at their function and use.

Again, there would appear to be a further clear separation between the main body of the long cairn and a tail segment which has also been perforated, the consequent depression revealing a further stone setting of uncertain significance. This tail-cairn element is polygonal in form and has attached to it, apparently, on a rather different axis (10°N.), two horns.

The cumulative nature of this monument and its positively intimidating complexity to the excavator's eye are most impressive, as is the close relationship between this site and the other sites described below.

CAT. 56 Torr Ban na Gruagaich (Mon. No. FOR 373) (fig. 2). It is with considerable hesitation that the writer presents the surveyed evidence from this site, set about 200 m. ESE of Tulach Buaile Assery. Formerly thought to be a simple round cairn, inspection by a surveying team suggested that this monument may be altogether more complex. The round cairn itself has a large depression in its centre which reveals stone elements which may suggest that the cairn conceals a megalithic chamber. The cairn also has a stepped outline, which may possibly indicate that its construction is of more than one phase, while on its

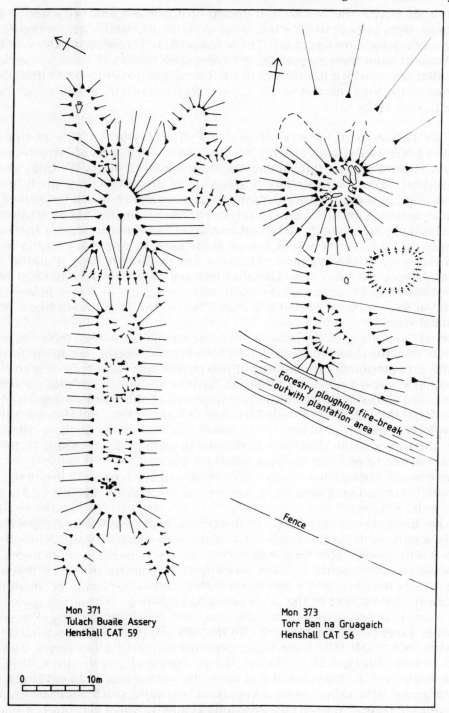

Mon 371
Tulach Buaile Assery
Henshall CAT 59

Mon 373
Torr Ban na Gruagaich
Henshall CAT 56

Forestry ploughing fire-break
outwith plantation area

Fence

0   10m

FIG. 2

E. flank the barest traces were recognized of possible horns. Attached to its S. side there does appear to be a much ruined structure which may represent the vestiges of a long cairn structure. The situation here is rendered more confusing by a band of deep forestry ploughing to provide a fire-break outside the nearby plantation fence, which has truncated what structure does survive to indicate the presence of the long cairn. A small, apparently more recent, structure stands just to the E. side of the cairn.

CAT. 59 Tulach Buaile Assery (Mon. No. FOR 371) (fig. 2). This monument is oriented ENE–WSW with, at the ENE end, a 4-m. high cairn of broadly circular form. It is possible that this mound has been damaged on its W. side, where a considerable 'scoop' into its face appears to be present, with a small bank of pre-existing cairn material at its foot. There is evidence for the existence of a chamber access in the NE sector of this cairn, where a marked depression exists. Miss Henshall, recording her site visit in August 1956, states: 'About halfway up the steep NE side . . . a hole has been made recently and it is possible to look down into part of the chamber. The roof has partially collapsed and it is not possible to see the plan. The chamber has apparently been orientated NNE–SSW. Two pairs of large upright slabs are visible; the end pair have a lintel resting on them, the other pair are about 2 m. to the S. and look like a pair of divisional slabs.'

There is something of the impression in the stepped outline of the cairn on this NE side, with the chamber described by Miss Henshall being 'set up' in the cairn, that this great terminal cairn may be of two phases, one cairn built over an earlier existing example—a suggestion that can have no resolution without excavation. Curle noted horns attached to the proximal end of this cairn during his visit in 1910 (RCAHMS 1911), and while Henshall during her visit, made in the 'difficult undergrowth' month of August, felt unable to be certain of the existence of these, the survey team, deployed on this site in spring 1982, and myself, felt that it was possible to plot the features noted by Curle.

There would appear to be further disturbance of this terminal cairn in the form of a small terraced enclosure built, apparently secondarily, against and into the cairn on its S. side.

As has been noted in other sites of this type already, this terminal cairn is quite clearly separated from the main body of the long cairn by quite a broad gully some 3–4 m. wide. The long cairn itself shares a number of features with examples already described. It lies askew to the alignment of the ENE terminal cairn and its horns (*c.* 8° S.) and bears within itself a bi-partite inconsistency in alignment, the W. half of the cairn swinging slightly S. Within the spine of the long cairn is a series of spaced 'disturbances' of a type already observed at Brawlbin Long (CAT. 6, Mon. No. FOR 396) and at Cnoc Freiceadain (CAT. 18, Mon. No. FOR 90). Here these depressions are of a regularity, and bear traces of stone uprights to an extent, that strongly militates against Curle's view (RCAHMS 1911, p. 136) that 'it had been pillaged for stone'. Miss Henshall felt that 'a group of 4 stones placed 8 m. from the W. end of the cairn seems to represent a chamber aligned along the long axis of the cairn and entered from the W. end . . .' (Henshall 1963, p. 296). The writer entirely concurs with Miss Henshall's general view here, but would suggest an alternative detailed constructional hypothesis to the effect that the two major rectilinear indentations within this cairn are the remains of small corbelled chambers now collapsed in—built within the long mound—features which would have given the cairn in antiquity a camel-like two-hump appearance, a feature possibly reflected in the ultimate elevation of Camster Long. It will be observed that the more easterly of the two depressions does display possible traces of a short entrance passage to the S. side of the cairn. Such an hypothesis would mesh quite neatly with the noted discontinuities of alignment within the long cairn's length. If such a possibility can be accepted in this instance, then it may also be extended to other sites producing similar phenomena. From the W. end of the long cairn two horns, axial to its length, obtrude.

CAT. 6 Brawlbin Long (Mon. No. FOR 396) (fig. 3). This site lies on a crest on open moorland. Very sadly the site is now contained within a forestry plantation, which apparently was not the case in 1956 at the time of Miss Henshall's visit. This plantation has unfortunately quite severely damaged this important monument and, while it was clearly the intention of forestry managers in the area to respect the cairn, it would appear that, owing to a lack of archaeological supervision, the delineation by the forester of the edge of the cairn has been somewhat haphazard. As a result some 12 m. of the 'tail end' of the long cairn, including the horn arrangements observed there by Miss Henshall in 1956, have been very severely damaged, if not destroyed. Elsewhere, particularly on the NW and E. flanks of the cairn, forestry ploughing has approached the cairn far too closely, riding right up on to its flanks and doing considerable damage. This monument is, or was, one of the most impressive of its class in northern Scotland and one of the most important prehistoric monuments in the area. It is a scheduled ancient monument and it is nothing short of tragic that a monument of this calibre, protected by the Secretary of State, could have been so seriously damaged by an agency of Central Government. The damage, of course, can in no way be made good.

The cairn is oriented NE–SW with a cairn that would appear to be more oval than round at its NE end. The axis of the oval cairn would appear at the present day to lie somewhat to the E. of the main axis of the cumulative cairn. The oval cairn would appear to have been the victim of disturbance both at its summit and on its S. and SW flank. A sharp and clearly defined gully separated the long cairn from the oval cairn, a feature recurrent on a number of similar sites. It was encountered by Corcoran at Tulach an t' Sionnaich and is apparent from detailed survey at Cnoc Freiceadain (CAT. 18, Mon. No. FOR 90)—where it was noted by Corcoran—and at Tulach Buaile Assery (CAT. 59, Mon. No. FOR 371). This feature renders difficult the clear perception of any specific priority relationship between both elements of the cairn in terms of field survey, and indeed, as Corcoran tells us, during excavation.

Running away to the SW, and now sadly curtailed, lie the remains of the long cairn. It would appear to be a simple one with roughly parallel sides (with revetment walling visible at the SW extremity of the cairn), although there might be some suggestion of quadri-lobate form in cairn outline—suggesting that even this ostensibly simple element could be cumulative in some measure. The precise form of the SW end of the cairn was, of course, not available for record in

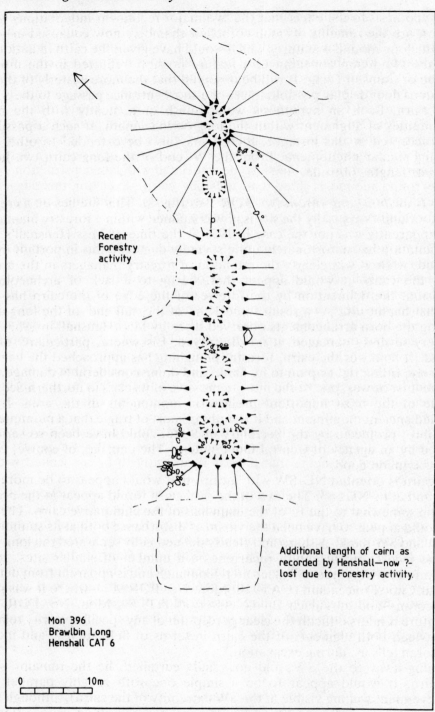

Recent
Forestry
activity

Additional length of cairn as
recorded by Henshall—now ?-
lost due to Forestry activity.

Mon 396
Brawlbin Long
Henshall CAT 6

0   10m

FIG. 3

1982. Miss Henshall also notes 'The [long] cairn has been robbed down the centre' and Curle, visiting the site on 11th August 1910, noted also 'The body of the cairn . . . has been removed for the sake of its stones'. The writer is not entirely happy with this explanation, and Curle does not make it clear whether his note is based upon his own general supposition or upon any independent evidence. The phenomenon is a recurrent one, occurring in very similar form at Cnoc Freiceadain (CAT. 18, Mon. No. FOR 90) and at Tulach Buaile Assery (CAT. 59, Mon. No. FOR 371), in all instances in isolated positions where there is no apparent objective for such robbing and where stone is not anyway in short supply. Two possibilities occur to the writer which can only be tested by excavation: (1) that this robbing is to be associated with late construction *on site*, i.e. the round mound is later than the long cairn—even for this suggestion, however, the process would appear to be too orderly; (2) that the activity is of an altogether different and at present unknown kind.

In summary, a number of points of a detailed nature can be made at this preliminary stage:

1. Miss Henshall accepted 'for the sake of argument' (the writer's words) that the proximal round cairn element of these monuments was primary to the long cairn, which was thereafter attached in secondary chronological position. Much of the work described above suggests that in a number of instances this was not the case and that the round cairn (Mon. Nos. FOR 90, 92 and 371) appears to truncate or overwhelm the end of the long cairn element. That this has been shown *not* to be the sequence at Tulach an t' Sionnaich (Corcoran 1963) by excavation is an argument that loses some force in the face of the fairly clear fundamental differences of form and design between that cairn and those under consideration.

2. That the concave-sided long cairn element and the parallel-sided element can be clearly differentiated as functionally distinct, with a range of possible internal structural elements that appear recurrently to be associated with the parallel-sided type.

3. That equally clearly the long cairn element of these constructions has been generally subjected to considerable dilapidation, possibly with the later construction of some round cairn elements as an objective. Recognition of this depletion element in cairn construction may enable us to reassess the relationship between sites like Na Tri Shean, South Yarrows (South) and Camster Long.

It has become clear during survey conducted in 1983 that further monuments, originally drawn by Anderson in the 1860s and never replanned since, are significantly inaccurate, and a full reconsideration of the evidence related to this well-known cairn group will appear in the publication of the 1982 and 1983 survey due to be published in 1984.

BIBLIOGRAPHY

Cherry, J. F., Gamble, C. and Shennan, S. 1978. *Sampling in Contemporary British Archaeology*, BAR 50, Oxford.
Clarke, D. L. 1977. *Spatial Archaeology*, Cambridge.

Corcoran, J. X. W. P. 1966. 'The excavation of three chambered cairns at Loch Calder, Caithness', *Proc. Soc. Antiq. Scot.* xcviii [1964–66], pp. 1–75.

Crawford, O. G. S. 1953. *Archaeology in the Field*, London.

Crowther, D. 1983. 'Old land surfaces and modern ploughsoil: implications of recent work at Maxey, Cambs.', *Scot. Arch. Rev.* ii, part 1, pp. 31–44.

Fowler, P. J. 1972. 'Field archaeology in future', in Fowler, P. J. (ed.), *Archaeology and the Landscape*, London, pp. 96–126.

— 1981. 'The Royal Commission on Historical Monuments (England)', *Antiquity*, lv, pp. 106–14.

Groube, L. 1981. 'Black holes in British prehistory: the analysis of settlement distributions', in Hodder, I., Isaac, G. and Hammond, N. (eds.), *Patterns of the Past*, pp. 185–209.

Henshall, A. S. 1963. *The Chambered Tombs of Scotland*, I, Edinburgh.

— 1972. *The Chambered Tombs of Scotland*, II, Edinburgh.

HMSO 1973. *Field Archaeology in Great Britain*, 5th edn.

Hodder, I. and Orton, C. 1976. *Spatial Analysis in Archaeology*, Cambridge.

Hogg, A. H. A. 1980. *Surveying for Archaeologists and other Fieldworkers*, London.

Lockyer, Sir N. 1909. *Surveying for Archaeologists*, London.

Mercer, R. J. 1980. *Archaeological Field Survey in Northern Scotland*, I, Univ. of Edinburgh Dept. of Arch. Occ. Pap. 4.

— 1981. *Archaeological Field Survey in Northern Scotland*, II, Univ. of Edinburgh Dept. of Arch. Occ. Pap. 7.

— 1982. 'Field survey: a route to research strategies', *Scot. Arch. Rev.* i, part 2, pp. 91–7.

— forthcoming a. *Archaeological Field Survey in Northern Scotland*, III.

— forthcoming b. 'Site identification and nomenclature—a theoretical basis', paper given during the Theoretical Archaeology Group meeting at Durham 1983.

RCAHMS 1911. *Inventory of Monuments and Constructions in the County of Caithness*, Edinburgh.

RCHM 1978. *Survey of Surveys*.

Survey Work in Eastern England

David Hall, F.S.A.

This paper describes the techniques used in various parts of lowland England during the past 20 years. The principal areas investigated lie in Cambridgeshire, Northamptonshire and Yorkshire. Approximately 2,025 sq. km. (500,000 acres) have been surveyed. There will first be a description of regional fieldwork techniques, and then an example of the results, giving a summary of what is known of early prehistoric settlement in Northamptonshire.

In spite of a long history of fieldwork in England[1] and an increase in the use of aerial photography since the 1940s, large-scale ground assessment has received little attention. Published county inventories are little more than a collection of data from earlier literature and aerial photographs, with an occasional plan of medieval earthworks, and are not very suitable for regional analysis. The view taken in the 1950s was that most site locations were known; but work in the next decade showed that there was much Roman and Iron Age settlement on heavy Midland clays,[2] most of which consist of soils unresponsive to aerial photography. During the 1970s it was shown that lithic scatters and Saxon sites existed on light soils,[3] even though cropmarks were rarely encountered at the findspots. News of these discoveries reached the archaeological literature, and the view then changed, and it was considered that sites of all periods occurred in all locations.[4] This tenet is as untrue as the earlier one. It is quite clear that settlement occurs in very specific areas, as will be shown below.

The main part of the present field-survey programme, a study of the former wetlands that drained into the Wash, is organized by the Fenland Project, based at Cambridge and supported by the Department of the Environment. Until the seventeenth century the south and western parts of the region were nearly all marsh, but in previous millennia the water-table was lower, so there were settlements that became drowned and buried. The total area of the Wash Fens is about 4,000 sq. km. The other regions surveyed, Northamptonshire and Yorkshire, consist of lowland rising to 200 m. in a few places. All three terrains are used for intensive arable farming, which continually destroys the evidence. In the fens there is also a problem of soil erosion and lowering of the water-table, with threat to waterlogged environmental remains.

25

Objectives

The objective of the fenland work is to identify sites and monuments that are still in a good state of preservation because of partial burial.

Fen soils include marine deposits as well as peat, and by mapping them the fen extent at various times over the last six millennia can be reconstructed. The approach is to record the complete landscape, not just isolated sites, with the aim ultimately of understanding something about the cultural systems that have left their transient remains. The survey is multi-period, but excludes material later than A.D. 1500. Few areas of England can offer such material, and survey is urgently needed to identify remains for preservation or excavation before they are lost.

On the uplands (i.e. ground higher than the fen), sites are not as well preserved, unless they occur in medieval woodland, or are buried under alluvium lying in flood plains of larger rivers. However, so little accurate information is available about the settlement patterns that survey is still essential.

Sampling

Several criteria affect the sampling design used for the Fenland Survey, the most important being the cost. Public money is involved, and the results must be cost effective. Time-consuming parts of the operation are finding out who owns or tenants farmland, seeking permission for land entry, and travelling to and from the area. It is therefore imperative that, having finally arrived, everything be investigated and recorded. Except for important areas there will only be a single visit, and there is little likelihood of such a large-scale survey being undertaken again in the foreseeable future. Indeed, the visitation of every field in this manner is almost certainly the first such occasion since the original Ordnance Survey mapping of *c.* 1860–85, and there is every possibility that the same length of time will elapse again, by which time much landscape evidence will have vanished. It is clear, therefore, that as many present-day and future needs as possible must be satisfied.

From this it follows that the survey must be multi-period, including the medieval period. For an analysis of the medieval landscape there are historical surveys which can effectively be combined with the ground evidence. This is only possible if the whole parish (or township) is available for study, because historical surveys usually deal with these land units, and little can be done if the whole is not treated. A parish must, therefore, be the minimum sample unit.

The Fenland Survey work began as a one-year investigation of the Cambridgeshire part of the fens.[5] Six regions with different underlying geology, and variable degrees of previously known information, were investigated. Subsequently it was decided to look at the whole of the Cambridgeshire fen, and more recently the Fenland Project was set up to study the former wetlands of the counties of Lincoln and Norfolk.[6] Samples forming elongated blocks running from the fen edge towards the Wash have been chosen. In Northamptonshire and Yorkshire the sample unit is the parish or township (*c.* 300–1,500 ha.), because medieval field-systems are one of the main research themes.

Much has been written about probabilistic sampling, and the original work in America was designed to study cultural remains in a context very different from the varying topography of the East Midlands of England.[7] Much of the discussion is centred on detailed 'non-site' techniques that take 4–12 man days per sq. km. to complete. Such a procedure is not applicable for the problem of the fens, and is really a halfway stage between regional survey and excavation, i.e. it will be the next level of data recovery for limited selected areas of importance. An example of such an approach has recently been published by Crowther.[8]

Sample design should always include some geological weighting. Experience over a wide area with differing terrains shows that settlement pattern is largely determined by soil type and the presence of water. It is therefore pointless to spend a lot of time on barren terrain if the manpower available is limited. Samples should always be large: a transect 1 km. wide, or a statistical scatter of kilometre squares, are not large enough. Many important sites in Cambridgeshire would have been missed by such an approach. If half, or less, of a region is to be covered then it is better to know what there is in a few large samples than to have a myriad of small samples and not be sure of anything.

Methods in the field

Preparatory work is necessary before going into the field. The main requirement is a copy of a 1:10,000 scale map with all previously known archaeological information marked on. For fenland studies a plot of old drainage channels, made from vertical aerial photographs, is necessary so that they can be checked on the ground.

Having selected the area to be studied there is the problem of how actually to study the land surface. An intensive grid-walk will give much information about a small area, and a cursory view will miss important and subtle aspects. The present survey aims to be somewhere in between, collecting all relevant pieces of data, but not attempting to make a detailed study of 'non-site' archaeology.

The conditions of agriculture are critical. Ideally, fields should be ploughed and well weathered. Much can still be observed, however, in land sown with winter corn, although soil colour cannot be seen at any great distance. Daylight conditions are relevant; diffuse light is better than bright sunshine. If the latter cannot be avoided, then it is better to work with the sun behind, when soil colouration is clearer.

The identification of upstanding monuments is relatively simple. Barrows are the most common early features, there being few earthworks of other prehistoric or Roman sites now surviving. Fairly common are the strip fields and earthworks around 'shrunken' medieval villages. More difficult to find are monuments in ploughed fields. Occupation areas can be detected as concentrations of artifacts, often associated with building debris, domestic refuse, and an area of dark soil.

A record of the soil type should be made for a settlement site. In the fenlands a complete map of soil types must be made to reconstruct the former fen area. From such soil evidence it is possible to determine the history of the fenland landscape since *c.* 8000 bc.[9]

Field techniques have been discussed previously.[10] The method chosen is to walk in strips 30 m. wide up and down a field. This ensures that nearly all sites and monuments are detected, as few features are less than 25 m. in diameter. The most difficult sites to find are those of the early prehistoric (flint artifacts) and Saxon periods. Such sites usually yield no cropmarks, so there is no indication that they exist apart from the ground evidence.

Any known or reputed site is checked to confirm its accuracy, or otherwise, and to improve the information. Often it will be found that a reported site has been inaccurately plotted or may not exist at all! Cropmark sites usually yield artifacts that will enable a date or classification to be assigned.

The checking of known information and the recording of soil boundaries will cause deviation from the 30-m. strip method, so giving additional coverage. When a site is discovered, close walking methods are required to ascertain its extent, and to collect a representative sample of artifacts, etc. Walking lines are reduced to 3–4 m., over the area in which artifacts are concentrated. The finds are bagged and labelled, and the settlement area marked on the map.

Rapid survey techniques

The success of the method described above lies in its rapidity. The routine 30-m. lines can be walked quickly until something is found. Even so, the rate of 10,000 ha. per year could not be achieved without several methods of making 'short cuts'. Experience has shown that sites earlier than the Iron Age do not occur on clay soils. A high proportion of eastern England consists of clay which preserves a dark occupation stain of organic matter at site locations. It is thus possible to see a settlement of Iron Age, or later date, as a dark patch in ploughsoil at some distance, e.g. 200 m., or as far off as 1 km. on undulating landscape. It is therefore not necessary to walk in 30-m. lines, 100 or 200 m. being quite adequate.

Fieldwork techniques can also be speeded up in fenlands. There are large areas of deep peat and other soils that have always been wet and so could support no occupation. All that is needed is a check to see if there are buried islands visible in modern drainage dikes, and to interpret any soil sections. Having also recorded the soil types in the main area of the field, the task is complete. By such means large areas can be surveyed and thoroughly interpreted.

The above methods explain how soils and settlements can be discovered. The topography itself must be understood. The existence of small valleys, too small to be picked out by contours, should be recorded, since these are important boundaries for such features as medieval field systems, as are the flood-plains of brooks and rivers.

Medieval fields

In many parts of England, especially the Midlands, medieval strip-fields can be seen surviving as ridge-and-furrow in old pasture. Survival of medieval field boundaries in the modern landscape makes it possible to reconstruct the complete physical layout in many parts of the country. The techniques have been described in full and will not be further covered here.[11]

Village earthworks are also recorded where they survive, although this is a rather different exercise from the rest of the fieldwork described. At the rapid level all that is noted is the area involved. Large-scale detailed earthwork survey will probably be necessary later.

Recording

The field record is made on the working copy of the 1:10,000 map. Soil boundaries, medieval fields and settlement areas of all periods are sketch-plotted. When a feature such as a barrow needs to be recorded accurately, then a surveyor's pocket compass is used. Artifacts are bagged and labelled on the spot.

The condition of every field is noted, i.e. whether ploughed, planted, etc., because it is important to know which are in bad condition so that a return visit can be made if necessary. Photographs are made of significant features. Farmers often have unrecorded artifacts which need examining.

It is essential to write up each day: otherwise information accumulates and is forgotten. Some form of identifying label is placed with finds bags in the field; in the evening the site is given its final number and eight-figure grid reference. Notes should be made about each site and the soils, the landscape, etc. A second copy of the 1:10,000 map is used to mark up findspots, soil types, field condition, etc. The lines of walking in the field are indicated. In the notes about sites and artifacts, numerical data needed for sites and monuments records are included, such as height above sea level, area of occupation in hectares, etc.

Nature and form of data

A more permanent record is prepared during the summer, when fieldwork is not possible. Base maps at 1:10,000 are prepared showing modern features only. Transparent-film copies of these are used to prepare period maps of the fen landscape and settlement at various archaeological times. All the numerical information gathered is added to a computerized data system. Finds are washed and a preliminary table made of the contents of each bag. Specialist help may be required for some of the material, and limited numbers of items may need drawing for publication.

Published examples of the Fenland Survey work are available.[12] The final results will be presented in a series of volumes with maps.

EARLY PREHISTORIC SETTLEMENT IN NORTHAMPTONSHIRE
(with Paul Martin)

Introduction

The following is an example of the results obtainable by a regional approach to fieldwork. About half of Northamptonshire has now been surveyed by the techniques described above. An immense amount of data of all periods awaits full analysis. In this paper we confine ourselves to discussing the distribution of lithic scatters. A full synthesis will not be attempted here, but we shall discuss some of the points immediately arising from the distribution map and the tables of flint categories (fig. 4 and pp. 36–43). Although we shall draw upon other published information, pottery or metalwork will not be discussed. Most of these finds were discovered by quarrying, and are therefore not a uniform sample.

In presenting these data we have tried to overcome the serious deficiencies present in most publications of distribution evidence. For instance, references in the literature to lithic scatters are deplorably lacking in numerical information;[13] on the rare occasions that numbers of finds are given there are no grid references.[14] This we have remedied in table 1. Distribution maps are completely useless unless they indicate the areas of land studied, and the regions of destruction; otherwise it is impossible to assess the significance of regional data. At an early stage in the fieldwork it became clear that geology had a marked influence on site location, so fig. 4 shows a representation of the semi-permeable soils in the county. The lithic scatters marked show all those revealed by the present work. Findspots of less than 20 flints in a limited area have not been plotted; to do this on small-scale maps gives a misleading impression of activity.

Table 1 gives a numerical analysis of flint types. It can be seen that large numbers have been recovered, a total of 11,657 coming from 108 findspots. Sites have been assigned a period (or periods) in spite of the uncertainty involved and at risk of being over-precise. Generally the period stated in the table is based on the presence of supposedly 'diagnostic' forms, and also on the nature of the flint-working and patination. Readers with a different view on the dating of a given flint type can modify the classification by consulting the table. Further work could be done by preparing length : breadth histograms, etc., but the value of this on surface collections, where material from more than one period may be mixed up, is doubtful.

The evidence from Brixworth (SP 7470) is not published here as it is already available.[15] Since 1980 further numbers of lithic artifacts have been recovered from there, bringing the total to about 20,000.

Nature of the assemblages

The source of the flint material is glacial 'river' gravel pebbles, except for imported axes of exotic stone. Most of the sites lie on acid soils and yield Mesolithic flints which are patinated, and later material which remains fresh. It is thus possible to identify reworking performed in later periods, because of the darker colour of the rejuvenation. On alkaline soils such a distinction could not be made, all the artifacts being of a uniform white patination.

Lithic scatters appear to represent settlements. It has been suggested that they are flint-knapping sites not associated with settlement, even though most of them lie on locations well removed from the gravel sources. If the flints represent industrial activity it is odd that *all* the material is worked away from its place of origin. Another interpretation is that the flints represent the transient stopping places of hunting parties. However, this does not seem likely when the site distribution and composition of flint types are considered. The large number of sites discovered cannot easily be explained away as representing industrial or hunting activities, because there then arises the problem of where the people involved came from.

The flint assemblages yield a range of tools, waste flakes, fire-cracked flints, and an occasional saddle quern, etc., and are generally of the same composition as material from excavated occupation remains. The assemblages are of a similar nature to groups deriving from the Isleham region of the Cambridgeshire fens.[16] Here the state of preservation is good because material was drowned by the fen soon after deposition, and has not been ploughed out until recently. The Isleham assemblages have been spared four millennia of winters and agricultural disturbance; most of them produce pottery and animal bone, and seem to be domestic settlement sites. The Northamptonshire material differs only in that frost has destroyed pottery, and constant admixture with acid soil has destroyed the bone. It will be assumed in the rest of this discussion that all the lithic scatters represent settlement. This does not preclude the existence of other types of prehistoric activity that did not leave lithic remains, and cannot therefore be discovered by this type of fieldwork.

Lithic distribution

A glance at fig. 4 shows that sites of all three lithic archaeological periods lie on light soils (shading on the map), clay being avoided. This conclusion is quite inescapable, in spite of assertions in the literature over the years that it is merely a matter of more careful work to find flints on clay soils.[17] Recent claims that large lithic scatters occur on clay at Marston St. Laurence (SP 5342) are incorrect. Familiarity with the local topography would have shown that the sites lie on permeable limestone soils. Light soils were presumably preferred because they are well drained and suitable for dwellings, and easier to work by the techniques of primitive agriculture.

Figure 4 shows how striking is the way in which the sites lie close to a brook offering a water supply. Sites of the historic period have a similar distribution for their prominent settlements, in spite of an apparent spread of lesser and specialized sites over all the landscape. One of the main reasons, in the case of the later periods, is the practice of mixed farming, the requirement of large quantities of water for animals and the presence of rich grazing meadows. Springs that could supply the small needs of humans are inadequate for thirsty herds. An implication of the distribution of lithic sites is that their occupants, too, were keeping considerable numbers of domestic animals. While this interpretation could be accepted for the Bronze Age and Neolithic periods, it is difficult in the case of the Mesolithic period. There are suggestions that red deer and gazelles were brought under man's control,[18] and at Oakhanger, Selborne, Hants, one of the interpretations of an unexpected concentration of ivy pollen was that the evergreen was used as winter fodder for animals in 5,600 bc.[19]

However, nowhere in Europe is there clear evidence of animal bones morphologically altered by selective breeding, with the exception of the dog.[20] Perhaps the best interpretation is that Mesolithic people were closely aware of the territorial movements of animals, including their drinking places, which would have occurred at regular spots next to brooks.

Excavations have proved the large-scale use of domesticated animals in the

Neolithic and Bronze Age periods; they were introduced from the Continent. At Fengate, near Peterborough (TL 2199), a proportion of the bone derived from farm animals of the third and second millennium bc.[21] In southern England, similar results have been obtained at Windmill Hill and elsewhere. It seems that the arrowheads of these two periods, so frequently found, did not contribute significantly to the provision of meat, but were used to hunt animals for sport, to control pests, and for such activities as culling and warfare, etc.

It might be argued that in the complex microtopography of Northamptonshire, the abundance of brooks and the tendency of light soil to be exposed in bands near to them inevitably mean that settlements will be near water, given that light soils are a determining factor. Comparison with other parts of the country, where there are extensive terrains of well-drained soils such as chalk or sand, shows that waterless high ground is devoid of lithic scatters, and sites huddle along the side of brooks (or fen). Such a distribution is particularly apparent on the Yorkshire Wolds (chalk) and the Chippenham and Snailwell area of Cambridgeshire (sand).[22] Water is thus demonstrated to be a determining factor in man's choice of site, as well as light soil. This would not be easy to see in the Northamptonshire evidence alone, except perhaps at Guilsborough (SP 6772), with its more extensive exposures of ironstone.

Land use

Without environmental sampling the state of the landscape remains uncertain. As only a few sites have been excavated within the county which provide environmental data,[23] the results are necessarily at an early stage. All of the Northamptonshire sites show activity in the third millennium and indicate that the surrounding countryside was open grassland. However, as all of them are adjacent to the major valleys, of either the Nene or the Welland rivers, the result comes as no surprise; these territories were doubtless opened up at an early date.

Boulder-clay regions away from the valleys were presumably densely forested in the Mesolithic phase, and became gradually encroached upon. The existence of a drowned Mesolithic forest (the 'bog oaks') buried under the areas of the Wash Fens that have a clay base gives an idea of the former appearance of the Midland claylands.

Neolithic axe distribution might be supposed to measure the extent of woodland at that time, if it be assumed that axes were used for cutting down trees. However, the distribution of axes recently sectioned and catalogued at Northampton Museum 'shows a marked preference for light well-drained soils . . . and a tendency to avoid clay formations'.[24] It is thus doubtful whether axes were primarily used for woodland activities, and they rather represent exotic tools most frequently found at settlements. All our finds of axes and fragments (except five) occur in lithic scatters, and were not isolated. Although axes can deal with small trees, and excavation of carpentered planks proves that large trees were used when required,[25] it is unlikely that they were used to clear mature woodland on a large scale. Much more likely means of clearance would be fire and the ringing of bark. Animals would prevent the regeneration of woodland by grazing.

Ecological studies show that there was a deterioration of soil structure in the

Mesolithic period, and an elm decline in the early third millennium bc.[26] These changes can be equated with forest clearance. Soils on acid rocks, which were stable and alkaline under forest conditions, became leached when the landscape was opened up, changing their pH to acidic values. This may explain why most of the Northamptonshire Mesolithic flints are patinated. They were originally dropped on alkaline soil, which caused patination; flints of subsequent periods fell on a degraded acid soil and remained fresh.

The Northamptonshire site distribution suggests a planned land-use of light soils, because there are distinct areas of such soils that are devoid of lithic scatters. The peninsula now occupied by the villages of Mears Ashby (SP 8466) and Wilby (SP 8666) has many hectares of sandy ironstone, and a topography very similar to the Guilsborough-Teeton (SP 6773–SP 6970) area. Whereas the latter has a dense settlement, at Mears Ashby there is not one site. This parish has been investigated in detail by a local worker over 20 years. It has produced on odd occasions scrapers, an axe, and a few arrowheads, but never more than one at a time. Our own survey was in accord with this, i.e. that there are no flint sites. It seems that the land was opened up, but used for grazing, not settlement. Marston St. Laurence (SP 5342) has been similarly studied and also only yielded a thin background activity, when examined on a single occasion by our techniques.

Another feature of the lithic settlement distribution is the way in which areas of barrows and cropmarks are avoided. The only upstream gravel-terrace of any size is at Grendon-Wollaston (SP 8661–SP 8964), where there is a small barrow field (SP 8761), but no flint scatters nearby. Yet, away from the barrows, six lithic scatters occur, ranging in date from Mesolithic to Bronze Age (sites Wollaston 21–26). The next barrow field downstream, a fine earthwork set at Irthlingborough meadows (SP 9671), has no known flint site nearby. The well-known ritual area at Maxey (TF 1207) has produced little flint material, the nearest site being at Nunton (TF 1107, site Maxey 18). Another large barrow-field lies in Borough Fen (TF 1805), and another around the county boundary-peninsula of Catswater (TF 2506). Only one flint site has been found. Admittedly the last two areas are partly covered by fen deposits, and there is still a chance of buried occupation being identified.

In complementary manner, at specific flint sites the incidence of cropmarks is slight. Only two of the sites at Brixworth (SP 7470) have cropmarks, and these are not proven to be contemporary. It is for these reasons that lithic sites have remained unrecognized for so long.

Other regions offer the same kind of organized land-use evidence. The Yorkshire Wolds, long known for their barrows and cropmarks, produce very few concentrations of flints.[27] In the Chippenham area of Cambridgeshire there are no flint sites near barrows, yet at Isleham twenty-five occupation sites have no cropmarks and no barrows near to them.[28] The case of Mears Ashby (SP 8466), Northamptonshire, mentioned above, is probably a smaller-scale example of this phenomenon: there are a few cropmarks, some linear and some of ring-ditch barrows; one barrow remains as an eroded earthwork.

It is concluded that there was a deliberately controlled land-use. There were clear areas without settlement (i.e. lithic remains) that seem to be reserved for grazing, occasionally with a cropmark that could be a cattle byre. These grazing regions are also the preferred areas for the burial mounds, placed out of the way on what was in many cases marginal ground. Might it be that the ditches of barrows served to keep out animals as well as being quarries for the mound material?

The land use of the areas with lithic remains might be expected to be agricultural in the Neolithic and later periods. Detailed consideration of the flints from Brixworth (SP 7470) has shown that there are two Mesolithic sites (with patinated flint), but most of the later ones have a quantity of reused early material. This is interpreted as possible evidence of ploughed land, the Mesolithic sites being turned over to reveal flints which were then picked up for reworking.[29]

Nevertheless, the scale of arable farming was probably small[30] (as with all periods until Saxon–medieval times). The exits of the major rivers into the fen around Peterborough leave a record of what was happening to the landscape upstream. On the present-day fen-surface there is extensive river alluvium, produced by soil erosion, transport, and deposition downstream largely as a result of clearance and ploughing in medieval times. It is the only such large-scale deposit, there being nothing equivalent dating from earlier periods. For the Neolithic and Bronze Age phases the prevailing economy must have been animal husbandry.

Causewayed enclosures and their functions are still much debated. If they are market centres, then they ought to occur in regions with considerable settlement. The enclosures at Etton and on the other side of the Welland would appear to serve the Peterborough region. Two enclosures west of Northampton (Briar Hill, SP 7358, Hardingstone, and a recently discovered one in Harlestone)[31] are also near settled areas. The fourth enclosure, at Southwick (TL 041929), has not been examined by us.

Comparison of data and future work

The evidence discussed above has been produced by single visits to sites, except for the case of Brixworth (SP 7470). Repeated study here for 10 years shows how much material is potentially obtainable from the other lithic sites. The total is in excess of 20,000 flints and, to be comparable with sites visited but once, this should be divided by 9. An estimate of the number of flints recovered from ploughsoil has been made at Maxey (TF 1207), where perhaps as little as 2 per cent of the artifacts in the ploughsoil were exposed for fieldwalking.[32] A similar figure has been calculated elsewhere.[33]

Some comment is necessary on a previously published lithic distribution for Northamptonshire, which shows as important parishes which do *not* stand out significantly, as adjudged by our techniques. No published figures are available for the number of flints discovered at Marston St. Laurence (TF 5342);[34] to be comparable with our data they should be divided by 17 to account for 20 years of collection and the law of diminishing returns. Mears Ashby (SP 8466) is also reckoned as significant, but checking with the fieldworker there showed that only *c.* 300 flints have been found in 20 years.[35] As mentioned before, little was found in either parish by our methods. Both these areas have a background scatter that can be found on most light soils. The repeated collection magnifies the amount of material, as at Brixworth (SP 7470), and makes them difficult to compare with other data, until a correction factor is applied.

The real lithic distribution is therefore seen to be as on fig. 4, with a strong preference for light soils. Brixworth, Flore (SP 6462), Guilsborough (SP 6773), and Welford (SP 6380) are significant areas for intensive activity. The collections of flint in Northampton Museum indicate that the parishes of Duston (SP 7261) and Hardingstone (SP 7358, on the site of the causewayed enclosure) were also important lithic areas, before they were built over.[36]

More fieldwork will doubtless extend specific data in the county. What is really needed is excavation, especially at sites with the prospect of waterlogged remains, to establish the nature of the lithic scatters and the surrounding landscape. All the sites are threatened by ploughing, which will remove surviving traces of structural and environmental evidence. Lithic scatters represent one aspect of prehistoric land-use, and data should be used in conjunction with ecological evidence and that produced by other scientific disciplines.

We believe that the regional fieldwork has demonstrated the wealth of prehistoric activity present in the Midlands, and further similar studies are required to obtain a national view.

Acknowledgement

We are grateful to the Northamptonshire Archaeological Unit for the information on areas quarried and built up, used on the plan.

TABLE 1. Analysis of Northamptonshire flint types (see *key*, p. 42)

Site	G	P	T	RM	BF	FA&F	SA&F	H	T&BA	TA	L-LP	LA	P-CK	S	U/S F&B	WF&B	RC	BC
						P/NP			P/NP P/NP	NP	NP	P/NP	P/NP	P/NP	P/NP	P/NP	P/NP	P/NP
Astwell SP 628 438	g	M N	138		1							2		10	15	93		17
Bainton 5 TF 0880 0680	g	N	49					1						7	13	27		2
Barnack 5 TF 0604 0424	l	N B	69		2					2				1 2	6 10	36 6		3 1
Barnack 6 TF 0594 0384	l, i	N B	264	16	12			1				2 1		21 3	7 3	165 13		12 2
Benefield 3 SP 9939 8963	s		64	3	10									1	1 3	28 3		12 3
Bradden 1 SP 6527 4744	i	N	60		3									7	14	28	2	1 5
Bradden 2 SP 6453 4906	g	M N	21												2 4	4 4		2 5
Bradden 3 SP 6622 4828	g	N	40											5	1 12	1 17	4	
Brington 1 SP 6460 6370	g		52	1	3								1	3	12	32		
Castle Ashby 1 SP 8560 6090	B	B	101	4	2									7	1	83		4
Cold Ashby 1 SP 6475 7570	i+s	N B	93		6			1		1		1		11	15	5 38	10	2 3
Creaton 2 SP 7355 7148	g	M N	180		6									11	31	32 81	10	9
Denton 2 SP 8415 5856	s	M N B	111	12	11									2	9	28 33		3 13
Draughton 4 SP 7680 7798	i	M N	126	18	5									4	5 19	29 43	3	3
Draughton 5 SP 7695 7784	i	N	67	10	2									4	8	8 17	9	1 8

Site	Data
East Haddon 2 SP 6608 6775	7 8 5 64 3 6 2 2 6 107 N i
Flore 2 SP 6412 6165	1 3 38 4 10 1 3 1 1 2 2 5 71 N 1
Flore 4 SP 6475 6190	3 41 58 1 5 4 1 2 1 9 21 146 N 1
Flore 5 SP 6435 6272	15 10 69 67 2 17 3 1 1 24 26 237 M N 1
Flore 10 SP 6365 6135	15 5 128 72 4 3 1 3 20 23 274 M i
Flore 10 SP 6460 6190	5 7 4 130 69 5 3 1 1 1 43 23 292 N i
Flore 11	1 2 55 33 1 3 3 1 16 15 136 1+i
Flore 12 SP 6475 6200	1 3 87 19 2 3 2 1 23 16 158 N 1
Glinton 2 TF 1356 0288	9 4 14 50 7 6 2 10 102 M N B g
Glinton 3 TF 1470 0600	14 2 71 44 4 11 2 11 1 1 21 12 194 M N B g
Guilsborough 1 SP 6717 7220	9 3 6 26 38 2 5 1 2 8 8 108 M N i
Guilsborough 2 SP 6613 7363	4 1 2 78 26 11 2 14 138 M N s+i
Guilsborough 4 SP 6631 7172	1 4 3 32 17 5 3 65 N B g+i
Guilsborough 5 SP 6705 7473	3 2 7 14 1 30 M B g+i
Guilsborough 7 SP 6695 7185	7 1 2 8 9 3 5 1 4 46 M N s+i
Harringworth 2 SP 9330 9542	7 10 214 11 7 1 2 10 10 272 N B 1
Harringworth 4 SP 9338 9821	12 5 37 23 6 5 3 1 2 9 104 M N 1
Harrowden Lit. 1 SP 8786 7181	17 17 4 6 121 63 20 22 2 3 9 1 20 73 379 M N i
Harrowden Lit. 3 SP 8653 7115	9 1 26 10 7 4 3 1 2 3 8 76 M i
Helpston 5 TF 1258 0644	6 8 13 6 33 N B g

TABLE 1. *cont.*

Site	G	P	T	RM	BF	FA&F (P/NP)	SA&F	H (P/NP)	T&BA (P/NP)	TA (P/NP)	L-LP (NP)	LA (P/NP)	P-CK (P/NP)	S (P/NP)	U/S F&B (P/NP)	WF&B (P/NP)	RC (P/NP)	BC (P/NP)
Helpston 8 TF 1144 0296	l	N	31	1	2	2								1	1 4	10 7	3	5 12
Holdenby 2 SP 6968 6939	i	M N	267	9	22			3			1			2	25	21 149	2 15	3 3
Holdenby 3 SP 6940 6938	i	N	82	4	7		1							6	1	12 36	9	1 3
Holdenby 4 SP 6990 6906	i	M	26	1	1										1	4 11	4	2 5
Hollowell 1 SP 6968 7171	s+i	M N	99	2	7					1		1		8	5	12 49	1 6	6 4
Hollowell 3 SP 6968 7123	s+i	M N	133	4	9							1		1 3	1 10	46 38	1 9	11 1
Hollowell 4 SP 6788 7215	i	M B	136	11	5			3	1					5	5 5	61 17	9 1	3 2
Hollowell 5 SP 6785 7134	s	M N	36	1	1			2						1	4	10 12		3 2
Long Buckby 5 SP 6780 6883	i	B	101	4	3					1				5	6	73	14	
Long Buckby 5 SP 6462 6848	i	B B	56					2						8	12	24	13	
Long Buckby 6 SP 6470	i	B B	46												17	12	6	2
Long Buckby 7 SP 6336 6958	g	B	17													16	16	1
Maidwell 2 SP 7500 7623	i	N B	65	2	2									9	13	29		10
Maidwell 8 SP 7305 7640	i	B	85	3										10	8	53	11	
Maidwell 10 SP 7522 7822												Data not currently available						
Maxey 16 TF 1246 0809	g	M N	99	6	9									3	5	50 6	2 2	15 2

Site	Grid Ref	Finds (as tabulated)	Total	Class	Type
Maxey 18	TF 1192 0742	3 14 4 8 1 1 2	37	N	g
Northborough 2	TF 1455 0755	3 22 8 1 6 5 2	47	B	g
Oakley Little 4	SP 8940 8540	2 1 17 6 2 1 2 9 12	60	M N	s+l
Oundle 3	TL 0270 8818	2 7 34 1 1 5 2 2 4	60	N	l
Oundle 6	TL 0080 8835	6 7 11 84 13 3 2 8 7	148	N	s
Overstone 1	SP 8095 6747	8 103 13 19 10 2 1 3 8	177	N B	s+i
Rothwell 2	SP 7897 7986	5 3 1 7 37 62 2 16 4 1 16 6	163	M N B	s+i
Southorpe 4	TF 0787 0234	8 47 12 8 5 1 1 19 5	108	N	l
Spratton 2	SP 7290 6910	4 33 28 1 1 2	95	N	i
Stanion	SP 9255 8670	5 5 1 31 58 1 19 2 7 6	135	M N	l+i
Sulby 1	SP 6605 7965	2 9 6 2 37 18 6 3 2	86	M N	g
Sutton 2	TL 0992 9898	2 10 35 1 16 5 1 4 5	79	N B	g
Teeton 1	SP 6876 7046	7 9 6 23 18 3 19 2 3 1 1 1 11	107	M N	s+i
Teeton 2	SP 6980 7117	8 9 14 53 11 4 1 9 10	123	N	s+i
Thornhaugh 6	TF 0870 0080	9 84 11 1 10 5 2	123	N B	l
Thornhaugh 7	TL 0646 9940	4 36 3 4 1 1 7	57	N	l
Thorpe Achurch 3	TL 0198 8220	4 1 55 2 4 1 1 1 7	75	N	l
Thorpe Achurch 5	TL 0207 8215	8 75 3 1 6 2	98	N	l
Thorpe Achurch 6	TL 0215 8202	12 3 4 99 6 5 1 13 16	159	N	l

TABLE 1. *cont.*

Site / Grid ref	G	P	T	RM	BF	FA&F P	FA&F NP	SA&F	H P	H NP	T&BA P	T&BA NP	TA P	TA NP	L-LP NP	LA P	LA NP	P-CK	S P	S NP	U/S F&B P	U/S F&B NP	WF&B P	WF&B NP	RC P	RC NP	BC P	BC NP
Titchmarsh 19 TL 0206 8123	s+g	M N	109	12	5									2					1	2	3	14	10	49			5	5
Titchmarsh 20 TL 0193 8115	s	M N	219	6	21															2	6	6	106	54		3	10	4
Titchmarsh 21 TL 0190 8110	s+g	M N	361		26		1			1									1	8	3	56	44	148	1	15	15	38
Titchmarsh 22 TL 0199 8102	g	M N	153	2	8					1												30	18	52	2	5	14	17
Titchmarsh 23 TL 0195 8097	g	M N	29		1															3		11	2	8				3
Towcester 4 SP 6734 4630	l	N	168		9		1										1			7		9		118		11		12
Upton 3 TF 1059 0131	l	M B	167	10	1														5	4	3	6	98	17	2	8		12
Upton 8 TL 1088 9965	l	N	91	4	5															4		4	71	2				5
Watford 6 SP 6176 6872	i	B	80	1	2					2	1	1		1						6			5	59				3
Watford 7 SP 6158 6884	i	N B	116	4	10					1	2	1								6	1	17	3	51		12	1	2
Watford 8 SP 6193 6900	i	M B	268	7	14					6										15	6	46	21	99		21	16	15
Welford 1 SP 6264 8192	g	N B	73	4	1															2		21		33		8		3
Welford 2 SP 6260 8210	g	M N B	52																	1		13		25		3	1	9
Welford 3 SP 6270 8210	g	N	30	1	1			1		1												7	3	11				5
Welford 4 SP 6284 8212	g	N B	177	2	4			2						2						9		34	7	88		18		12

Site	Grid Ref	Counts (reading order)	Total	Fabric	Type
Welford 5	SP 6267 8174	4 9 31 9 4 2	59	N B	g
Welford 6	SP 6315 8195	1 22 18 6 128 1 38 17 1 1 7 1	246	N	g
Welford 7	SP 6317 8192	8 3 37 16 3 1	68	N B	g
Welford 8	SP 6317 8170	2 3 3 19 17 4 1 1 2	52	B	g
Welford 9	SP 6312 8145	9 3 35 17 5 1 3	73	N B	g
Welford 10	SP 6313 8140	4 5 24 8 3 1	45	N B	g
Welford 11	SP 6315 8132	2 5 25 9 1	42	N B	g
Welford 12	SP 6339 8109	6 3 10 12 4 1 1	40	B	g
Welford 13	SP 6347 8108	1 5 15 62 27 5 1 1 3 2	123	N B	g
Welford 14	SP 6347 8116	1 8 41 23 5 2	80	B	g
Welford 15	SP 6351 8123	10 27 7 3	47	N B	g
Welford 16	SP 6357 8120	1 17 70 18 3 2 2	114	N B	g
Welford 17	SP 6455 8040	4 3 3 8 1	19	N B	g
Welford 18	SP 6472 8035	1 1 1 19 8 3 4 1	39	N	g
Welford 19	SP 6490 8030	1 7 19 7 1	36	N B	g
Welford 20	SP 6435 7862	4 8 9 2 1	24	N B	g
West Haddon 2	SP 6463 7170	2 3 2 25 1 19 3 2 1 1	60	M N	s+g
West Haddon 3	SP 6195 7290	3 3 1 6 1 19 3 16 5 1 1 3	62	M N	l+g
Whilton 1	SP 6427 6566	7 9 20 36 106 17 1 5 2 5 1 17 20	246	N B	g

TABLE 1. *cont.*

Note: the table is printed sideways. The columns FA&F, H, T&BA, TA, LA, P-CK, S, U/S F&B, WF&B, RC and BC are each sub-divided into patinated (P) / non-patinated (NP), shown below as "P NP"; L-LP is non-patinated (NP) only.

Site	G	P	T	RM	BF	FA&F	SA&F	H	T&BA	TA	L-LP	LA	P-CK	S	U/S F&B	WF&B	RC	BC
						P/NP		P/NP	P/NP	P/NP	NP	P/NP	P/NP	P/NP	P/NP	P/NP	P/NP	P/NP
Whilton 2 SP 6291 6453	g	N B	34		2									5	5	1 13		3 4
Wittering 2 TF 0475 0157	i+s	M N	252	19	7					1					4 2	196 5	1 4	14
Wollaston 21 SP 9037 6440	i	N	85		4	1		2				1		1	4	7 55	6	1 4
Wollaston 22 SP 9018 6378	i	N	179	8	6			2						18		23 106	6	4 4
Wollaston 23 SP 8969 6469	s	M N B	590	9	39	6		2	1			2	1	14	8 44	111 318		10 17
Wollaston 24 SP 8960 6442	g+s																	
Wollaston 25 SP 8924 6420	g+s	N						Data not currently available										
Wollaston 26 SP 8885 6371	g+s	M N	49		1									1	2 7	3 28		7
Total of sites 108			Total of flints (not including burnt material) 11,657															

Key
BC = blade cores; RC = rough cores; WF&B = waste flakes and blades; U/S F&B = utilized/serrated flakes and blades; S = scrapers; P-CK = plano-convex knives; LA = leaf arrowheads; L-LP = laurel-leaf points; TA = transverse arrowheads; T&BA = tanged and barbed arrowheads; H = hammerstones; SA&F = stone axes and fragments; FA&F = flint axes and fragments; BF = burnt flint; RM = reworked material; T = total; P (in main head) = period; M = Mesolithic; N = Neolithic; B = Bronze Age; l = limestone; g = gravel; i = Northampton sand and ironstone; s = sand. NP = non-patinated; P (in sub-head) = patinated; G = geology. The total column includes the rare types listed in table 2.

TABLE 2. Rarer tools

Barnack 5	1 asymmetrical arrowhead NP
Barnack 6	3 burnt scrapers, 1 scalene triangle P
Draughton 4	1 microlith P
Flore 5	1 backed blade P
Flore 10	1 scalene triangle NP
Guilsborough 1	1 oblique point P
Guilsborough 7	1 fabricator NP
Harringworth 2	1 fabricator P
Harringworth 4	1 scalene triangle P
Harrowden, Lit. 1	1 backed blade P
Harrowden, Lit. 3	1 backed blade P, 1 point P
Hollowell 1	1 hollow backed arrowhead P
Hollowell 3	1 oblique blunted point P
Hollowell 4	1 geometrical arrowhead P
Long Buckby 6	1 fabricator P
Maxey 16	1 microlith NP
Oakley, Lit., 4	1 Horsham point
Southorpe 4	1 rejuvenated axe
Thornhaugh 6	1 fabricator P
Rothwell 2	1 microlith P, do. NP
Thornaugh 7	1 fabricator P
Teeton	1 scalene triangle P, 1 tranchet flake P
Thorpe Achurch 5	1 fabricator P
Titchmarsh 19	1 geometrical arrowhead P
Titchmarsh 20	1 rod form P
Titchmarsh 21	1 oblique blunted point P, do. NP, 1 trapeze P, do. NP
Titchmarsh 22	1 rod form P, 2 backed blades P, 1 rejuvenated flake NP
Titchmarsh 23	1 backed blade
Upton 3	1 hollow based point
Watford 8	1 microlith P, 1 fabricator NP
Welford 1	1 discoid object NP
Welford 4	1 bifacial tool NP
Welford 6	1 fabricator NP, 1 backed blade NP
Welford 16	1 bifacial tool NP
Welford 18	1 bifacial tool NP
West Haddon 2	1 microlith P
Wittering 2	1 backed blade P, 1 scalene triangle P
Wollaston 23	2 microliths P, 1 tranchet axe fragment P, 1 backed blade NP, 1 microlith NP, 1 polished edge blade

NOTES

[1] Beginning with Camden, Aubrey, and Stukeley. See P. Ashbee, 'Field archaeology: its origins and development', in P. J. Fowler (ed.), *Archaeology and the Landscape* (London, 1972), pp. 38–74; also R. J. C. Atkinson, *Field Archaeology* (London, 1946), and M. W. Beresford, *History on the Ground* (London, 1957).

[2] D. N. Hall and N. Nickerson, 'Sites on the North Bedfordshire and South Northamptonshire Border', *Beds. Arch. J.* iii (1966), pp. 1–6.

[3] P. W. Martin and D. N. Hall, 'Brixworth, Northamptonshire: new evidence for early prehistoric settlement and agriculture', *Beds. Arch. J.* xiv (1980), pp. 5–14; and *id.*, 'Brixworth, Northamptonshire—an intensive field survey', *JBAA* cxxii (1979), pp. 1–6.

[4] RCHM, *Northants.* IV (1982), pp. xxiii–xxiv.

[5] Organized by the Cambridgeshire Archaeological Committee.

[6] J. M. Coles and D. Hall, *Antiquity*, lvi (1982), pp. 51–2.

[7] J. F. Cherry, C. Gamble and S. Shennan (eds.), *Sampling in Contemporary British Archaeology*, BAR 50 (Oxford, 1978).

[8] D. R. Crowther, 'Old land surface and modern ploughsoil: implications of recent work at Maxey, Cambs.', *Scottish Arch. Rev.* ii (1983), pp. 31–44.

[9] R. S. Seale, *Soils of the Ely District* (Sheet 173), Memoirs of the Soil survey (HMSO, 1975); D. N. Hall in R. T. Rowley (ed.), *The Evolution of Marshland Landscapes* (1981), pp. 52–73.

[10] C. Hayfield (ed.), *Fieldwalking as a Method of Archaeological Research*, D.o.E. Occ. Res. Pap. 2 (HMSO, 1980).

[11] D. Hall, *Medieval Fields*, Shire Publications (1982).

[12] D. N. Hall in Rowley, *op. cit.* (n. 9), and D. Hall, 'The changing landscape of the Cambridgeshire silt fens', *Landscape History*, iii (1981), pp. 37–49.

[13] RCHM, *op. cit.* (n. 4), pp. 98–101.

[14] *Ibid.*, appendix to vol. III under Guilsborough, Haselbech, Hollowell, and Welford.

[15] See note 3.

[16] D. N. Hall, in A. Lawson (ed.), *European Wetlands in Prehistory* (Oxford, 1985 forthcoming).

[17] RCHM, *op. cit.* (n. 4), pp. xxiii–xxiv; vol. III (1981), p. xxiv.

[18] E. S. Higgs, *Papers in Economic Prehistory* (Cambridge, 1972).

[19] Discussed in G. Dimbleby, *Plants and Archaeology* (St. Albans, 1978), p. 140.

[20] J. Murray, *The First European Agriculture* (Edinburgh, 1970), pp. 17–29.

[21] F. Pryor, *Excavation at Fengate, Peterborough, England, The Second Report*, Royal Ontario Museum Monograph 5 (1978), pp. 177–8; *id.*, *The Third Report*, ROM Monograph 6, Northants. Arch. Soc. Monograph 1 (1980), p. 180.

[22] *Op. cit.* (n. 16).

[23] Fengate, *op. cit.* (n. 21); Etton, F. Pryor, pers. comm.; and Ecton (SP 8361), W. G. R. Moore and J. H. Williams, *Northants. Arch.* x (1975), pp. 3–30.

[24] W. G. R. Moore and W. A. Cummins, 'The petrological identification of stone implements in the south-east Midlands', forthcoming, copy available at Northampton Museum.

[25] J. M. Coles, *Experimental Archaeology* (London, 1979), pp. 101–4.

[26] I. Simmons and M. Tooley (eds.), *The Environment in British Prehistory* (London, 1981), pp. 134–6, and 106–7.

[27] D. N. Hall and P. W. Martin, in Wharram Percy fieldwork monograph, edited by C. Hayfield, forthcoming.

[28] Hall, *op. cit.* (n. 16).

[29] Martin and Hall, *op. cit.* (n. 3).

[30] I. F. Smith in C. Renfrew, *British Prehistory, a New Outline* (London, 1974), p. 123.

[31] For Etton, see F. M. M. Pryor and I. A. Kinnes, *Antiquity*, lxvi (1982), pp. 124–6; Briar Hill, see H. M. Bamford, in *Northants. Arch.* xiv (1979), pp. 3–9; Harlestone, discovered in 1979 by J. Pickering, SP 725 635.

[32] Crowther, *op. cit.* (n. 8).

[33] Similar results were obtained in Devon, R. Silvester, pers. comm., 1984.

[34] RCHM, *op. cit* (n. 4); county summary in P. J. Fowler and P. Sinton, *Northamptonshire, an Archaeological Atlas*, RCHM (1980).

[35] W. Callis, pers. comm.

[36] W. R. G. Moore, Northampton Museum, pers. comm.

Fieldwork Techniques in the Lincolnshire Fens 1968–1978

Brian Simmons, F.S.A.

The retrieval of the archaeological record in the Lincolnshire Fens can be studied in, perhaps, three distinct phases: the work of C. W. Phillips and, later, Mrs. S. H. Hallam, covering the period up to the 1960s (mainly dealt with in *The Fenland in Roman Times*[1]), the work of the Car Dyke Research Group between 1968 and 1978 (from 1975 incorporated into the South Lincolnshire Archaeological Unit) and, since 1981, funded by grants received from the Department of the Environment. A brief word regarding the latter research should be sufficient in the context of this paper. Over a number of years, and through the lobbying of the South Lincolnshire Archaeological Unit, the Lincolnshire fenlands have been recognized as an area of outstanding archaeological importance. Since 1981 more government money has been put into greater and more intensive fieldwork and two field officers were appointed for the county in 1982.

Before this recent interest in the Lincolnshire Fens, however, fieldwork was carried out on a random system, based, from the 1970s, on a carefully worked-out sampling programme. The problem of studying such a large area as the Lincolnshire Fens (approximately 500 square miles) is one of logistics. It is impossible for a small group of unpaid workers, operating mainly at weekends, to examine field by field 500 square miles in a relatively small time-span, say 5 years. The equation is a simple one to determine. There are some 50,000 fields in the Lincolnshire Fens, and with a regular work force of ten people it would mean that each person would have to examine 5,000 fields, or, if the time-limit of 5 years is set, 1,000 fields per person per year. This is clearly a superhuman task, especially when the availability of the fields is considered, which is, by and large, in winter only, perhaps in theory for 25 weeks each year. Even this estimate of availability is optimistic, as the effects of weather have not been allowed for: a more realistic figure would be 20 weeks. Thus, each fieldworker would have to look at some 50 fields each weekend, a target never likely to be achieved. Clearly a different approach has to be sought.

However, before this approach can be discussed, the original purpose of the fieldwork should be mentioned. When the Car Dyke Research Group first came

45

into being in 1968 its sole aim was to study the Car Dyke itself, and not the surrounding landscape.

The Car Dyke has not been systematically recorded in modern times and it was felt that the first task should be to walk the entire (Lincolnshire) length, some 56 miles (90 km.), noting the width of the channel, the height of the existing banks, the state of repair, and landowners' and farmers' names. This was accomplished. At the same time, it was agreed that one field on either side of the Car Dyke should be carefully walked, looking for evidence of settlement which might be related to the Car Dyke. It was during the course of this latter research that a change of policy came about, and only about half the length of the Lincolnshire Car Dyke, 30 miles (48 km.), was finished field by field.

As the early fieldwalking progressed it became apparent to those involved that the fields beyond the environs of the Car Dyke would also have to be examined. There were several reasons for this change in policy. Some of the early fieldwork had revealed that there were Roman roads or tracks crossing the Car Dyke. As these roads could well be part of a larger scheme of land settlement, it became necessary to examine the direction which they took. Associated with the roads were settlement sites which, in turn, were apparently related to the Car Dyke and the other Roman watercourses which were beginning to be recognized through the fieldwork.

A new difficulty was then encountered. How could the programme of field-walking be truly representative of the whole area of research when only a small part was to be studied? The solution to the problem appeared to lie in what was already known and in laying down some basic guide-lines. First of all it was thought important to ensure that Roman settlements should be studied in their relationship to various geological patterns. At the same time some sites were known from aerial photography, and a proportion of these should be seen. Equally, other sites had been reported by earlier workers and it was thought essential that some of these should be revisited. The bulk of the land, however, was unknown, archaeologically.

Although the primary objective of the study was to examine the Roman landscape, the first principle of fieldwork, as seen by the Group, was to recover all possible information of all periods from the surface of the fields. Secondly, it had been noted that some other fieldworkers had been selective in their fieldwork: only rims, samian ware and decorated sherds had been picked up, or, even worse, the fact that Roman pottery was present, but not collected, had been noted. Sometimes a Roman site was claimed on the basis of a few sherds with little or no supporting evidence. The Group decided that a Roman site could only be recognized if there were at least 100 sherds (perhaps an arbitrary decision), together with other information, for example, marks on aerial photographs, soil discolorations, humps and bumps in the field. On the other hand, if only a few sherds of unusual pottery (for instance, Middle Saxon or Bronze Age) were found, then this information was treated differently and sites were claimed on more slender evidence for some periods other than Roman.

But despite the use of these simple rules and methods of recording and process-ing the results of the fieldwork, the original question of which fields to survey still had to be answered. Of the number of fields (50,000) in the area, 600 (in round figures) looked interesting from aerial photographs. Another 800 had been visited and recorded by earlier workers. A third archaeological consideration was all the chance finds which had been reported from time to time, a single coin from here, or piece of unusual pottery from there; in all some 400 fields were included in this category. This then left 48,200 fields where there was no information of any sort.

The other variables to be considered were those of topography and geology, and type of agriculture (grassland or arable). In the case of the Group's area these categories can be listed as:

TABLE 1

1. Topography	(a) Upland	10,000 fields (20%)
	(b) Fenland	40,000 fields (80%)
2. Geology	(a) Fen coarse silts	15,000 fields (30%)
	(b) Fen clays	14,000 fields (28%)
	(c) Fen peats	6,000 fields (12%)
	(d) Fen edge gravel	5,000 fields (10%)
	(e) Upland limestone/clay	10,000 fields (20%)
3. Agriculture	(a) Arable	45,000 fields (90%)
	(b) Pasture	5,000 fields (10%)

The final choice of which fields to visit can then be tabulated (table 2).

In order to understand the table, and repeating what has already been said in a slightly different way, if the first line, 'Aerial photos', is considered as an example, several points can be made. First of all there are 600 fields which show some archaeological potential in the area. Of this number, only 10 per cent (60) should be visited, 54 of which are arable and the balance pasture. The total number is then split between the various types of soils and topographical situations (in the case of the Lincolnshire Fenlands, the topography equates more or less with the geology and soils; for instance, the limestone occurs entirely in the uplands and not in the fens). In the 'Fen coarse silts' category, 16 arable fields (30 per cent) should be surveyed out of the total of 54, and 2 pasture fields out of the total of 6, and this practice continues throughout the complete table.

This type of sampling technique is an ideal which is difficult to achieve in the field for various reasons. The table assumes that the ratio of archaeological sites seen on aerial photographs is the same throughout all the variations of topography, geology and agriculture, but this is not so; there are more sites to be seen in the silt fens than anywhere else. It also assumes that chance finds are consistent and that other workers have followed the same trends as laid down in the table. In fact, there are no regular patterns to be seen. For instance, in the Witham peat fens it was known before the sampling took place that there were no known aerial photographs of archaeological marks, nor had there been any report of chance finds or finds made by other fieldworkers. Consequently, all the fields examined in these peat fens came under the 'Unknown' category, and, because of the unusual nature of the archaeology (or lack of it) more than the required number of fields were eventually surveyed (1,000, all with negative results). Similarly, the portion of arable to pasture land is given as 9:1 throughout the area. In the fenlands this ratio is somewhat higher, 19:1, and, therefore, lower in the uplands.

TABLE 2

	Total no. of fields in area 50,000	Total no. of fields to be visited 10% (i.e. 5,000 of 50,000)	Geology/topography				
			Fen coarse silts 30%	Fen clays 28%	Fen peats 12%	Fen edge gravel 10%	Limestone/clay 20%
Aerial photos	600	60	18	17	7	6	12
Arable 90%		54	16	15	6	6	11
Grassland 10%		6	2	2	1	–	1
Other workers	800	80	24	22	10	8	16
Arable 90%		72	22	20	9	7	14
Pasture 10%		8	2	2	1	1	2
Chance finds	400	40	12	11	5	4	8
Arable 90%		36	11	10	4	4	7
Pasture 10%		4	1	1	1	–	1
Unknown	48,200	4,820	1,446	1,350	578	482	964
Arable 90%		4,338	1,301	1,215	520	434	868
Pasture 10%		482	145	135	58	48	96
Total	50,000	5,000	1,500	1,400	600	500	1,000

Nevertheless, it was felt that the table was more than a useful guide, and any further fieldwork done should be based on such a model, providing it was used in a reasonably flexible manner.

There are also one or two pitfalls to avoid when using this system. The size of fields, of course, varies considerably over the general area. It is pointless looking at large arable fields and small grass fields; it might be found that the average field is 12 acres and, therefore, if an arable field of, say, 50 acres needs to be surveyed this should be counted as 4 average fields. Similarly, if pasture fields are smaller than the norm (grass paddocks, for example) then the acreage should be made up to the average. Common sense plays a great part in determining what should be examined and what should be left alone. There is little point in visiting every field which has produced Roman coins and ignoring those fields where only Roman tiles have been found. As much of a balance ought to be struck between different types of sites as between pasture and arable and various categories of soils.

It should also be borne in mind that the final product of the sample will only be as good as the people who are doing the sampling. Inevitably, and in spite of the rules laid down, fieldworkers will return to the same site several times for a number of reasons; it may be spectacular in the number of coins found there, or it may be close to where the fieldworker lives. Whatever the reason, the number of visits to a particular field, together with the finds from each visit, should be carefully noted in the record so that in the eventual interpretative processes the fact that more coins (or whatever else may have been found) were noted in a particular field than anywhere else may be seen in its true light.

It is a relatively simple task to list all the sites found during the past ten years. However, the very term 'site' is misleading and the word can be applied variously to a single Roman hut, for example, or the entire Lincolnshire silt fenlands. Is the entire Wash basin a 'site' in the sense that the area was occupied during one period and deserted during another? In considering the Roman period it was often difficult to decide where one settlement finished and another commenced. Similarly, analysis of the Bronze Age finds suggests that we are not looking at twenty different and isolated sites but at a settlement pattern stretching for at least 20 miles (32 km.) on a north–south line, and in one area (Billingborough) for 4 miles (6·4 km.) east–west. Where do we say that this occupation begins and ends? How do we put boundaries around it? The answers to these Bronze Age problems are not easy to find. On the other hand, however, it is now possible to say, with some degree of certainty as a result of our fieldwork, that during the Roman period there were many off-shore islands each with its settlements.[2] Is it safe to assume that each of these islands constitutes a 'site'?

The one clear fact which emerges from the fieldwork is that nothing can be viewed in isolation, whether it is a long, linear earthwork such as the Car Dyke, or a single field, or a separate archaeological period, or one excavation. The settlement and alteration of the landscape by man leaves a complex and difficult record for the modern archaeologist to interpret. These difficulties and complexities, however, are not insuperable, and apart from the methods described above, and used in South Lincolnshire, new techniques have been developed over the past few years to decipher the clues which have been left behind by previous ages. In the case of South Lincolnshire perhaps the most important new approach was the involvement of soil scientists.[3] In strictly archaeological terms there is nothing new in asking soil scientists for their help in examining excavated layers; what is new in South Lincolnshire is that it is now being realized that the later (Iron Age, Roman and medieval) sedimentation has possibly masked the earlier cultural settlement patterns. It is these earlier patterns which cannot be seen from fieldwalking programmes or aerial photography. A different research approach has, therefore, to be determined in order to examine the buried soil horizons.

NOTES

[1] C. W. Phillips (ed.), *The Fenland in Roman Times* (London, 1970).

[2] B. Simmons in F. H. Thompson (ed.), *Archaeology and Coastal Change*, Soc. Antiq. London Occ. Pap. n.s. I (1980), pp. 56–73.

[3] I am grateful in this respect to the Soil Survey of England and Wales. Dennis Robson, in particular, head of the Section in Lincoln, has been for many years an enthusiast in his assistance to the archaeologists. Equally, Dr. Helen Keeley of the Department of the Environment's Ancient Monuments Laboratory has given much valuable help and advice.

Archaeological Field Survey:
a Cornish Perspective

Nicholas Johnson

Since 1977 Cornwall Committee for Rescue Archaeology has been engaged on various field survey projects, the most notable being those in the Land's End Peninsula (West Penwith) and on Bodmin Moor. Most have been undertaken in advance of development and, in particular, improvement of moorland for pasture. They involve surveying in featureless moorland, rocky and overgrown terrain, steep cliffland, amidst modern fields fossilizing prehistoric fields as well as typical lowland farming landscape. Not surprisingly, resources have not been large, with staff seldom numbering more than two, but nonetheless the investment in such work has been considerable. The Department of the Environment has borne the lion's share, with a substantial contribution coming from the Royal Commission on Historic Monuments (England). The purpose of this work is simple: to record upstanding remains in advance of known or perceived development for the purposes of enhancing the County Sites and Monuments Register (SMR), and the better conservation and management of those archaeological remains. All archaeological decisions in Cornwall will in future be influenced by the collective and cumulative wisdom of the SMR and set in a national perspective through the growing offices of the National Monuments Record (NMR). It is the development of county SMRs that has forced a complete rethink of the nature and purpose of field survey.

An SMR is a growing record of evidence of man's past activity. If pursued to its logical conclusion an SMR should include all structures, artifacts and processes associated with past activity before yesterday. In practice this is restricted by available resources and limits are set on what goes into this data ark; thus, what we perceive to be the more obvious archaeological remains, such as prehistoric sites and finds, medieval buildings, industrial works, etc., are likely to be recorded before, for example, field-names, modern farm boundaries, post-war buildings, public utility works and forestry plantations. In much the same way that the County Record Office holds a county's documentary archive, and the museum holds its artifacts, so an SMR holds its archaeological 'sites'. This never-ending task has two immutable requirements: (1) the record must be

51

internally consistent; (2) it must be possible to enter and extract information in a systematic, efficient and usable form.

Archaeological information must be recorded and entered into the SMR in a way that is consistent with these requirements. It follows that if all archaeological information should properly be in a county SMR and the NMR, then no matter who collects the data they should be collected with these rules of entry firmly in mind. It is these 'rules of entry' that determine in what form data are collected.

Excavators have long recognized the need for internal consistency in records, and it is generally accepted that, for instance, three-dimensional measurements are essential and that the relationship of one feature with another must be noted even if that relationship is obscure. Horizontal and vertical plans are necessary, and photographs of the site or features within that site must be clearly tied into the spatial and temporal phasing of it. Records of contexts are kept on context cards and, together with the plans and photographs, are the written representation of a two- or three-dimensional form. It goes without saying that failure to abide by these rules does not improve the confidence of colleagues, and a further invitation next season may not materialize. The same may be said of buildings records, where for many years it has been accepted that there are certain measurements that must be taken, and many structural 'thesauri' exist giving standard definitions of architectural forms.

Sadly, this is not always the case for field survey and, in particular, the subject of this paper: the survey of visible, upstanding features. There are no generally accepted scales, definition of structural terms or even agreement as to what minimum measurements should be taken. It is extraordinary that this discipline, with its roots in the work of John Aubrey and William Stukeley, should still be carried out to widely differing standards. Yet the survey of individual sites and the mapping of historic landscapes represent one of the greatest and most exciting challenges facing archaeologists today.

Translating heroic words into action is not easy, but a look at what is missing in so much fieldwork can indicate where improvements should be made. Field survey should be based on the premise that the surveyor may be the last person to see the remains before they are removed. On that basis, as on an excavation where most of the site is destroyed in the process of recording, future workers, by examining the survey records, should have a fighting chance of understanding as much of the site as the original surveyor. It follows that it should be possible to reinterpret the evidence in the light of more recent experience. This is rarely the case because of failure to abide by the first of those SMR requirements:

1. Internal consistency of the record

a. *Descriptive terms*. There are few accepted descriptive terms in field survey. Site types *are* gradually being standardized so that barrow, cairn, longhouse, deserted medieval village, engine house, windmill mound, and so on, are accepted terms. The same is not the case for features such as walls, ditches, banks, lynchets, hollow-ways and the like. If we divide what we are surveying into positive and negative features there are any number of discrepancies in description. For example:

Positive features. When is a wall a wall? Does it have to be faced on both sides to be a wall? If what used to be a wall is tumbled to such an extent that none of the original facing is visible then should it be called a wall or a stone bank? When surveying a substantial wall that is faced on both sides and filled with stones is it adequate simply to call it a wall when a drystone wall, only one stone thick, can also be called a wall? To go further, if a boundary is faced on one side and is a bank on the other, one surveyor may call it a wall and another a stone-faced bank.

Negative features. When is a ditch a hollow-way or a gully or dyke? There are often different dialect terms in many areas of the country.

The problem is not the dialect variation of description but the lack of definition of those terms. It is crucial that definitions are consistent and defined within an SMR.

b. *Standard measurements.* Do surveyors consistently measure height, width, thickness, depth, diameter, length and area, where appropriate, on *each* feature surveyed? Consistent minimum measurements are accepted practice on excavations.

c. *Structure and materials.* Both these descriptions are essential in comparing one feature with another, but are rarely noted throughout a field survey. Structure has been tackled by vernacular building specialists, identifying, for instance, walls that are random or coursed. We should be able to distinguish between 'built' or 'piled' structures, i.e. banks of cleared stones that never had a formal structure and those features that do have a formal structure.

It is also desirable to know whether a bank is earthen or stone, whether a mound is an earthen barrow or a stone cairn, not just in the obvious cases but in situations where the word 'stone' means, for instance, entirely of stone or 'mostly of stone'. These may appear to be finer points of detail but they are at the heart of distinguishing the date and function of features.

d. *Relationships.* One of the most serious omissions is a consistent record of the relationship of features one with another. In the majority of cases it is difficult to make comment, but in some instances it is possible and desirable to note the relationship. So many plans show walls finishing on others and it is tempting to carry them on with other walls on the same alignment. Comment should be made on whether it is certain that a wall stops and does not continue, or, for instance, that one wall overlies another.

e. *Reliability of evidence.* To some extent this is dependent on the proficiency of the surveyor, the scale used, weather conditions, and the like. In moorland areas in particular, the vegetation cover is a major factor in reliability of evidence. Damage through ploughing, trample and other activities can cause features on the plan apparently to terminate or suddenly diminish in size. This is not of archaeological significance but due to extraneous circumstances.

f. *Standard representation of detail.* There are no standard ways of representing walls, lynchets, natural slopes, banks, etc. It is a difficult problem and is at present taxing the combined thoughts of aerial archaeologists, when they consider how to show cropmarks in a consistent form. Clearly the scale at which the feature is shown is important here, where at a small scale it is not possible to distinguish between different types of features. However, many surveys are at a large scale and it is essential that, even if national agreement is a long way off, at least at a local level ditches, for example, are represented on a plan in the same way.

At the end of the survey, too often, all that is produced is a map with varying features depicted and a description of the site. It is exceptionally difficult for one archaeologist to be sure that another archaeologist's work is compatible with his or her own work.

At a more basic level we are often confronted with a survey plan showing lines, dashes, dots, blobs, hachures and fuzzy areas. There may well be a supporting level 3 archive that explains what these are, but in many cases this is not so. Instead it is rather like being confronted with an Ordnance Survey map of a modern farming landscape (where the surveyor's notes had been lost in the Blitz), defining fields and routeways and with black rectangles depicting buildings. From this we are expected not only to identify the different types of field boundary and buildings, but also identify what their functions were. It would be extraordinarily difficult to say whether a farm was an arable farm, a mixed farm, or a farm specializing in animal husbandry, let alone purely in pig husbandry, on the map evidence alone. It is this that we are faced with in archaeological field survey plans. More thought on how to represent features on a plan can go some way to solving this extremely difficult problem.

The six factors outlined above all determine what is described and how it is presented in order to ensure internal consistency of the record. In addition to this, it is necessary to record the information in such a way that it can be entered into an SMR, stored conveniently, and retrieved in a manner that is useful. This is the second immutable requirement, and is to a large extent dependent on the successful completion of the first:

2. Data storage and retrieval

a. *Scale*. The choice of scale is often the crucial decision determining the amount of detail to be recorded. Four factors influence this choice:

(i) *Convenience*—a small board may necessitate a smaller scale; if the area to be covered is large then a small scale may be the only practical solution.

(ii) *Accuracy required*—sketch plans of features are either drawn as divorced surveys or drawn onto existing Ordnance Survey map detail at 1:25,000, 1:10,000, or 1:2,500 scale. Accurate survey seems hardly worthwhile at any scale less than 1:2,500. If one pays for visiting an area and surveys it accurately it is a gross misuse of money if the result shows only the barest detail because of the small scale chosen.

(iii) *Detail required*—at scales smaller than 1:2,500 it is possible to show only the bare essentials of a site, and even here hut circles and longhouses are mere dots or rectangles; again, 1:2,500 is the minimum scale. Even at this scale it is difficult to show hut details, such as internal and external facing, or the structure of field walls and so on. At 1:1,000 most details can be represented on a plan, but for individual monuments such as cairns, kists, hut circles, and other settlements or ritual monuments, structural details become difficult to distinguish at less than 1:500.

(iv) *End user requirements and costs*—1:2,500 is convenient, as the survey details can be easily based on the OS 25 in. maps; 1:1,250 is a popular choice of scale, as many surveyors find it easier and cheaper to double the size of 1:2,500 maps; others prefer 1:1,000 where the facilities for accurate enlargement are available. Above 1:1,000 it is not advisable to use expanded 1:2,500 OS maps. An important consideration is how the survey will be stored and used in the SMR. Most SMRs use 1:10,000 and 1:2,500 maps as a base; consequently many surveys will have to be reduced and redrawn. This stage of the post-survey work is often forgotten by surveyors not connected with SMRs. It would save an enormous amount of time if surveys were handed into an SMR at the appropriate scale for that archive. The original drawings would of course be stored at their original scale.

b. *Recording format.* It is not possible, even when using a large scale, to note all necessary details on the plan itself. A record sheet, context sheet or notebook provides a suitable addition, especially if the format of the sheet forces one to note details in a systematic and comparable form. Surveying in upland areas is often only possible in the winter months, when bracken growth has died down. The weather makes note-taking a difficult and often impossible task. It is also difficult to assign context numbers to a feature if the whole site has not yet been surveyed. In consequence, such essential note-taking often has to be done in the office as soon as possible after the survey. Simple information on, for instance, vegetation cover, relationships between features, measurements and so on, is often forgotten and is difficult to reconstruct after the survey has finished.

c. *Descriptive terms.* These have been discussed already and it should only be emphasized that standard terms used in field surveys should be compatible with the SMR thesaurus.

d. *Storage details.* It is often assumed that it is relatively easy to store an excavation archive in an SMR. Storing notebooks and plans is no problem; the difficulty is retrieving particular parts of the archive in a manner which ensures that it can be compared with other excavation data held in the archive. This is rarely considered to be the province of the excavator, but rather is regrettably left to the Sites and Monuments Officer, who usually has no detailed knowledge of the site. The same is true for field survey, except that often only the site plan is deposited.

e. *Post-survey proposals for site conservation.* Field survey should not be viewed simply as an academic exercise. The archaeological remains are too precious for it to be left to others to sort out priorities for conservation. Surveyors should be aware that sites surveyed may be important enough to warrant protection. Whether this involves direct statutory protection via the provisions of the Ancient Monuments and Archaeological Areas Act, 1979, or the less binding sentiments of County Structure Plans and other local government directives, detailed recommendations are needed. This involves deciding what is important, what are the threats and how these threats can be averted. It may require suggestions for future management, such as scrub removal from settlement sites, removal of unsightly debris, a change in grazing regime, and such like. The surveyor has an obligation to make suggestions in consultation with the appropriate archaeological body which will have to supervise the work and to submit these problems to the archive as a supplement to the academic report.

f. *Publication*. Large-scale field surveys covering many hectares create difficulties for publication. Perhaps the two main considerations are to avoid having to reduce or expand many plans because of the added expense that this causes, and, secondly, to ensure that a full field survey record will involve only a summary publication of the results, with the level 3 archive being stored in the SMR for future consultation by researchers.

The Sites and Monuments Record is the pivotal point in the process of recording monuments. It is no longer acceptable to survey the sites and leave a lot of the post-survey work to others. Indeed, it is the recognition that there *is* post-survey work that marks a change in the attitudes to field survey in recent years. In many cases it is not possible for someone not directly involved in the survey to carry through the process of recasting a record into an SMR-compatible form and make a detailed proposal for protection. It seems futile if the efforts of field survey are not carried through beyond mere academic appreciation to the realms of public display and long-term conservation management.

All the factors and considerations discussed above must inevitably be weighed against those influences that affect all decisions on what and how to survey:

3. Research strategy

a. *Academic/rescue priorities*. Ideally, it is possible to outline academic priorities through both time and space. This is certainly made easier through the computerization of many SMRs and the NMR. Inevitably, many surveys have been justified for reasons of dire threat to the safety of monuments and landscape. Whilst rescue may be the catalyst for action, the academic justification for work must be strong. Too many other calls on slender resources militate against weak academic justifications for action.

b. *Resources available*. Shortages of time and money are by far the most influential factors in determining the scale and detail of field survey. However, no matter how urgent a survey is it should always try to be a standard format, in the same way that rescue excavation and watching briefs try to maintain standards of recording compatible with more leisurely and technically well-equipped excavations. A standard format forces one to remember to record details that would otherwise slip from memory in the heat of the moment.

c. *The nature of the area to be surveyed*. Survey of earthworks in farmland presents very different problems to surveys in rocky moorland. In the latter areas work is only possible at certain times of the year, damage is more likely, and gaining permission for access can take a very long time owing to lack of knowledge of who owns large stretches of common land and moorland. It is not unusual to have to walk for at least an hour of the working day to get to the survey area and, taking into account short daylight hours and several hours of driving, the working day can be reduced (assuming half an hour for lunch) to five hours or even less.

Surveys in farmland can use the OS 25 in. maps as a base, but this is often not possible in upland areas where OS 25 in. cover is not always complete. Lack of identifiable survey points results in divorced surveys, or perhaps the choice of a smaller than normal survey scale.

Differences in vegetation cover not only restrict useful activity to certain times of the year, but also reduce the reliability of the survey, when dense vegetation such as heather, bracken and gorse obscures the detail. Peat cover makes survey patchy, if not impossible, in places.

There are no binding rules for guidance, but a flexible approach will reduce unnecessary time-wastage and economize on valuable survey time.

FIELD SURVEY IN CORNWALL

An attempt has been made to standardize field survey recording on all projects carried out by CCRA. This involves work in the two moorland blocks of West Penwith and Bodmin Moor as well as on individual monuments found elsewhere, such as barrows, hillforts, cliff castles, etc. The system is the same for all, but the scales used are sometimes different. The method of work is certainly time-consuming and involves a lot of paper- and map-work. However, the results are useful, accessible, and will be able to be reinterpreted in the light of future research. Figures 5–9 give a brief introduction to this method.

It is not possible to describe here in detail the method of field survey and recording used, but a brief introduction will give a flavour of what is a developing and reasonably satisfactory methodology. Work is divided into various stages:

1. *Pre-survey preparation*—various permissions sought and gained; choice of survey scale and survey method; production of enlarged OS maps as survey base, if appropriate; division of the survey area into named blocks for descriptive convenience.

2. *Survey*—detail is recorded on survey plans so that features are identified using conventional mapping symbols. Thus a bank is defined by dashed lines, and a faced wall by continuous lines, and so on. Measurements and other information are written onto the plan where possible. Full details are recorded on context sheets either in the field or shortly afterwards.

3. *Post-survey*—the surveys are drawn onto gridded overlays with both 'detail' grids as well as 'explanatory' overlays being drawn. As a second stage the archaeological explanation of the surveys is drawn onto 1:2,500 grids and the detail condensed onto SMR sheets. The 1:2,500 maps and the SMR sheets are then the basic computer-compatible SMR record of that area. All the other records are stored. Finally, reports are written on the recommendations for future archaeological work (i.e. excavations, more detailed survey of certain features, palaeoenvironmental work, etc.), recommendations for statutory and non-statutory protection and proposals for conservation and management.

Scales

CCRA survey extensive sites such as fields at 1:1,000; large earthworks such as 'rounds', hillforts and cliff castles at 1:500; longhouses, hut circles, cairns, buildings, etc., at 1:200, 1:100 and, exceptionally, at 1:50. In order to

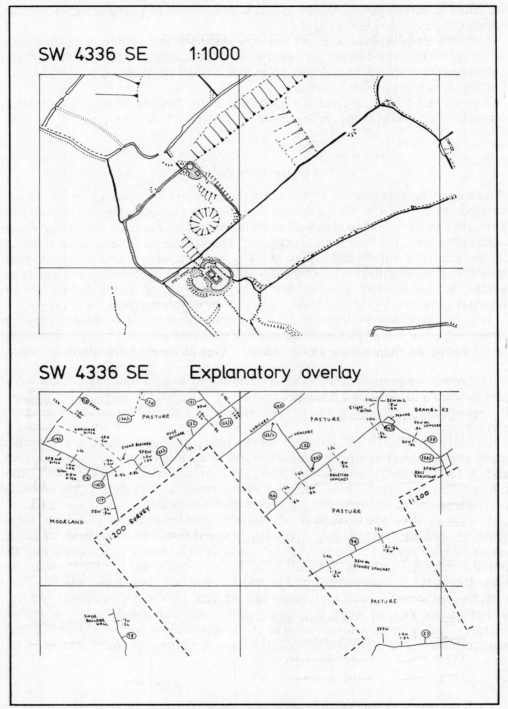

FIG. 5. Example of 1:1,000 survey plan with an accompanying explanatory overlay
(figs. 5–9 aligned to north, with north at top of page)

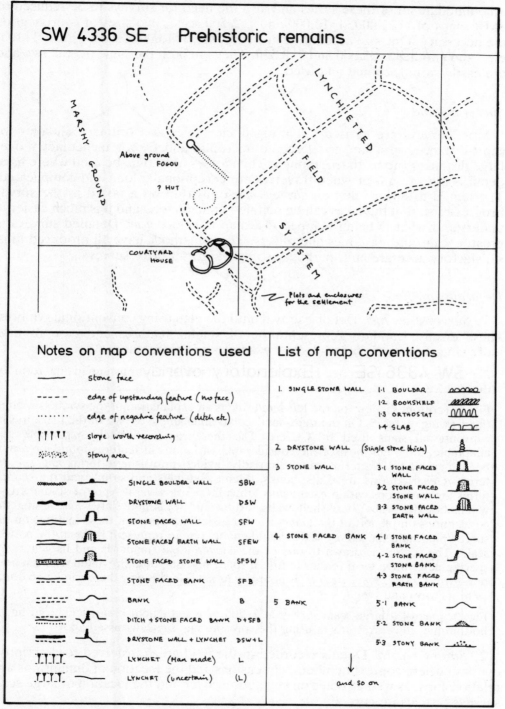

SW 4336 SE   Prehistoric remains

MARSHY GROUND

LYNCHETTED FIELD SYSTEM

Above ground FOGOU

? HUT

COURTYARD HOUSE

Plots and enclosures for the settlement

Notes on map conventions used

— — stone face

- - - - edge of upstanding feature (no face)

· · · · · edge of negative feature (ditch etc)

꜀꜀꜀꜀꜀ slope worth recording

꜀꜀꜀꜀꜀ stony area

SINGLE BOULDER WALL	SBW
DRYSTONE WALL	DSW
STONE FACED WALL	SFW
STONE FACED EARTH WALL	SFEW
STONE FACED STONE WALL	SFSW
STONE FACED BANK	SFB
BANK	B
DITCH + STONE FACED BANK	D+SFB
DRYSTONE WALL + LYNCHET	DSW+L
LYNCHET (Man made)	L
LYNCHET (uncertain)	(L)

List of map conventions

1. SINGLE STONE WALL
   - 1·1 BOULDER
   - 1·2 BOOKSHELF
   - 1·3 ORTHOSTAT
   - 1·4 SLAB

2. DRYSTONE WALL (Single stone thick)

3. STONE WALL
   - 3·1 STONE FACED WALL
   - 3·2 STONE FACED STONE WALL
   - 3·3 STONE FACED EARTH WALL

4. STONE FACED BANK
   - 4·1 STONE FACED BANK
   - 4·2 STONE FACED STONE BANK
   - 4·3 STONE FACED EARTH BANK

5. BANK
   - 5·1 BANK
   - 5·2 STONE BANK
   - 5·3 STONY BANK

and so on

FIG. 6. Examples of 1:1,000 survey archaeological interpretation plan and the conventional signs and descriptions used in survey and recording on fig. 5

accommodate all of these scales and also the need for surveys to be reduced to SMR maps of 1:25,000, 1:10,000 and 1:2,500 scale, two sizes of overlay grids are necessary. One size accommodates 1:10,000, 1:1,000, 1:500, 1:200, 1:100, etc., and another 1:25,000 and 1:2,500. They are both the same overall size and are easily stored, copied and used.

Survey method

Most surveys are carried out using plane tables and ordinary alidades for short-distance work and a telescopic microptic alidade for tacheometry over large distances (up to 100 m. radius). Theodolites need only be used where fixed detail is not present or when traverses are exceptionally long and complicated. The aim is to ensure that all surveys are drawn up on a board as the survey progresses so that mistakes can be rectified immediately, and it is much easier to understand what is being mapped if a map is before you. Detailed surveys at greater scales use baselines and offsets. These methods have all produced most satisfactory accurate and, perhaps as important, sensitive surveys.

Recording method

1. *Survey drawings.* Detail is drawn onto the plan using conventional symbols. These ensure standard representation of similar features and ease of final redrawing. Figures 5, 6 and 8 show examples of this method.

Fig. 5: (top section) part of a 1:1,000 survey with the details drawn up in final form for the archive.

Fig. 6: (bottom section) on the left-hand side is an explanation of the symbols used in the drawing on fig. 5. On the right-hand side is an example of part of the thesaurus of conventional signs used by CCRA. The thesaurus is infinitely expansible and adaptable, although most of the considerable variations in features found have now been identified. The terms can be broadly divided into *generic* terms and *specific* terms. *Generic* terms are walls, banks, ditches, lynchets and so on, and the *specific* terms are variations within each *genus*—thus there are several types of SINGLE STONE WALL: boulder walls, bookshelf walls, orthostatic walls and slab walls. Using the conventions on the left of the diagram it is possible to represent these features on the survey plan, and the survey scale should enable one to represent these at the correct scale. The feature is drawn to one of the conventional standards and its generic or specific descriptive term (either in full, if space permits, or abbreviated where it does not—STONE FACED WALL or SFW) is noted by its side. In this way there can be no doubt as to its form and type.

Fig. 8: part of a large-scale survey at 1:200 of a settlement area (defined in fig. 5, bottom half in centre) drawn using the conventional signs discussed above.

2. *Survey record.* Details recorded in the field are transferred to descriptive overlays where context numbers, dimensions and the location of dimensions and relationships, as well as notes on vegetation cover and the location of large-scale surveys, are also recorded.

Fig. 5: (bottom section) part of a 1:1,000 survey with all these details recorded on the explanatory overlay.

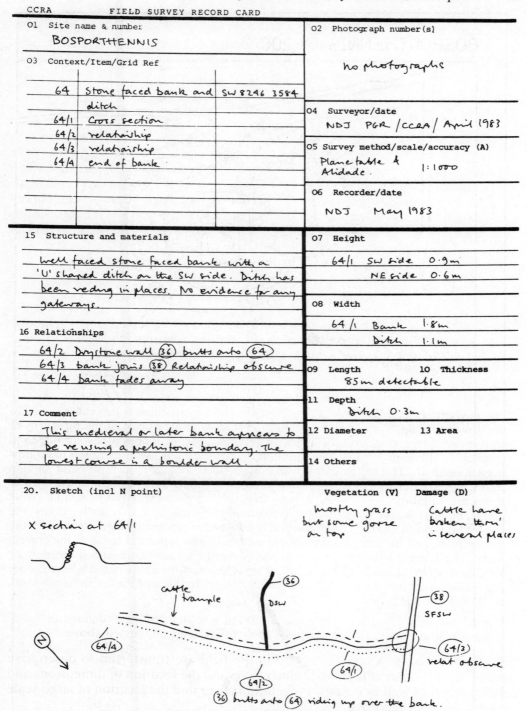

FIG. 7. Example of a standard Field Survey Record Card

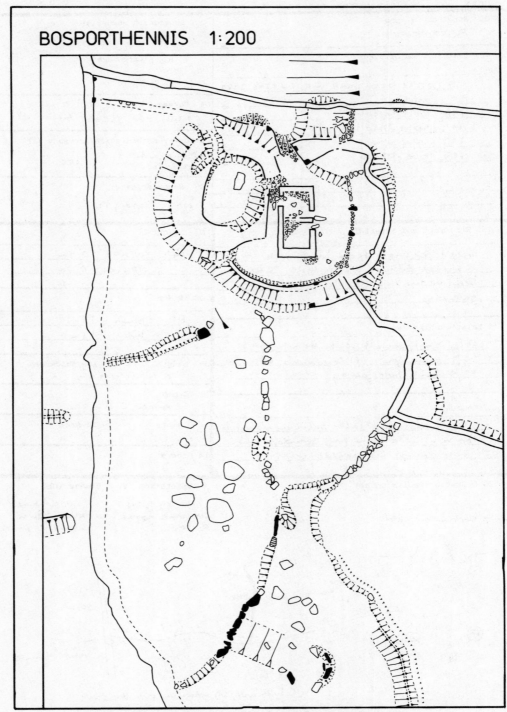

BOSPORTHENNIS   1:200

FIG. 8. Example of a 1:200 large-scale survey of a settlement site

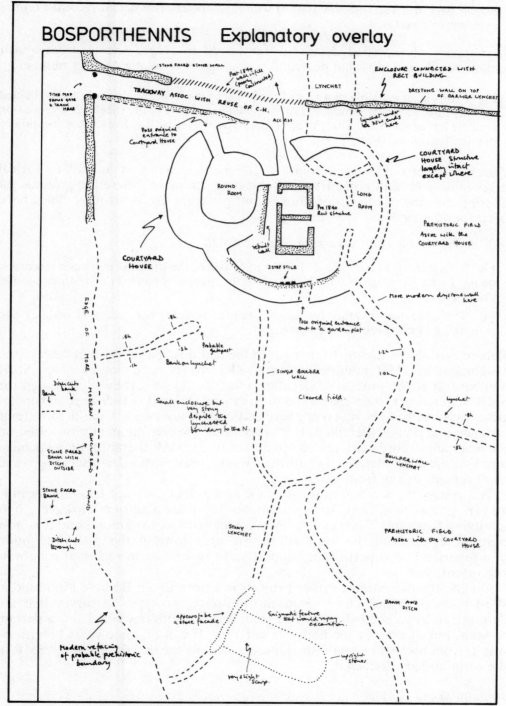

FIG. 9. Example of a 1:200 explanatory overlay for fig. 8

Fig. 8: part of a 1:200 survey (fig. 9) with many descriptive details recorded on the explanatory overlay.

A summary of recorded details is transferred to record sheets, where each feature requiring individual description is assigned a unique context number.

Fig. 7: this is an example of a record card, where the information recorded is divided broadly into: 1. Identification and survey details (top part of the sheet); 2. Description (middle left of sheet); 3. Dimensions (middle right of sheet); 4. Sketch and location of details (bottom of sheet).

The record card has been found to be indispensable as an aid to logical description and both objective and subjective comment. There are grounds for altering the size of the various boxes, but generally the descriptive fields have been found adequate.

3. *Interpretation and accession into the SMR.*

Fig. 6: (top section) part of a 1:1,000 survey where the prehistoric remains recorded on fig. 1 have been extracted. This is part of the process of putting the information into the SMR.

Fig. 9: explanatory overlay for fig. 8. Stippled features are medieval or later and everything else is prehistoric in date.

Record cards have already been made of the features of a survey that deserve the assignment of SMR numbers. Clearly all contexts need not be given SMR numbers. It is the process of deciding what should be retrievable through the SMR numbering system that is the most crucial stage. It is here that archaeological decisions have to be taken; here settlements are defined and field systems assigned and phases identified. It is crucial that the conventional terms used on the maps and record cards are compatible with the SMR thesaurus of descriptive terms. Recommendations for further work, preservation, conservation and management follow from here.

The system works, but although work in the field does not take appreciably longer, post-survey work is now considerably more onerous. However, it is gratifying that after a survey has been completed months beforehand it is now possible, by checking the maps and record cards, to recall the exact description of a feature. This is particularly important as several areas recorded have now been destroyed.

Finally, the two current survey projects in Cornwall, on Bodmin Moor and in West Penwith (Land's End peninsula) illustrate two types of survey that are determined by local conditions. The recording methods described above pertain to both, but the survey methods are different. It will be some years before the results from both will be published, but meanwhile the details rest in the SMR in the form already discussed.

Bodmin Moor

The reasons for surveying this relatively small area of moorland (200 sq. km.) are more fully described elsewhere,[1] and only a brief description is appropriate here. It was felt that the recording of sites in open moorland presented difficulties in survey control, and the variety and abundance of the remains to be mapped made rapid survey on the ground too daunting a task. It was also felt that this was an appropriate area to test the effectiveness of photogrammetry as a technique for recording remains in the uplands. A 1:2,500 scale photogrammetric survey of the moor has been undertaken by Ann Carter of the National Monuments Record (RCHM (England)). All significant archaeological detail has been plotted, as well as natural features that may help identification on the ground. The *c.* 200 1-km. sq. 1:2,500 plots are being checked for accuracy of detail by a Royal Commission survey team in order to test the reliability of the detail shown. The detail shown on the plots is checked, but only in a few sample kilometre squares are the areas thoroughly searched. CCRA are surveying at 1:1,000 scale selected areas in order to check the detail as well as interpret the results for publication. These ground surveys are providing good evidence of what sort of detail is missed on the photogrammetric survey—low ridge-and-furrow unlit by sympathetic sunlight or unemphasized by snow cover, low lynchets, and many features obscured by gorse, bracken and brambles. The 1:2,500 plots are enlarged to 1:1,000 and the details are very easily added in the field. The air photo plots provide a magnificent framework for ground survey and have been found to be metrically accurate. The results of the surveys will form an immense archive and the accession of it into the SMR will take a long time, but the significance of it for archaeological interpretation is huge.

West Penwith

This is the area of courtyard houses and chambered tombs where archaeological remains lie amongst and above the modern farming landscape. The archaeology is very complicated because it is often fossilized within modern fields, and the variety and state of preservation of the remains are well known as being of particular note. Many areas are covered in a low-growing variety of gorse that obscures features from the air, and there are a few areas of featureless moorland that make survey control difficult. In addition, because archaeological remains such as prehistoric field boundaries are often within or beneath modern boundaries, it is difficult to sort out which is which on an air photo. Air photographic surveys are therefore of limited value, but this loss is compensated for by the degree to which OS 1:2,500 detail can be used as a base for larger-scale ground survey. OS detail covers much of the area in the form of small irregular fields and it is a relatively simple matter to enlarge the 1:2,500 maps to 1:1,000 as a base for ground survey. Over a thousand acres of very complicated archaeological landscape have already been planned at 1:1,000 scale, with detailed surveys at 1:200 and 1:100 scale of settlements and ritual monuments. The examples of the survey method shown on figs. 5–9 have been taken from the West Penwith survey project and match exactly the survey and recording method used on Bodmin Moor, as well as many other surveys carried out elsewhere in the county. The most difficult task in each case has been to find the time and resources adequate to tackle the post-survey recording and analysis.

It requires a conscious shift in the allocation of resources allotted to field survey to ensure that the archaeological landscape is adequately recorded and that the record can be usefully retrieved. It is always embarrassing to rely on memory.

Acknowledgement

I would like to thank my colleague, Peter Rose, for much helpful discussion and advice.

NOTE

[1] N. D. Johnson, 'The result of air and ground survey of Bodmin Moor, Cornwall', in *The Impact of Aerial Reconnaissance on Archaeology*, ed. G. S. Maxwell, CBA Res. Rep. 49 (London, 1983), pp. 5–13.

The Maddle Farm (Berks.) Project and Micro-Regional Analysis

Vince Gaffney and Martin Tingle

'The methodology most appropriate for the task of isolating and studying processes of cultural change is one which is regional in scope and executed with the aid of research designs based on the principles of probability sampling' (Binford 1972, p. 135). 'The sampling universe for investigations of populations of cultural items is necessarily the site' (Binford 1972, p. 144).

Since Lewis Binford published his seminal paper on regional research, European archaeologists have displayed an increasing awareness of the utility of field survey as an analytical tool. Archaeological survey results were no longer regarded as evidence of a static settlement pattern; rather, they provided information on whole systems of settlement and the 'rules' that generated them in the first place (Flannery 1976). The scale at which these processes operate inevitably led to the use of probabilistic sampling techniques, as did the limited funding available for fieldwork. At the same time the development of analytical projects was encouraged by the growing realization that our archaeological heritage was vulnerable to the ravages of urban and agricultural expansion (Groube and Bowden 1982; Mercer 1982). Surveys of different regions were needed urgently if academic priorities for fieldwork were to be established. Where these surveys were taking place in 'terra incognita', they could hardly be conducted on a small scale or over a small area. The demise of more local projects, such as the parish survey, is notable when one compares documents such as Hayfield's *Fieldwalking as a Method of Archaeological Research* (1980) with the Wessex Archaeological Committee's planning document (Ellison 1981) or Roger Mercer's recent paper on research strategies (1982).

The changes were inevitable and for the most part desirable. However, it seems that in some cases the use of large-scale survey technique has merely followed fashion and some of its exponents have not paid enough attention to the implications of using probabilistic methods. It would appear that some workers persist in the idea that a regional sampling strategy will somehow provide a data base from which a suitable model of land use can automatically be extrapolated. This paper is not intended as an argument against probabilistic survey—such a

67

stance would be atavistic. If we seek to work on a regional scale, such techniques are a necessity. However, recent discussion of the character of survey data does suggest we should take stock of our progress (Thomas 1975, 1982).

Perhaps the most important change has been the weakening of our concept of the 'site' as the one unit of analysis employed in regional survey (Thomas 1975; Foley 1981). Permanent settlements were not used by all types of community and the traces of their activities may vary remarkably in their visibility (Gaffney and Tingle forthcoming). Moreover, where 'sites' did exist, there may also have been a range of off-site activities which occurs throughout the landscape as a whole (Foley 1981: Gaffney and Tingle forthcoming). The question of site visibility is obviously culture-specific and best dealt with on the basis of individual projects, but it is worth considering the implications of analysing survey results in terms of activities rather than 'sites'.

If one accepts that human activity may be represented by the presence, or indeed the absence, of artifacts, the minimum unit of analysis used by the archaeologist is most likely to be the individual object (Thomas 1975). It follows that in survey we do not sample archaeological *sites*; we sample human behaviour as represented by the artifacts distributed throughout a landscape. Such objects only peak in intensity at those locations we call sites. It becomes pertinent to examine the relationship between the results of surveys conducted at different scales and the types of past behaviour which they attempt to investigate.

In doing this it is worth considering the varieties of land use found in different socio-economic systems. The basic scales of activity have been considered by Robert Foley (1978). Although Foley was concerned with the problems of sampling Palaeolithic and Neolithic settlement, with some modification his scheme can be used in considering more complex societies. He distinguishes between:

(a) The site or residential core area—the area which is traditionally the central point of settlement (and also of archaeological activity!).
(b) The micro-region or home range—the area exploited for subsistence or immediate economic requirements.
(c) The region or total range—the system within which sites and micro-regions interlink to form a coherent and interpretable cultural or economic unit (after Foley 1978).

Whilst field survey does have a role to play, as in investigation of intra-site patterning (e.g. Crowther 1983), more attention should be paid to the broader spheres of human behaviour. Apart from parish surveys and the techniques of site-catchment analysis, little attention has been paid to work at the micro-regional level. Indeed, even these small-scale approaches have lost favour. Parish surveys provide only an arbitrary sample of a landscape, reflecting historic tenurial boundaries, whilst site catchment is based on an idealized model of land use, and its conclusions cannot really be tested. In its traditional form, site-catchment analysis ignores many of the complex social and economic decisions which regulate land use in complex societies, and in any case such models fail to account for the role of 'off-site' activities (C. Gaffney *et al.* in

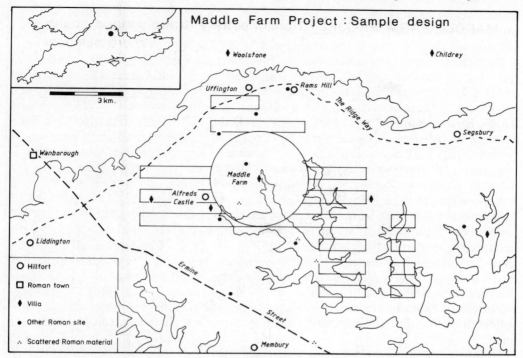

FIG. 10

prep.). However, recent work by the authors on the Berkshire Downs seems to provide evidence of the need to continue research at this geographical scale.

The Maddle Farm Project was initially undertaken to investigate a small Romano-British villa/settlement complex near Upper Lambourn, Berkshire, not only by excavation, but also by extensive fieldwalking. We recognized that such an aim could not be achieved by designing a large probabilistic survey in the area. It was felt that we did not have sufficient data to ensure that we knew what 'sites' would actually look like in the field. All too often the dots on distribution maps are a subjective summary of extremely complex quantitative evidence. Such maps rarely provide the negative evidence necessary to prove that an area was unoccupied.

It was decided that a multi-stage survey should be initiated. In the first stage a circle of 2 km. radius, centred on the villa, was to be investigated and all available land within this area was to be walked—a total of 8 sq. km. The evidence collected from this pilot survey was then to be used to design the second stage, a large sampling scheme composed of systematic transects 500 m. wide and located at 500-m. intervals. The sample scheme was designed to reflect the dominant topography of the area (fig. 10).

Collection occurred within the Ordnance Survey hectare grid located from 1:2,500 maps. Within each hectare, four 100-m. 'runs' took place at 25 m. intervals, always running north–south. Each run was subdivided into two 50-m. traverses, giving a total of eight individually recorded contexts within each hectare. The advantages of such a technique, which was pioneered by Peter

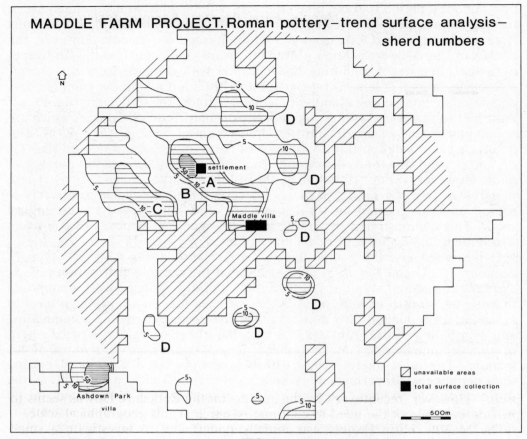

FIG. 11

Woodward (1978), is that the grid is not only permanent, but is standard and nationwide, allowing direct comparison between the results of surveys using the same method. Significantly, at least three other major surveys are using this technique within the Wessex region: the Stonehenge environs project conducted by Julian Richards, the Dorest Ridgeway project directed by Peter Woodward, and Sue Lobb's Kennet Valley project.

In the Maddle Farm Project, total collection on selected sites was also undertaken within the National Grid, using 5-m. squares, which later formed a framework for excavation in the same areas. This allowed the authors to relate surface and excavated data, and by this means to test the results of fieldwalking.

The patterns discussed in this paper are the product of the first season's work inside the circle of 2-km. centred on the villa. Figure 11 summarizes the trends shown by surface pottery within this area. Perhaps the most significant point is that the ceramic distribution is not confined to 'sites' at all. In fact the material is distributed over 500 ha. The nature of this distribution is unlikely to be the result of simple settlement drift, as the major period of discard is confined to a few centuries. Moreover, there is a demonstrable centre of settlement, the villa complex, shown by excavation to have been occupied from the immediate post-conquest period to some time after A.D. 340, possibly with continued use in the sub-Roman period. It seems likely that the majority of the material results from manuring undertaken from a centrally located settlement. However, the density of sherds does not show a straightforward gradient across the landscape, as if the intensity of manuring had declined with distance from settlement. Rather, the material demonstrates that the distribution is far more complex. It is composed of a dense ring of finds immediately around the settlement (fig. 11, A). Adjacent to this zone, with its high density of sherds, are other areas which are apparently devoid of any quantity of archaeological material (fig. 11, B). The latter are surrounded in turn by spreads of more intense sherd discard (fig. 11, c), and beyond this zone again there is an area with a much smaller number of finds. However, it does contain a series of low density *foci* (fig. 11, D). These patterns are not the results of biases affecting our field collection; a series of topsoil quadrats aligned on the fieldwalking grid were sieved to the natural chalk. This demonstrated that there were no significant deposits of colluvium which might have affected fieldwalking results.

It is argued elsewhere that this pattern resulted from a specific type of economy (C. Gaffney *et al.* in prep.), and that the ceramic distribution reflects carefully considered variations of land use within the study area. It is supposed that the decision to manure on such a large scale reveals a fairly high level of agricultural production. We must examine the arrangements for accumulating and distributing the basic material. It must have been necessary to place a herd of suitable animals near enough to the settlement to allow an efficient use of this manure. The most likely reconstruction would involve a dairy herd grazing semi-permanent or permanent pasture. The herd would be brought to the settlement to be milked. Their natural by-products would be collected, mixed with settlement refuse and eventually dispersed to the desired areas around the farm. Naturally, the permanent or semi-permanent pasture associated with such a herd would not show archaeological evidence in the form of sherd concentrations. This pattern may account for area B in fig. 11.

Beyond the zone easily provisioned by the settlement, the laws of energy efficiency would come into play. However, certain problems may have been offset by removing activities from land around the settlement to more peripheral areas, thus allowing less intensive use of those parts of the territory which were difficult to service from the centre. Concentrations of pottery in the outer zone may not be evidence of settlement *per se*; they need only be manure heaps! It would have been most efficient to locate such activity areas fairly evenly and it seems possible that this idea accounts for the minor *foci* located by survey (fig. 11, D).

This pilot survey provides evidence for an ordering of the landscape invisible to both site-based survey and to probabilistic sampling. Considering the evidence provided by the Maddle Farm Project, one may have reservations about the distributions of discrete 'sites' provided in so many surveys, for archaeologists can all too easily condense a vastly complex field record into an impressionistic sketch. This assumes a far more sedentary pattern of past activity than is warranted by much of the evidence.

The results of the Maddle Farm Project emphasize the need to investigate the discard of artifacts well outside the most obvious peaks in their distribution. We need to take greater account of lower-level scatters and negative areas. The latter achieve significance only when the whole field record is scrutinized at a micro-regional level of analysis.

Of course, the sampling strategies used by archaeologists in regional survey are meant to indicate broad systemic patterning and are not designed to identify *all* types of site within the landscape. They can only identify a sample of sites and non-sites. The chances of their detection will depend on the size of the total sample and the techniques used by individual projects (Plog 1976). The relationships between such sites are unlikely to be detected by most large-scale surveys. No doubt a sampling strategy could have been designed to recover the patterns presented here, but it would need to have investigated so much of the study area that the main point of sampling, its cost effectiveness, would have been lost completely.

Again, it must be emphasized that we do not wish to criticize the use of sampling techniques in field survey; indeed, publications of the sampling methods used by our project for survey and excavation will emphasize our firm commitment to such strategies. We wish to demonstrate that when fieldworkers choose the scale of their survey—even in historic archaeology—they are making certain assumptions about the distribution and character of past activities (Foley 1980). Such a choice should be explicit, since the adoption of regional samples will mean that they are investigating one set of behavioural patterns at the expense of others. In studying regional systems we may find ourselves poorly equipped to investigate the subsistence strategies associated with specific settlements or types of site. On the other hand, archaeologists who are working at a micro-regional level cannot expect to model entire settlement systems from a dozen kilometres of downland! Unless we realize the implications of survey decisions at every level, we may find ourselves in possession of data we cannot understand.

This paper opened with two quotations from Lewis Binford's paper on research design. We felt that they exemplified a view of sampling in archaeology that some fieldworkers have taken too literally. But it was in the same paper that Binford wrote: 'In any general discussion of method and theory there is an inevitable bias on the part of the writer. It should be pointed out that I believe the isolation and study of cultural systems . . . is the only meaningful approach to understanding cultural processes' (Binford 1972 (first published 1964), p. 136). Twenty years after that article first appeared, we too should try to be as explicit about the aims of our own research.

Acknowledgements

We would like to thank Richard Bradley, F.S.A., for his constructive comments on an earlier draft of this paper; Mark Bowden for preparing the illustrations, and Lorraine Mepham for typing the manuscript.

BIBLIOGRAPHY

Binford, L. R. 1972 (first published 1964). 'A consideration of archaeological research design', in Binford, L. R., *An Archaeological Perspective*, London, pp. 135–63.

Crowther, D. 1983. 'Old land surfaces and modern ploughing. Implications of recent work at Maxey, Cambridge', *Scottish Arch. Review*, ii, pp. 31–44.

Ellison, A. 1981. *A Policy for Archaeological Investigation in Wessex: 1980–1985*, Wessex Arch. Comm., Salisbury.

Flannery, K. V. 1976. Introduction to Chapter 6, 'Analysis on the regional level', part 1, in Flannery, K. V. (ed.), *The Early Mesoamerican Village*, London, pp. 161–2.

Foley, R. 1978. 'Incorporating sampling into initial research design: some aspects of spatial archaeology', in Cherry, J., Gamble, C. and Shennan, S. (eds.), *Sampling in Contemporary British Archaeology*, BAR 50, Oxford, pp. 49–65.

— 1981. *Off site Archaeology and Human Adaptation in Eastern Kenya*, Cambridge Monographs in African Archaeology 3, BAR S97, Oxford.

Gaffney, C., Gaffney, V. and Tingle, M., in prep. 'Settlement, economy or behaviour? Surface artefact patterns and land use interpretation', paper presented at the fourth annual conference of the Theoretical Archaeology Group, Durham 1982.

Gaffney, V. and Tingle, M., forthcoming. 'The tyranny of the site: method and theory in field survey', *Scottish Arch. Review*.

Groube, L. M. and Bowden, M. C. B. 1982. *The Archaeology of Rural Dorset, Past, Present and Future*, Dorset Nat. Hist. and Arch. Soc. Monograph 4.

Hayfield, C. (ed.). 1980. *Fieldwalking as a Method of Archaeological Research*, D.o.E. Occ. Pap. 2.

Mercer, R. 1982. 'Field survey: a route to research strategies', *Scottish Arch. Review*, i, pp. 91–7.

Plog, S. 1976. 'Relative efficiencies of sampling technique in archaeological surveys', in Flannery, K. V. (ed.), *The Early Mesoamerican Village*, London, pp. 136–58.

Thomas, D. H. 1975. 'Non site sampling in archaeology: up the creek without a site', in Mueller, J. W. (ed.), *Sampling in Archaeology*, Tucson, pp. 61–81.

— 1982. *The Archaeology of Monitor Valley*, 1: *Epistemology*, Anthrop. Pap. American Museum of Natural History 58.

Woodward, P. J. 1978. 'Flint distribution, ring ditches and Bronze Age settlement patterns in Great Ouse: the problem, a field survey technique and some preliminary results', *Arch. J.* cxxxv, pp. 32–56.

II. FRANCE

Iron Age Settlement and Society in Europe: Contributions from Field Surveys in Central France

Nigel Mills

Current research concerning the Iron Age in western Europe emphasizes internal development and the study of socio-economic processes as key factors in understanding the important changes that take place in Iron Age society during the second and first centuries B.C. The appearance of the fast potting-wheel, the development of specialist artisanal industries, the manufacture and use of coinage, the spread of large-scale long-distance trade and exchange systems, the construction of *oppida*, and documentary evidence from the Roman authors for well-defined social hierarchies, all show that this is a period of greatly increased socio-economic complexity. However, research has traditionally concentrated on the study of major settlements and burial sites, in isolation from their rural settlement and environmental contexts. Particular attention has been focused on the *oppida*, many of which have been classified as urban settlements owing to their large size, the presence of specialist artisanal quarters, the use of coinage, the complexity of buildings in social and functional terms, and other factors. In certain cases, as at Aulnat-Gandaillat (Clermont-Ferrand, Auvergne), and at Levroux (Indre), a proto-urban phase has been defined in low-lying settlements located adjacent to the *oppida* which succeed them. In Gaul, many of the *oppida* continue after the Roman conquest, before being replaced by new administrative towns created by Roman imperial needs.

This traditional research has failed to provide an adequate understanding of the broader social and economic context of the *oppida* and other major sites, since it is evident that the economic and socio-political changes that take place in the Late Iron Age cannot be understood without a firm understanding of rural settlement organization and development. For instance, what is the relationship

74

between the major settlements and contemporary rural sites? Is there a change in the overall organization of settlement between the Early and Late Iron Ages, or are the *oppida* superimposed on an otherwise unchanged settlement system? Do the *oppida* function as 'agricultural towns', with the majority of the population concentrated in them, or do they function rather as political and commercial centres outside the rural system?

Answers to these and similar questions can only be obtained through study of data samples which are representative of the distribution, organization, and development of rural settlement during the Iron Age. Adequate data samples are not available for most parts of Europe, and a programme of field survey has been started in two key areas of central France in order to obtain relevant evidence. This paper considers the methodology employed in the field surveys, and summarizes the methods and results of the first stage of the survey programme. Following general discussion of survey methodology, the areas are considered in turn, through presentation of the local background, survey methods, and results, concluding with a discussion of the wider implications of the studies.

Survey methodology

Field survey consists of a range of techniques designed to collect information concerning the nature, variability, and organization of artifact and settlement distributions across a landscape. Three principal problems are faced in designing a survey programme—that of scale (defining the limits of the area to be studied), that of the specific techniques or sampling design to be used, and that concerning bias in data recovery from different parts of the survey area due to post-depositional factors (soil erosion and deposition, differential weathering of artifacts, differences in modern land use affecting data recovery and comparability, etc.).

Survey programmes in Britain and Europe have tended to concentrate on particular landscape types (the Downlands or the river gravels in Britain, for instance), and to use modern or past political boundaries to define the survey limits. Thus in Britain, parish and county boundaries are often used, for administrative and organizational reasons. In Italy, various surveys (Dyson 1978; Jones 1962, 1963; Kahane *et al.* 1968; Mills 1981) have taken the political boundaries of Roman towns to define the survey areas. However, while these boundaries may be useful for organizational purposes, or be appropriate for studying certain aspects of Roman settlement where the administrative areas are known or can be assumed, they are not necessarily appropriate for looking at prehistoric settlement systems which were not subject to the same political controls. Surveys which concentrate on particular landscape types, or which use modern or past political boundaries to define the study area, may produce important biases in the evidence which must be considered in interpretation. Great care is needed in initial project design, and it is important to be explicit about how and why a particular approach was adopted.

A regional approach, as advocated by Binford (1964), seems most appropriate for initial research designs, since human behaviour tends to be regionally circumscribed. Settlement and land use in one part of a region tends to be closely tied with settlement and land use in other parts of the same region, since imbalances in resource distribution ensure that dependent relationships develop. Such ties are not static, but change through time, and the study of changing interrelationships between different parts of a region is a crucial guide to understanding processes of societal development. The different parts of a region cannot be understood in isolation, since settlement and land use in each will reflect, to a greater or lesser extent, activities and processes in other parts. The dynamic relationship between preferred and marginal areas of arable land during times of population pressure is one striking example of such ties (Mills 1980, 1983a, and in press a), information from both types of area being required to understand the processes involved. The first step in survey design will therefore often consist in defining an appropriate region for the study in hand, and breaking this region down into complementary ecological zones which offer contrasting opportunities for settlement and land use. In the case of agricultural societies, this initial research design is often assisted by analysis of historical settlement systems and their organization over the landscape.

The next step is to select an appropriate sampling strategy to ensure that representative samples are obtained of artifact and/or settlement variability within the different ecological zones. The need for sampling in this context has recently been considered by Cherry and Shennan (1978) amongst others (see also Cherry 1980; Flannery 1976; Mueller 1975) and requires no further elaboration here. However, it should be emphasized that there is no single survey technique or level of intensity that can be regarded as ideal, since more and/or different types of information can always be obtained by using different techniques. Thus immensely detailed and time-consuming surveys of small areas may yield little or no information concerning broader regional patterns. An important distinction here is between surveys designed to look at distributions of individual artifacts at regional and/or micro-regional scales (see, for example, Foley 1981), and surveys designed to look at distributions of permanent settlements (see, for example, Barker and Lloyd 1981; Cherry 1980; Mills 1980, 1981), since the scale of recording required may vary considerably. Multi-stage sampling strategies will usually be needed, initial rapid survey on a large scale being followed up by more intensive work, designed to answer particular problems. Even in initial rapid survey work, there are choices to be made. For instance, the study of Roman settlement systems may require less intensive work, since Roman settlements tend to be more easily recoverable through surface survey than prehistoric settlements (but see Mills 1981). However, such surveys may not give a valid picture of the distribution of prehistoric settlements. The methods employed depend on the questions being asked, and there is an obvious need to be explicit about the aims of any survey work, and the methods used, to enable valid comparison between results in different areas.

The third major problem area concerns bias in data recovery caused by differential preservation and surface visibility of archaeological material in different parts of the study area (see, for instance, Hayes in press; Mills in press b). In particular, it is vital to understand the geomorphological processes which have affected a study area, and geomorphological work should be integrated into survey programmes from the outset, since existing geomorphological data are rarely adequate for archaeological purposes.

A recurring example of bias in modern data samples, illustrated in the Auvergne area below, may be found in regions which possess different types of arable land which may broadly be classified as marginal, preferred, and poorly drained. Previous research designs, modern developments in the form of drainage and building programmes, and differential destruction of evidence through soil erosion and centuries of ploughing, have frequently led to data samples which are biased towards the marginal and poorly drained areas. However, by their nature, settlement and land use in such areas represent a particular adaptation to local conditions, and are usually dependent on processes of socio-economic development in the preferred areas. Settlement and land use in the marginal and poorly drained areas are not usually continuous, and cannot be seen as representative of settlement and land use in the preferred arable areas, although the evidence will provide important indications of processes of socio-economic development at the regional scale (Mills in press a).

These three major problems in survey design and implementation are considered and illustrated in the case studies presented below.

THE AUVERGNE

Background

The central Auvergne is ecologically and geomorphologically diverse, consisting of a long depression containing the Grande and Petites Limagnes and the Allier river valley, bounded by higher relief to the east and west (fig. 12). The volcanic chain of the Monts Dômes lies to the west, rising to a maximum height of 1,500 m., some 1,000 m. above the Grande Limagne. Arable land is scarce and poor over the volcanic mountains, but there are extensive areas of pasture suitable for grazing cattle and sheep. A series of lava-capped plateaux and volcanic outliers with poor arable soils lines the eastern edge of the mountains, dominating the Limagnes.

The vast plain of the Grande Limagne extends over the northern part of the central depression. This plain lies at an average height of 300 m. and is covered by poorly drained, black, silty soils called *terres noires*, underlain by marly limestones. These *terres noires* are several metres deep in places, and initial work on their origin and chronology suggests they have been laid down during the later Holocene, from the Neolithic onwards, but particularly from the Late Iron Age (Daugas and Raynal 1977; Daugas and Tixier 1977; Daugas *et al.* 1983; Gachon 1963; Collis *et al.* in press). The *terres noires* today provide some of the most productive cereal lands in France, but they require extensive drainage before they can be cultivated, and fairly large areas were marshy until recent times.

The Petites Limagnes lie to the south of the Grande Limagne, and comprise a series of more or less extensive basins divided by limestone hills and lava-capped plateaux. The relief forms in the lower parts of the basins include gentle piedmont slopes, low interfluves, broad stream valleys, and depressions. Soils are thin and stony over the tops of the interfluves and upper parts of the piedmonts, becoming deeper lower down, while the depressions are filled with

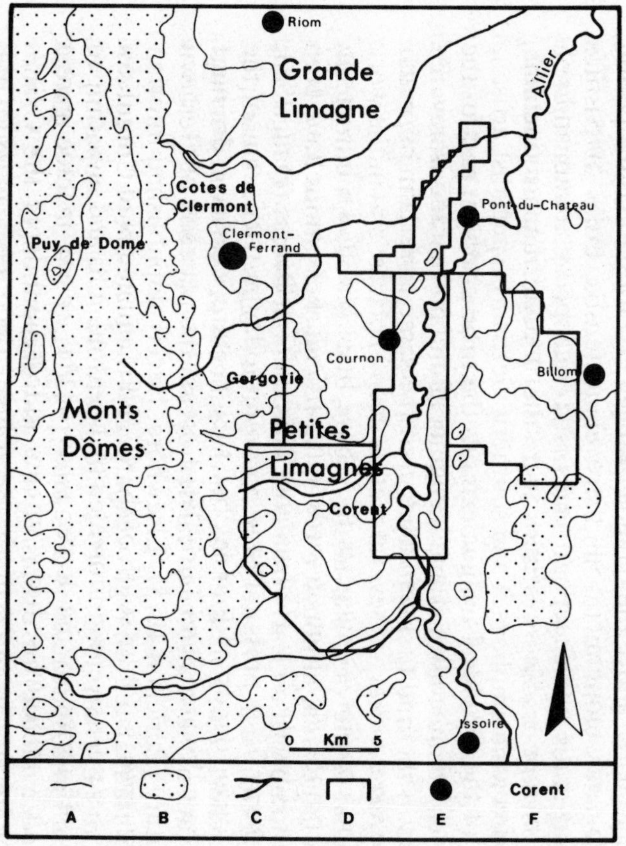

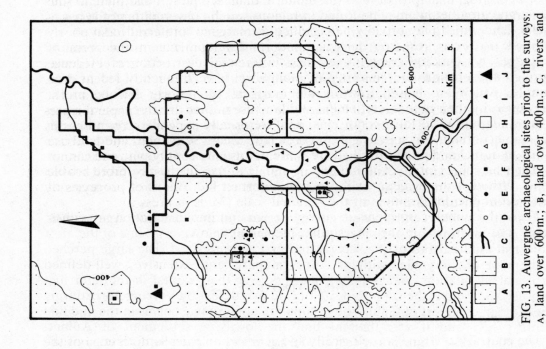

FIG. 13. Auvergne, archaeological sites prior to the surveys: A, land over 600 m.; B, land over 400 m.; C, rivers and streams; D, pre-Late Bronze Age settlements; E, Late Bronze Age settlements; F, Late Iron Age settlements; G, early Roman settlements; H, *oppida*; I, Roman settlements

FIG. 12. Auvergne, relief and survey area: A, contours; B, land over 600 m.; C, rivers and streams; D, survey areas 1979–82; E, major towns; F, major landscape features

terres noires similar to those of the Grande Limagne. The hill and plateau soils provide poor arable land and pasture, while soils in the lower parts of the basins are highly productive under cereals and almost entirely cultivated today.

The Allier valley is the third major geomorphic unit in the central depression. The valley forms a deep trench some 3 km. wide, with a series of gravel terraces in the bottom. The lowest terrace, up to 800 m. wide in places, is of recent date, as shown by finds of modern pottery in its upper levels, over 1 m. below the present ground surface. Finds of Palaeolithic artifacts show that the upper terraces date to various phases of the Quaternary. The terraces are covered by thin soils except where colluvial accumulations occur in footslope positions. These terrace soils are well-drained and extensively cultivated today, mainly with cereals.

The Limagnes and the Allier valley are dominated to the east by more broken hilly country composed of sand and clay-rich rocks. This area is presently devoted to pasture and forest.

This area of the central Auvergne is of great interest for Iron Age studies, since it lies at the heart of the territory occupied by the Arverni, one of the most powerful Gallic tribes of the second and first centuries B.C. The large perched settlement of Gergovie, with its stone ramparts and extensive, well-defined artisanal, habitation, and religious quarters, was their capital in the later first century B.C., and is the supposed site of Caesar's defeat by Vercingetorix during the Roman conquest of Gaul. The occupation at Gergovie begins in the mid first century B.C. and it was thought that the low-lying settlement of Aulnat-Gandaillat, some 6 km. north-east of Gergovie and on the southern edge of the Grande Limagne, may have been the earlier, proto-urban centre, subsequently abandoned in favour of Gergovie (Collis 1975, 1980).

The excavations at Aulnat-Gandaillat have revealed Late Iron Age levels which provide one of the most complete sequences in Europe for this period, running from the early third to the mid first century B.C. (Collis 1983). The richest occupation dates to the second and first centuries B.C., when there is evidence of important trading contacts with the Mediterranean (including numerous imported wine amphorae) and southern Germany, specialist artisanal workshops (bone-, glass-, and iron-working), the manufacture and use of coinage, and a rich ceramic assemblage including abundant painted wares. The site is abandoned in the mid first century B.C. at the same time as the *oppidum* develops at Gergovie.

Alunat-Gandaillat is the only site in the region that has been methodically excavated over a large area, although a few small rescue excavations have been done elsewhere, notably of an Early Iron Age settlement at Brezet (Daugas and Malacher 1975, 1976) and of Late Iron Age pottery kilns (Rue Descartes: Daugas and Malacher 1976; Eychart 1968) in the suburbs of Clermont-Ferrand. Small-scale excavations have also been carried out on the plateaux of Gergovie since the last century (Perichon 1975). Elsewhere, largely unpublished information suggests important Late Iron Age occupation on the plateaux of Corent and Côtes-de-Clermont (Eychart 1962, 1969), and Early Iron Age occupation on these and other hill and plateau tops (Fournier 1943; Hatt 1943). Recent work has also produced evidence for extensive use and occupation of the Grande Limagne in the Late Iron Age (Daugas and Raynal 1977; Daugas and Tixier 1977, 1978; Daugas et al. 1983).

Daugas and others (Daugas and Raynal 1977; Daugas and Tixier 1977; Daugas *et al.* 1983) proposed a cyclical model for the development of Iron Age settlement at a regional scale, using current evidence of Iron Age settlement distribution as their data base (fig. 13). According to this model, the main areas of occupation varied according to changes in groundwater conditions in the low-lying areas. Thus settlement was concentrated on the upland areas in the Early Iron Age, descending into low-lying ground in the later Iron Age as natural drainage of these areas improved, and returning to upland areas again in the later first century B.C. as the lower ground was invaded by marsh once more.

However, no systematic fieldwork had been done in the basins of the Petites Limagnes or in the Allier valley, which have been the main areas of agricultural settlement in the region from the Roman period onwards. It was therefore possible that the existing data sample was biased towards the Grande Limagne and the higher ground, and was not a true reflection of settlement distribution and development over the region as a whole.

The field survey was started with the aim of producing a satisfactory sample of settlement distribution and variability at a regional scale, which would both give a guide to changes in settlement organization and development in the Iron Age, and provide a firm basis for future research.

Research design and methods

The various ecological and geomorphic units provide contrasting opportunities for human settlement and land use which must be considered when interpreting settlement changes through time, and which were used in designing the survey programme. Apart from the Grande Limagne, there is no evidence to suggest that environmental conditions have altered so radically as to affect the essential contrasts in agricultural and settlement potential between the different parts of the region. The pattern of settlement and land use during the historical period therefore provides a useful framework for designing the survey programme.

The best arable soils lie in the area formed by the Grande and Petites Limagnes and the Allier valley, and it is here that agricultural settlements might normally be expected to concentrate. In particular, and apart from an apparent gap in the Dark Ages, agricultural settlements have been concentrated in the basins of the Petites Limagnes, on the terraces of the Allier valley, and on the edges of the Grande Limagne from the Roman period onwards. However, the interior of the Grande Limagne, and the upland areas within the central depression and surrounding it, are special cases which seem only to have been occupied under particular economic environmental, and/or demographic conditions.

Although agriculturally rich, the Grande Limagne is only likely to have been exploited extensively for agricultural purposes either when natural changes in groundwater conditions made the area more attractive for settlement, or when socio-economic conditions favoured drainage and cultivation. Such human conditions would include a sufficient degree of centralized control or co-operative interest to allow major drainage programmes to be established, and, since it is unlikely that such programmes would be undertaken solely for subsistence ends, while the produce itself would have been specialized, access to a redistribution system with demand for agricultural produce.

The upland areas form a second special case, since they are covered by thin soils which provide poor arable land and/or rough pasture. These upland areas frequently have abandoned medieval and later field systems and/or settlements which seem to correspond to the major periods of recorded demographic increase, involving the expansion of the settled and cultivated zone onto marginal arable soils. A similar process may have operated in the prehistoric period, and the occupation of the uplands at particular periods may therefore be an index of population pressure on the more favourable arable land below. The uplands may also have provided particular opportunities for human settlement and economy within the regional system. For instance, the primary economic basis of the volcanic country has traditionally been stock-raising, dependent on access to markets for the livestock and their produce. It is also possible that occupation of the hills reflects a need for defence, while sites such as Gergovie are obvious central places. However, such sites are particular cases and should be differentiated from a more general spread of settlement and land-use over the uplands.

Whether as marginal land, or as a source of particular agricultural produce or raw materials, occupation in these areas must be seen in relationship to human settlement and land use in other parts of the region, particularly in the Limagnes and the Allier valley. In this context, the uplands may themselves be sub-divided, including, on the one hand, the sub-regions of the volcanic country and the hills east of the Limagnes, and, on the other hand, the hills and plateaux that border and divide up the Allier valley and the Limagnes themselves.

Given the potential biases in the existing data sample, the first objective of the survey programme was to establish the pattern of settlement over the historically preferred occupation zone of the central depression. It was therefore decided to carry out a programme of systematic fieldwalking over ploughed land, concentrating on the three major basins of the Petites Limagnes (Sarlième, Ruisseau d'Assat, and La Sauvetat), and a section of the Allier valley (figs. 14, 16). Little work was done in the Grande Limagne apart from a trial survey along the south-eastern edge, since the accumulation of *terres noires* precludes normal surface survey work here. However, the initial work already done in the Grande Limagne provides a broad outline of settlement development in this area.

It was neither possible nor desirable to cover all the designated area, which extends over some 250 sq. km. Following a trial survey in 1979 (Mills 1983b), a combination of judgement and formal sampling techniques was used, taking the three basins, the Allier valley, and the south-east edge of the Grande Limagne as discrete areas or populations to be sampled. These different areas were stratified using basic agricultural criteria and incorporating two main strata: stratum 1—good arable/gentle slopes/basin floors and lower slopes; stratum 2—poor arable/pasture/steep slopes/upper slopes of basins and hilltops. A third stratum comprising accumulations of *terres noires* was added where appropriate in the 1981 season.

The first stage of the fieldwalking programme was designed to assess the distribution pattern of later prehistoric (Neolithic to Iron Age) and early historical (Roman to early medieval) settlements, and the fieldwalking and

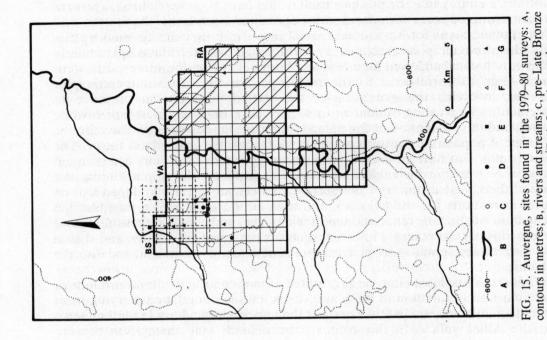

FIG. 15. Auvergne, sites found in the 1979–80 surveys: A, contours in metres; B, rivers and streams; C, pre–Late Bronze Age settlements; D, Late Bronze/Early Iron Age settlements; E, Late Iron Age settlements; F, early Roman settlements; G, Roman settlements

FIG. 14. Auvergne, grid and sampling design for the 1979–80 surveys: A, contours in metres; B, rivers and streams; C, survey areas (BS: Bassin de Sarliève; VA: Val d'Allier; RA: Ruisseau d'Assat); D, 1979 survey grid; E, 1980 survey grid—stratum 1; F, 1980 survey grid—stratum 2; G, squares surveyed; / transects surveyed

recording methods were chosen accordingly. Settlements were defined as centres of permanent or semi-permanent occupation with substantial habitation and other domestic and/or agricultural structures. Archaeologically, such settlements are frequently recognizable by surface scatters of artifacts, particularly pottery, and concentrations (see below) of pottery within the survey area were classed as probable settlements as defined above. Rescue excavations carried out over two concentrations of prehistoric pottery confirmed the presence of settlements by revealing evidence of pits, hearths, floors and post-holes, while the settlement of Aulnat-Gandaillat was originally found using similar criteria.

A rigid definition of a settlement in terms of the density and size of the artifact scatter was not considered useful, since the surface scatter may vary according to a range of factors which differ according to local conditions, including the relative density of artifacts in the survey area (either locally, or at a regional scale), conditions of artifact visibility, such as the state of the soil surface (ploughed, weathered, etc.), and the depth of the site below the present ground surface. The relative density of artifacts across the areas as a whole, and within individual sampling units (1,000 and 500 m. squares) proved crucial, and discrete concentrations of prehistoric pottery showed up sharply against a low background level of isolated sherds. Most of the Iron Age settlements shown in figs. 14–20 have produced at least 100 sherds from a well-defined area (varying from about 10×20 m. to 80×100 m.). A few diagnostic sherds found together were not considered sufficient to define a settlement, but such concentrations were recorded and revisited at different times of year to check whether more material had appeared.

Record cards (fig 21) were completed for each square walked, giving details of the topography, geomorphology, survey conditions, and artifact spread (relative density, type/variety, particular items of note, etc.). Separate cards were completed when discrete concentrations of artifacts were encountered. These concentrations were bagged separately within each square, while other artifacts were bagged according to scatter units which varied greatly in extent. These scatter units were defined by natural and artificial boundaries such as streams, roads, etc., and were used to allow some spatial control over the locations of isolated finds within the squares, while at the same time restricting as far as possible the time spent in recording, labelling, and bagging in the field. This method resulted in a loss of detailed information concerning distributions of isolated finds within particular fields, this loss being more than compensated by the increase in the area covered in the time available (see below). It is the intention to publish more quantitative information on the background scatter at a later stage.

Experimentation with different fieldwalking techniques led to a change in fieldwalking strategy between the 1980 and 1981 seasons. In 1980, kilometre square survey units were used (fig. 14) except in the Allier valley, where an interval transect technique was employed to provide a sample across the different terraces of the valley floor. A 20 per cent stratified random sample was selected in the Ruisseau d'Assat area, but the extent of built-up land in the Bassin de Sarliève meant that squares had to be selected on a judgement basis according to accessibility. Each fieldwalking team consisted of four people, with a ratio of one experienced to three inexperienced walkers, each team aiming to

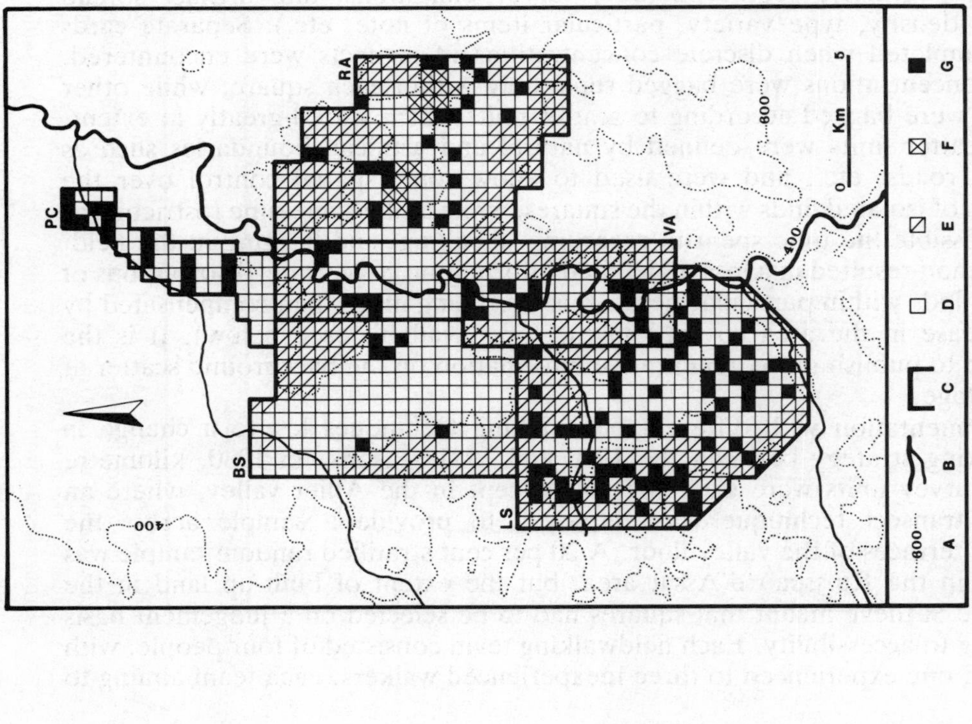

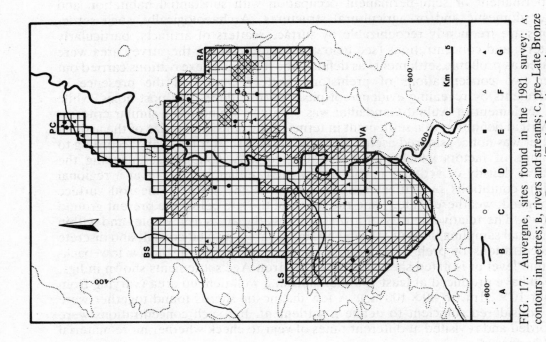

FIG. 17. Auvergne, sites found in the 1981 survey: A, contours in metres; B, rivers and streams; C, pre-Late Bronze Age settlements; D, Late Bronze/Early Iron Age settlements; E, Late Iron Age settlements; F, early Roman settlements; G, Roman settlements

FIG. 16. Auvergne, grid and sampling design for the 1981 survey: A, contours in metres; B, rivers and streams; C, survey areas (BS: Bassin de Sarliève; PC: Pont-du-Château; RA: Ruisseau d'Assat; VA: Val d'Allier; LS: La Sauvetat); D, 1981 survey grid—stratum 1; E, 1981 survey grid—stratum 2; F, 1981 survey grid—stratum 3; G, squares surveyed

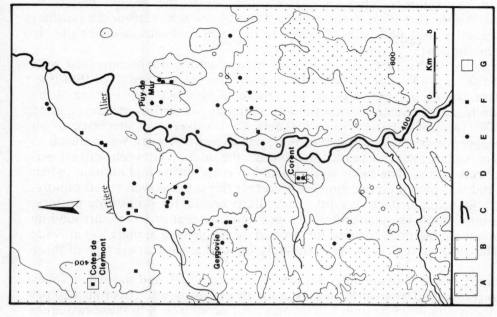

FIG. 19. Distribution of prehistoric settlements in the central Auvergne (all finds up to 1982): A, land over 600 m.; B, land over 400 m.; C, rivers and streams; D, pre-Late Bronze Age settlements; E, Late Bronze/Early Iron Age settlements; F, Late Iron Age settlements; G, *oppida*

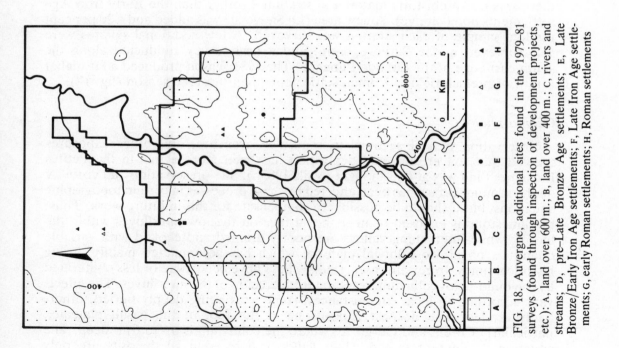

FIG. 18. Auvergne, additional sites found in the 1979–81 surveys (found through inspection of development projects, etc.): A, land over 600 m.; B, land over 400 m.; C, rivers and streams; D, pre-Late Bronze Age settlements; E, Late Bronze/Early Iron Age settlements; F, Late Iron Age settlements; G, early Roman settlements; H, Roman settlements

cover one kilometre square per day, with an interval of 10 m. between each walker. The fieldwalking was carried out over a period of two weeks, with two teams, in late summer, after the harvest but before the ground had been ploughed. Although not ideal, these ground conditions were considered satisfactory, as good results had been obtained in the 1979 trial season under similar conditions (fig. 14).

The results of the 1980 season proved unsatisfactory when compared with those of 1979 (fig. 14), and the fieldwalking techniques were altered for 1981 (fig. 16). 500 m. square units were used, since these allowed better dispersion of the survey units across the area using random sampling, as well as increasing edge effect. The ratio of experienced to inexperienced walkers was increased to an equal proportion of each per team of four, and the rate of work was reduced to two 500 m. squares per day per team, although the interval between walkers was also reduced to 5 m. The fields were walked in early spring and autumn, when the ground was ploughed and rain ensured that the soil was weathered rapidly, thereby enhancing artifact visibility, particularly crucial for prehistoric pottery, which is often badly abraded and similar in colour and texture to the surrounding soil. Each team member covered the ground by zig-zagging along a 2–3 m. wide band. The 1981 surveys took approximately six weeks, with an average of three teams.

Stratum 1 of the Ruisseau d'Assat area was resurveyed, and the Allier valley was also resurveyed by stratifying it as in the three basins, and covering a 20 per cent random sample of stratum 1. This emphasis on stratum 1 in these two areas resulted from the 1979 and 1980 surveys, which did successfully demonstrate that there was less prehistoric material in stratum 2 (other than the Early Iron Age settlements noted above). A new area (La Sauvetat) was added and a 20 per cent random sample of each stratum was surveyed. A few additional squares were also surveyed in the Sarliève basin, and a trial survey conducted along the south-east edge of the Grande Limagne. The 1981 season produced a far higher return of prehistoric and Roman settlements than the 1980 season (fig. 17).

Geomorphology

Observation of soil sections in roadsides, trenches, and other exposures showed that soil erosion and deposition has been more active in the Petites Limagnes than was at first thought (Mills 1983b). Site preservation and visibility on the ground surface has been affected by these processes in certain topographic situations, but it should be possible to compensate for this in future work. Thus, the limestone is exposed or near the surface on the low interfluves within the basins, while intervening valleys are poorly drained and choked with variable quantities of alluvio-colluvial material which has accumulated mainly during historical times. In certain cases, small valleys have been more or less obliterated by the build-up of colluvium resulting from erosion of the interfluves. The effects vary according to local circumstances, some sites being deeply buried, others badly eroded. The deepest deposits lie at the foot of the basalt plateaux, particularly Corent and Gergovie, where the colluvium is up to 6 m. deep. The situation is different in the Allier valley, where colluvial deposits are only extensive in footslope positions at the valley sides. Elsewhere, and apart from the lower terrace with its covering of recent silts, the terrace soils are thin and it is likely that some sites have been destroyed by plough action. Pottery found on the terraces tends to be in poorer condition than in other areas. The mapping of zones of soil erosion and accumulation is intended in future seasons, in order to assess more clearly the influence of these factors on data recovery.

Results

Over eighty new prehistoric and Gallo-Roman settlements have been found in the surveys, giving a total of over 120, including those previously known (figs. 19, 20). The most positive and useful results concern the Iron Age and Roman periods, for which the settlements can be adequately dated. The rescue excavations at Clermont-Ferrand and on one of the survey sites near Cournon

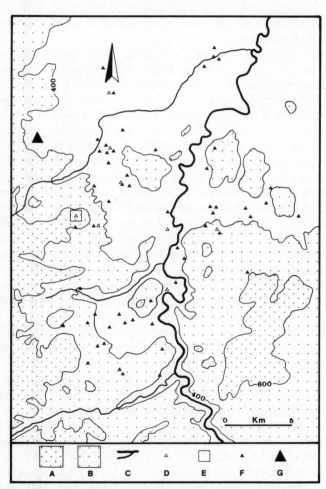

FIG. 20. Distribution of Roman settlements in the central Auvergne (all finds up to 1982): A, land over 600 m.; B, land over 400 m.; C, rivers and streams; D, early Roman settlements; E, *oppidum*; F, Roman settlements; G, Roman town of Augustonemetum

allow definition of Late Bronze/Early Iron Age assemblages, but without more detailed phasing. The assemblages from Aulnat-Gandaillat and Gergovie permit secure dating of the Late Iron Age assemblages, while the material remains of the Roman period are relatively well known through the fine wares.

Thirty-three sites have evidence of occupation in the Late Bronze/Early Iron Age, twenty-four of these being found in the surveys. Almost all the survey sites are located in stratum 1, on the good arable soils of the basins and on the terraces of the Allier valley. However, there are also several sites of this period on the hills and plateaux, and a few sites along the southern margins of the Grande Limagne. Although there is probably some chronological conflation, these data contrast markedly with the traditional view of settlement distribution in the Early Iron Age. The new data suggest a high density of settlement over the prime agricultural areas, other than the Grande Limagne, during the Late Bronze/Early Iron Age, which may have been correlated with an expansion of settlement and cultivation into the marginal arable land of the hills and plateaux within the central depression.

There are marked changes in the distribution and density of settlement in the Late Iron Age, up to the time of the Roman conquest in the mid-first century B.C. Only twelve settlements are known for this period, four of which were found in the surveys. The settlements are relatively numerous along the southern margins of the Grande Limagne, where Late Iron Age levels have been found buried beneath up to to 2 m. of *terres noires*. Isolated finds and burials have also been found well out into the plain of the Grande Limagne. Elsewhere the settlements are rare and widely dispersed, but there are also two major perched sites at Corent and Côtes-de-Clermont, although upland settlement is otherwise less evident than for the Early Iron Age. At least three of the lower-lying sites have produced material similar to Aulnat-Gandaillat, including imported amphorae, and two of these sites continue to be occupied in the later first century B.C., although Aulnat-Gandaillat itself is abandoned at this time.

The post-conquest pattern of settlement appears similar, with a small number of sites widely dispersed over the better arable soils of the basins and the Allier valley. The *oppidum* of Gergovie clearly develops as an important central place at this period, although the main occupation here is short-lived, lasting for about 30 years from the mid first century B.C.

The settlement pattern again changes markedly in the first and second centuries A.D. when numerous Gallo-Roman sites appear, spread widely over the main agricultural areas and over the Grande Limagne. However, while the total number of settlements is considerably greater than during the Late Iron Age (pre- and post-conquest), there is some evidence to suggest continuity of occupation at certain sites from the second century B.C. into the Gallo-Roman period. The Gallo-Roman sites vary greatly in size and extent, from small scatters of tile and rubble with scarce pottery, to scatters covering several hectares and producing abundant building and ceramic remains. No sites have evidence of rich architectural embellishments such as columns, dressed stone, and/or mosaics, although some have produced painted wall-plaster and floor-tiles. The *oppidum* of Gergovie seems to have been replaced as a central place by the town of Augustonemetum (modern Clermont-Ferrand), where recent excavations have revealed remains of fine monumental architecture, including bath-houses with mosaic floors (Sauget 1980 and in press).

Area: Commune: Zone: Square:

Date: Team:

Sites: Period: Collection areas:

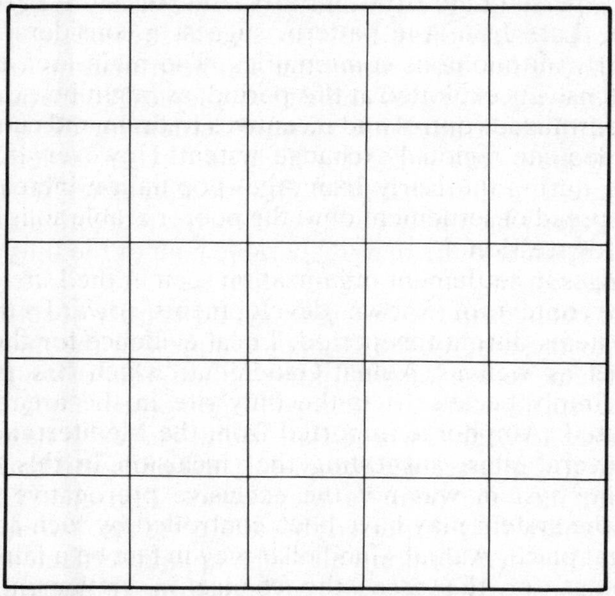

ENVIRONMENT: (Topography, soils, erosion, vegetation, crop)

SURVEY CONDITIONS: (Surface visibility - SA, SB, SC, SD.
Object visibility - OA, OB, OC. Vegetation cover, plough
condition, weathering, dust, stones)

    SA etc. = extent of soil surface visible. SA - 100%
              (e.g. plough), SD - less than 25% (e.g. thick
              growing crop in rows).
    OA etc. = ease of seeing objects in soil (weathering etc.).

ARCHAEOLOGICAL MATERIAL: (Surface features, type & extent
of scatters, soil discolourations, condition/preservation)

FIG. 21. Auvergne/Levroux: survey record card

Discussion

The data are beginning to reveal long-term trends in the development of settlement and society during the Iron Age and into the Roman period. These trends allow us to develop hypotheses concerning the nature of these developments which must be assessed by future work.

The numerous dispersed Late Bronze/Early Iron Age sites, particularly when compared with the Late Iron Age pattern, suggest a considerable population living in small, fairly autonomous communities. The main area of the Grande Limagne is not extensively exploited at this period, as might be expected without a high degree of centralized control and incentives to drain and cultivate the soils generated by an adequate regional exchange system. However, it appears likely that at some stage during the Early Iron Age, population increased to a level which enforced a spread of settlement onto the poorer arable soils of the uplands within the central depression.

The radical changes in settlement organization seen in the Late Iron Age may be placed in the context of known developments towards more complex socio-economic systems during this period. Local evidence for these changes is seen at other sites as well as Aulnat-Gandaillat, which has probably been over-emphasized simply because it is the only site in the area to have been extensively excavated. Amphorae imported from the Mediterranean area have been found on several sites, suggesting that inclusion in this extra-regional exchange or trading system was not the exclusive prerogative of a few key centres, although the system may have been controlled by such centres. Rather than a major central place, Aulnat-Gandaillat may in fact be a fairly typical Late Iron Age settlement for the area, the change in settlement organization suggested by the surveys reflecting the appearance of fewer, larger, more structured 'village' type settlements, each possessing artisanal industries and being integrated in regional and extra-regional exchange networks.

The Grande Limagne seems to be fully integrated into the settlement and land-use system in the Late Iron Age, whereas this area was little used in earlier periods. We know from historical sources that the Late Iron Age in the Auvergne is associated with the rise of the Arvernian Empire, probably involving increased stratification of society as a whole, and increased control by the ruling élite over both social and economic relations. At the same time there is abundant archaeological evidence for the development of complex exchange systems. The large-scale exploitation of the Grande Limagne would have required an organized system of drainage, and outlets for the specialized produce, and both these conditions seem fulfilled. It may be that produce from the Grande Limagne constituted the principal wealth of the Arvernian society, permitting the extensive trade with the Mediterranean area.

We might expect these changes in social and economic organization to be associated with the appearance of central places of some form, and Corent and Côtes-de-Clermont would fit well here, Côtes-de-Clermont perhaps developing after Corent, associated with the expansion of settlement and land use into the Grande Limagne, Corent being better located to service the main settled areas of the Petites Limagnes and the Allier valley. Gergovie lies between these two sites and may have developed as a rationalization of preceding central places due to socio-political factors after the Roman conquest.

The changes in settlement pattern seen for the first and second centuries A.D. are obviously associated with the Romanization of the area. However, the organization of the Roman system, and the way in which the local population was incorporated into it, are poorly understood. Given the absence of rich villas, it may be that the landowning class resided mainly in Clermont-Ferrand, where there is abundant evidence of fine monumental buildings. It is interesting that Augustonemetum develops on the edge of the Grande Limagne, confirming the crucial importance of this zone for the subsequent development of the region, an importance that first appears in the Late Iron Age.

LEVROUX

Background

The area round the modern and Iron Age settlement of Levroux contains two strongly contrasted ecological zones (fig. 22). The Boischaut to the north is a hilly area composed of fairly humid sands and clays, with large areas of woodland and a history of mixed agriculture based on medium-sized landholdings. The Berrichonne plain lies to the south, and is limestone-based with a gentle relief of low interfluves and numerous broad, dry valleys. A few larger valleys have water in them during all or part of the year, and there are several springs, but surface water is generally scarce. Most of the plain is covered with thin, dry, calcareous brown soils which have a high stone content in places. However, many of the interfluves in the southern part of the plain are capped with wind-blown silts which give rise to locally thicker, siltier, more humid soils. There are also fairly extensive accumulations of alluvium in the bottoms of the larger valleys, and Gratier (1974) suggests this alluvial build-up has occurred from Neolithic times onwards. Colluvial deposits were noted in some footslope positions during the surveys, but did not appear extensive or deep, although some masking of archaeological levels has probably occurred.

The present settlement pattern over the plain consists mainly of large dispersed farmsteads, interspersed with a few villages and based since the Middle Ages on the rearing of sheep and goat. However, the introduction of artificial fertilizers and the spread of mechanization has led to major changes in the exploitation system, and the plain is now largely devoted to cereal agriculture, leaving vast expanses of open, hedgeless countryside.

The town of Levroux is of great interest for Iron Age studies in France since, with Aulnat-Gandaillat, it is only the second major low-lying site of this period that has been excavated on a large scale (Bouyer and Buchsenschutz 1983; Buchsenschutz 1981). In addition, a large *oppidum* with *murus gallicus* rampart (Ralston and Buchsenschutz 1975) is located on the hill adjacent to the town, also the site of the medieval castle, while the remains of a small Roman town lie under the modern settlement (Bouyer and Buchsenschutz 1983). The site is located at the interface between the Boischaut and the Berrichonne plain, at a point adjacent to a major communication route through the Boischaut. Excavation in the southern part of the modern town has revealed an extensive settlement of the second and earlier first centuries B.C. The remains include

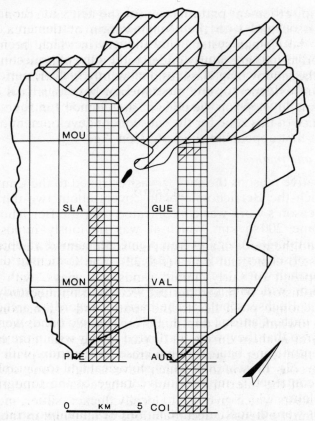

FIG. 22. Levroux: limits of the Canton, major landscape units, survey grid, and sampling strata. The shaded area to the north represents the Boischaut, with the Berrichonne plain unshaded to the south. The two bands surveyed are subdivided into 500 m. squares, each 2 × 5 km. unit having a 3-letter code. The shaded squares represent the stratum with silt-based soils, the open squares that with limestone-based soils. The town of Levroux is marked in the centre

numerous pits and post-holes, with evidence of artisanal industries, and abundant imports of amphorae. The settlement appears to have been abandoned in the mid first century B.C., at the time of the conquest, and replaced by the *oppidum* to the north which has produced indications of occupation in the later first century B.C., as at Gergovie. If so, the *oppidum* is itself replaced by the Gallo-Roman town which develops at the foot of the hill during the first and second centuries A.D. This town is by no means comparable in size and importance to Augustonemetum in the Auvergne, although the remains of a small theatre have been located in the southern part of the settlement.

The excavations at Levroux have been associated with an extensive programme of data collection over the whole of the Canton, including the creation of a sophisticated computerized sites and monuments record (ADEL 1972). This programme of data collection has been based primarily on aerial survey, place-name evidence, chance finds made by local farmers, and existing published sources. Other than the excavations of the Late Iron Age settlement at Levroux, the existing data base comprised mainly isolated finds for the later prehistoric period (Neolithic onwards) and four Gallo-Roman settlements of the first and second centuries A.D. No extensive fieldwalking surveys had been carried out. A survey project was therefore initiated with the aim of collecting evidence for settlement patterns and development in the later prehistoric period which would help place the Late Iron Age settlement at Levroux in its local context. It was also hoped that comparative data could be obtained for the situation in the Auvergne.

Research design and methods

For administrative reasons the survey was restricted to the Canton of Levroux (fig. 22), in which the Berrichonne plain covers about two-thirds of the total area. The first season's work was concentrated over the Berrichonne plain. The plain covers some 200 sq. km, which it was obviously impossible to cover entirely, so a sampling strategy was implemented aimed at obtaining a repre-sentative sample of settlement distribution and development at different periods as a guide for further work.

Two bands 2 km. wide and 18 km. long were selected for study from the grid established by O. Buchsenschutz as the basis for recording archaeological sites and monuments in the Canton (ADEL 1972). The two bands were selected on a judgement basis, so that they were distributed evenly within the eight grid bands covering the Canton, one band running close to Levroux, with the next some 4 km. distant (fig. 22). It was noted from geological and topographical maps that the two bands contained a representative range of the topography and soils present in the plain.

The two bands were divided into 500 m. squares, and two strata were defined, comprising the limestone-based soils on the one hand, and the silt-based soils on the other. This stratification was made since the contrasting agricultural qual-ities, particularly in respect of water retentiveness in a dry area, might have had significant effects on the distribution of settlement at certain periods, which it would be useful to assess. No particular account was taken of the major stream valleys except to check that these were adequately represented when the samples were drawn. This decision was made in the interests of keeping the strategy simple, and because it could not be assumed that the water supply was as severely restricted in prehistoric times as today. Had the water-table been higher, and the dry valleys contained permanent streams, water would have been in abundant supply.

Twenty-five per cent random samples were then selected for survey within each stratum, and within each band. The squares were then fieldwalked using the same technique as described above for the 1981 season in the Auvergne. The survey was carried out with three teams over a period of three weeks in September 1982 (figs. 23, 24).

Results

Twenty-two new sites were found, including twelve concentrations of prehis-toric pottery, and ten concentrations of Gallo-Roman material (figs. 23 and 24).

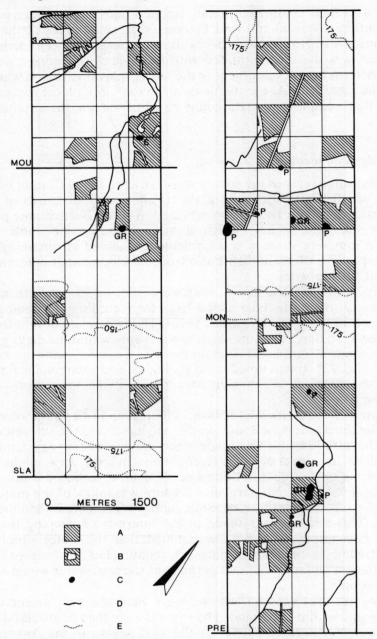

FIG. 23. Levroux, western survey band 1982: A, squares surveyed; B, clear areas within surveyed squares denote zones not covered owing to buildings, etc.; C, sites found in the surveys (S: flint scatter; P: prehistoric pottery scatter; GR: Gallo-Roman site); D, major water-courses (water flows all or part of the year); E, contours in metres

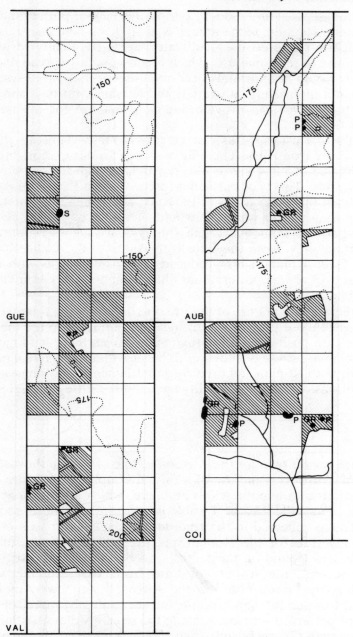

FIG. 24. Levroux, eastern survey band 1982: key as for fig. 23

The prehistoric concentrations are difficult to date since the material is usually rare (twenty to thirty sherds or less), and badly eroded, with few diagnostic sherds. Indeed, a remarkable feature of the area is the almost total absence of a background scatter of either prehistoric or Roman sherds away from sites, while even historical and modern remains are extremely rare other than round the farms. For the historical and modern period this lack of pottery may reflect the traditional land-use system of the area, based on sheep- and goat-raising. Human occupation debris scattered over cultivated areas frequently results from the addition of refuse to farm manure, which is subsequently spread over the fields. Such a process would not normally occur in a sheep/goat-based system in which the fields are not intensively cultivated, and in which, through simple rotation, the animals themselves can provide adequate manure for the needs of local cereal production.

Three of the prehistoric sites can be provisionally dated to the Neolithic, Bronze, and Early Iron Ages. The only evidence for occupation during the Late Iron Age consisted of a few sherds mixed with later material on two of the richer Gallo-Roman sites. This is of particular interest, since Late Iron Age pottery is well known from the excavations at Levroux, and is generally better made and longer-lasting than earlier wares. It would therefore be readily recognizable if present elsewhere. As in the Auvergne, this evidence suggests continuity of occupation at certain sites, from the Late Iron Age into the Gallo-Roman period. Most of the Gallo-Roman sites produced poor assemblages with rare samian, a few fragments of coarse pottery, and tile fragments. Only four sites produced richer assemblages.

The most remarkable feature of the site distribution is the relative rarity of the sites, and their marked preference for locations adjacent to the major streams. Only four sites are positioned more than 800 m. from these, and most are much closer. The sampling strategy allows us to be sure that this is a real pattern which is apparent for both Roman and prehistoric settlements, and suggests that in fact general conditions of water availability have altered little since later prehistoric times.

Discussion

The data are poorer than for the Auvergne, since only one short season's work has been done. However, the use of a formal sampling procedure allows some initial conclusions and hypotheses to be made, which complement the work in the Auvergne. First, the area as a whole is agriculturally much poorer than the Auvergne. This is reflected in the traditional sheep/goat-based economy, and appears equally true for the Roman and prehistoric periods, judged by the poverty of remains found on most sites, and by the relative rarity of the sites themselves. Second, the scarcity of Late Iron Age settlements other than Levroux reflects the trend noted in the Auvergne for fewer, more nucleated settlements at this period. This requires further testing by more selective survey in the areas of preferred settlement along the stream valleys. Although less rich and important than Gergovie and Augustonemetum, the settlement of Levroux seems to stand out against its poor hinterland in a more marked way than the major sites of the Auvergne. A tempting hypothesis, and one which could be tested against data from rural sites and Levroux itself, is that the town developed as the redistributive and controlling centre for the extensive pasture-lands of the Berrichonne plain. The new market outlets of the period provided a foundation for a specialized sheep/goat economy which has continued down to recent times.

General discussion and conclusions

The results of the Auvergne and Levroux surveys illustrate both the failure of previous Iron Age research to consider adequately the underlying processes operating at a regional scale in the development of west European societies during this period, and the potential of organized fieldwalking surveys to provide answers to some of the questions and a firm basis for generating hypotheses and related further research. In both cases, it is evident that major sites, whether the *oppida* or plains settlements such as Aulnat-Gandaillat and Levroux, cannot be understood in isolation from their local and regional contexts.

In the Auvergne and at Levroux, there is evidence for significant changes in the overall organization of settlement between the Early and Late Iron Ages. These changes seem to be associated with the observed trend towards greater socioeconomic complexity and interdependence of communities at a regional scale. In this context, it is likely that settlement locations, and in particular the abandonment or survival of particular sites as centres of occupation, become increasingly dependent on access to communication and exchange routes at local, regional, and extra-regional levels. At the regional scale, such a trend is seen in the gradual emergence of Augustonemetum as the centre in the Auvergne, and the earlier establishment of Levroux as the local centre controlling and servicing the local economic system. One implication of this is that survey work must take account of such variables in second-stage studies to ensure that an adequate picture of Late Iron Age settlement patterns is produced. A further implication is that the precise role of the *oppida* within these emerging systems can only be understood by detailed studies of a range of settlements representative of different parts of the regional system—what sites, for instance, are included at different levels in the regional and extra-regional exchange and production systems?

The surveys also enable us to see long-term changes in the rhythm and pattern of settlement at a regional scale, and in both cases there are indications of the establishment in the Late Iron Age of underlying trends which continue into historical times: in the Auvergne, the emergence of the Grande Limagne as a key zone within the regional economy; at Levroux, the establishment of the settlement of Levroux as the local centre controlling the local system. In both areas there are now important indications of continuity of occupation from the Late Iron Age into the Gallo-Roman period at certain sites. These trends emphasize that while certain aspects seen in the development of Late Iron Age societies may have extra-regional implications, each area will have its particular characteristics dependent on geographical position, and its local/regional agricultural potential.

In a more general context, the surveys illustrate the importance of regionally based research designs for the collection and analysis of data concerning the settlement and land-use systems. In the Auvergne in particular, the existing data base was heavily biased towards two ecological zones (the uplands and the Grande Limagne), which provided a misleading sample of settlement distribution and development over the region as a whole. In fact, the area of most continuous settlement is precisely that which was least well known archaeologically. We can be certain that similar biases exist in other parts of Europe, including Britain, suggesting that our current data bases are inadequate to provide answers to fundamental questions concerning settlement distribution and development. In many cases, the areas least well known archaeologically are those areas of good-quality arable soils which have been preferred areas for agricultural settlement throughout historical times, and were probably so used in later prehistoric times also. These are also areas which are under increasing threat from modern agricultural, industrial, and housing developments, which are least well considered in research and rescue archaeological programmes, and yet which are critical to our understanding of regional settlement and land-use patterns.

The surveys also demonstrate the efficacy and cost-effectiveness of rapid initial surveys designed to obtain a broad picture of archaeological potential, which can then be followed up by more detailed work designed to answer particular questions. In the Auvergne and Levroux surveys the rate of work was approximately 6 man hours per 10 ha. (with a 5 m. interval between walkers), which may be compared with figures for line-walking ranging from 10 to 100 man hours per 10 ha. (intervals from 30 m. to 3 m.) given in Fasham *et al.* (1980, p. 9). In both the Auvergne and Levroux surveys, the low-level resolution of the locations of individual finds was more than compensated for by the rapidity with which an overall pattern of artifact concentrations was developed, enabling second-stage research to be designed more cost-effectively. Thus the whole of the Auvergne survey could have been accomplished in five to six months by a permanently employed team of four, composed of two experienced fieldwalkers and two trainees. This time estimate includes basic finds processing, data sorting and summary reports, but not final analysis and publication.

Acknowledgements

During 1981 the author held a Centre National de la Recherche Scientifique/British Council Research Fellowship. The fieldwork teams in the Auvergne were supported by grants from the Maison des Sciences de l'Homme, the British Academy, the Royal Anthropological Institute, the Explorer's Club, Sigma Xi Scientific Research Foundation, the Ernest Cassell Educational Trust, the Conseil Supérieur d'Archéologie, the Prehistoric Society, and the Wenner Gren Foundation for Anthropological Research. M. Poursat (Directeur, Direction des Antiquités Historiques, Clermont-Ferrand) authorized and encouraged the surveys, and J.-M. Sauget and J.-P. Daugas gave invaluable assistance. R. Perichon and J. Collis encouraged and made possible the survey programme in association with their excavations at Aulnat-Gandaillat, and gave crucial assistance. J.-M. Sauget and G. Loison carried out rescue excavations on two of the sites found during the surveys. M. Desfeuilles provided accommodation and finds-processing facilities at Mirefleurs. E. Arduini, C. Chopelin, and J.-P. Maillard and his family provided help in innumerable ways.

The fieldwork at Levroux was carried out as part of the research programme of the Association pour la Défense de Levroux (ADEL), directed by O. Buchsenschutz (CNRS), with additional funding through the Délégation Générale à la Recherche Scientifique et Technique. Accommodation and other facilities were provided by ADEL.

The fieldwork teams were composed of undergraduates and postgraduates, mainly from Sheffield University. Particular thanks are expressed to the team supervisors: Fiona Cameron, Ian Cumming, Dave Fine, Dick Grove, Colin Green, Peter Hayes, Dave Hosking, James Monnington, Grahame Mountenay, Simon Piéchaud, Sue Stallibrass, Sheila Sutherland, and Claire Soyer.

Note on figs. 13, 19 and 20

The number and locations of sites known prior to the 1979–82 surveys are based either on published data or on personal communications by local archaeologists. The information shown in fig. 13 is largely correct for the Petites Limagnes and the Allier Valley, but provides a considerable underestimate of the number of Late Iron Age settlements and isolated finds known from the Grande Limagne. This is because the data for the Grande Limagne have not yet been satisfactorily published.

BIBLIOGRAPHY

ADEL (Association pour la Défense et l'Étude du Canton de Levroux). 1972. *Carte archéologique du Canton de Levroux, Indre*, CNRS.
Barker, G. W. W. and Hodges, R. (eds.). 1981. *Archaeology and Italian Society*, BAR S102, Oxford.
Barker, G. W. W. and Lloyd, J. A. 1981. 'Rural settlement in Roman Molise', in Barker and Hodges 1981, pp. 289–304.
Binford, L. R. 1964. 'A consideration of archaeological research design', *American Antiquity*, xxix, pp. 425–41.
Bouyer, M. and Buchsenschutz, O. 1983. 'La chronologie du village celtique des Arènes à Levroux, Indre', in Collis *et al.* 1983, pp. 72–89.
Buchsenschutz, O. 1981. 'L'apport des habitats à l'étude chronologique du premier siècle avant J.C.', in Melkon, A. (ed.), *L'Âge du Fer en France septentrionale*, Mém. de la Soc. Arch. Champenoise 2, CNRS, pp. 331–8.
Collis, J. R. 1975. 'Excavations at Aulnat, Clermont-Ferrand', *Arch. J.* cxxxii, pp. 1–15.
— 1980. 'Aulnat and urbanisation in France: a second interim report', *Arch. J.* cxxxvii, pp. 40–9.
— 1983. 'La stratigraphie du chantier sud d'Aulnat', in Collis *et al.* 1983, pp. 48–56.
Collis, J. R., Duval, A. and Perichon, R. (eds.). 1983. *Le Deuxième Âge du Fer en Auvergne et en Forez*, Sheffield University, Centre d'Études Foreziennes.
Collis, J. R., *et al.* (in press). 'Fouilles de sauvetage dans la Grande Limagne', *Rev. arch. du Centre.*
Cherry, J. F. 1980. 'Towards the definition of site distribution on Melos', in Renfrew, A. C. and Wagstaff, J. M. (eds.), *An Island Polity: the Archaeology of Exploitation on Melos*, Cambridge, pp. 10–23.
Cherry, J. F. and Shennan, S. 1978. 'Sampling cultural systems: some perspectives on the application of probabilistic regional survey in Britain', in Cherry, J. F., Gamble, C. and Shennan, S. (eds.), *Sampling in Contemporary British Archaeology*, BAR 50, Oxford, pp. 17–48.
Daugas, J.-P. and Malacher, F. 1975. 'Premiers éléments sur la fouille du gisement protohistorique (Bronze Final/Halstatt) du Brezet III à Clermont-Ferrand, Puy-de-Dôme', *Bull. de la Soc. Préhistorique Française*, lxxiii, 3, p. 66.
— 1976. 'Les civilisations de l'âge du Fer dans le Massif-Central', in Guilaine, J. (ed.), *La Préhistoire française*, II: *Civilisations néolithiques et protohistoriques*, CNRS, pp. 734–52.
Daugas, J.-P. and Raynal, J.-P. 1977. 'Remarques sur le milieu physique et le peuplement humain en Auvergne à la fin des temps glaciaires', *La Fin des temps glaciaires*, CNRS, pp. 545–62.
Daugas, J.-P., Raynal, J.-P. and Tixier, L. 1983. 'Variations du milieu physique et occupation du sol au second âge du Fer en Grande Limagne d'Auvergne', in Collis *et al.* 1983, pp. 10–20.

Daugas, J.-P. and Tixier, L. 1977. 'Variations paléoclimatiques de la Limagne d'Auvergne', in Laville, H. and Renault-Miskovsky, J. (eds.), *Approche écologique de l'homme fossile*, CNRS, pp. 203–55.

— 1978. 'Les variations du paysage de la plaine de la Limagne durant l'Holocène, du tardiglaciaire à l'époque actuelle', *Bull. de l'Institut d'Études Latines et du Centre de Recherches A. Piganiol*, xiii, pp. 429–44.

Dyson, S. L. 1978. 'Settlement patterns in the Ager Cosanus: the Wesleyan University survey 1974–1976', *J. Field Arch.* v, pp. 251–68.

Eychart, P. 1968. 'Découverte d'un habitat celtique et gallo-romain, rue Descartes, à Chamalières', *Rev. arch. du Centre*, vii, 1, pp. 47–51.

— 1962. 'L'oppidum des Côtes, Clermont-Ferrand', *Ogam*, xiv, pp. 68–76.

— 1969. *Préhistoire et origines de Clermont*, Clermont-Ferrand.

Fasham, P. J., Schadla-Hall, R. T., Shennan, S. J. and Bates, P. J. 1980. *Fieldwalking for Archaeologists*, Winchester.

Fieller, N., Gilbertson, D. and Ralph, N. (eds.) (in press). *Palaeoenvironmental Investigations*, BAR.

Flannery, K. V. 1976. *The Early Mesoamerican Village*, London.

Foley, R. 1981. 'A model of regional archaeological structure', *PPS*, xlvii, pp. 1–17.

Fournier, G. and Fournier, P. F. 1943. 'Relève des stations à potérie halstattienne découvertes en Basse-Auvergne', *Bull. hist. et scient. de l'Auvergne*, lxiii, pp. 106–7.

Gachon, L. 1963. 'Contribution à l'étude du Quaternaire récent de la Grande Limagne marno-calcaire—morphogenèse et pédogenèse', *Ann. agronomiques*, xiv, 1, pp. 1–191.

Gratier, M. 1974. *Contribution à l'étude géologique et préhistorique de la région de Levroux*, ADEL.

Hatt, J. J. 1943. 'Les céramiques protohistoriques et gallo-romaines du Puy-de-Dôme. Essai de classification chronologique I: la céramique des plateaux', *Bull. hist. et scient. de l'Auvergne*, lxiii, pp. 95–105.

Hayes, P. (in press). 'Fen edge sediments, stratigraphy and archaeology near Billingsborough, South Lincolnshire', in Fieller *et al.*

Jones, G. D. B. 1962. 'Capena and the Ager Capenas: Part I', *Pap. Brit. School at Rome*, xxx, pp. 116–207.

— 1963. 'Capena and the Ager Capenas: Part II', *Pap. Brit. School at Rome*, xxxi, pp. 100–58.

Kahane, A., Murray Threipland, L. and Ward-Perkins, J. 1968. 'The Ager Veientanus, north and east of Rome', *Pap. Brit. School at Rome*, xxxvi, pp. 1–218.

Mills, N. T. W. 1980. 'Prehistoric Agriculture in Southern France—Case Studies from Provence and Languedoc', unpublished Ph.D. dissertation, Sheffield University.

— 1981. 'Luni: settlement and landscape in the Ager Lunensis', in Barker and Hodges 1981, pp. 261–8.

— 1983a. 'The Neolithic of southern France' in Scarre, C. (ed.), *Ancient France*, Edinburgh.

— 1983b. 'Prospections dans la campagne d'Auvergne', in Collis *et al.* 1983, pp. 22–8.

— (in press a). 'Regional analysis—contributions from archaeological field surveys in France' in Barker, G. W. W. and Gamble, C. (eds.), *Beyond Domestication*, London.

— (in press b). 'Geomorphology and regional archaeological research design', in Fieller *et al.*

Mueller, J. W. (ed.). 1975. *Sampling in Archaeology*, Tucson.

Perichon, R. 1975. *Les Découvertes archéologiques sur l'oppidum de Gergovie*, Pont-du-Château.

Ralston, I. B. M. and Buchsenschutz, O. 1975. 'Un murus gallicus à Levroux', *Gallia*, xxxiii, pp. 27–48.

Sauget, J.-M. 1980. 'Clermont Ferrand', in *Colloque International d'Archéologie Urbaine*, Tours.

— (in press). 'Les fouilles de la rue d'Assa à Clermont-Ferrand', in *Journées d'études sur l'archéologie urbaine*, Feurs.

The East Brittany Survey: Oust-Vilaine Watershed

Grenville Astill and Wendy Davies

A programme of fieldwork currently being carried out in eastern Brittany is part of a larger, multi-disciplinary study of the development and interrelationship of landscape, land use and settlement during the last 2,000 years, focussed on the communes of Ruffiac, Tréal, Saint-Nicolas-du-Tertre and Carentoir in the Morbihan; the four communes, covering an area of 190 sq. km., form a core for intensive study, but the seven surrounding communes will also be sampled in order to take in the whole Oust-Vilaine watershed (see fig. 25). The object of the study is to determine as fully as possible the nature of man's relationship with the land in a long-exploited part of Europe, and changes in that relationship; in simple terms, to investigate how much, what kinds of, and in what ways land was exploited to ensure the maintenance of life and how far individuals travelled in order to do this, both exceptionally and regularly. Work is accordingly aimed at understanding spatial relationships—at sites *and* their environments, and not simply at settlements. The project is therefore concerned with the basic rural economy of village communities, with the effects of exploitation upon the landscape and, conversely, upon the size and nature of the rural social group; hence, its concern is as much with the effects of the landscape upon man as with the effect of man upon the landscape.

The land in this part of Brittany is gently undulating, the folds running from west to east. The rocks are largely fine shales and schists, but some harder beds of quartz conglomerates give rise to a few outcrops; the soils are weakly acid, often podsolic. Nowadays land use is overwhelmingly arable, although there is some pasture and there are small woodland plantations. Settlements in the core include four principal villages (the commune centres) and about 350 subsidiary farms and hamlets; the nearest market towns are Malestroit, 10 km. to the west, and Redon, 25 km. to the south-east on the navigable waters of the River Vilaine. In human terms, this is a much-used and long-used landscape, a major factor in the selection of the area for study, for the project is aimed at investigating a typical agrarian economy rather than marginal conditions. Other factors which influenced the choice of this region are as follows: given the large

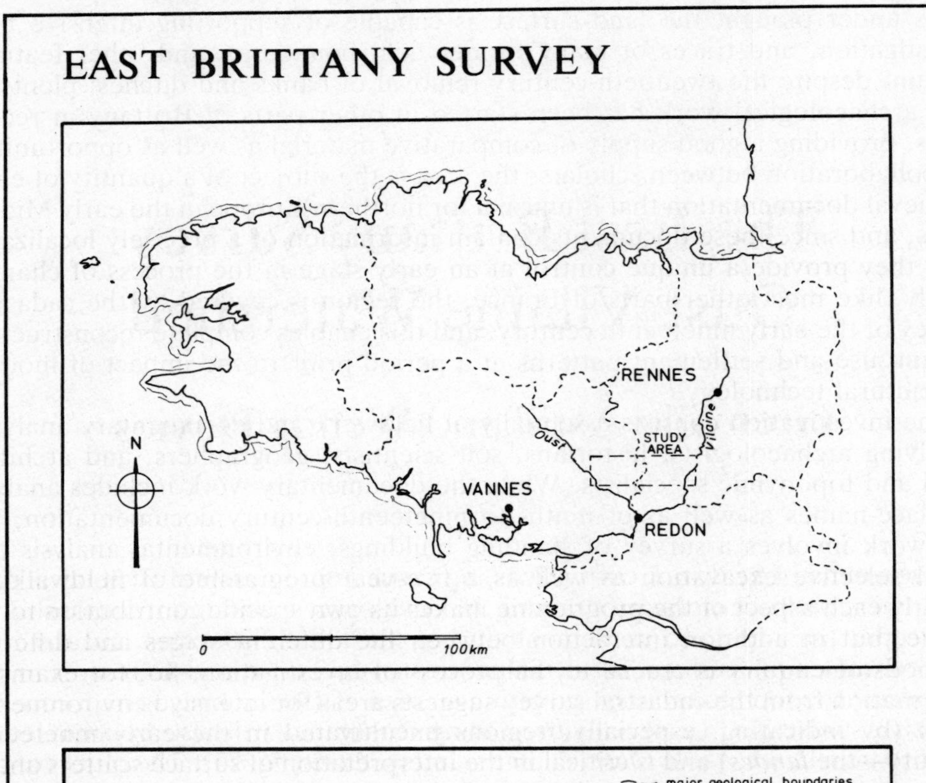

EAST BRITTANY SURVEY

FIG. 25. Above, the study area; below, transects in the core communes

areas under plough, the land surface is capable of supporting intensive field investigation, and traces of many former field boundaries and other features remain, despite the twentieth-century removal of banks and ditches; plenty of new archaeological work has been started in other parts of Brittany in recent years, providing a good supply of comparative material as well as opportunities for collaboration between scholars; the area is the subject of a quantity of early medieval documentation that is unusual for northern Europe in the early Middle Ages, and since these documents contain information of a precisely localizable type they provide a unique control at an early stage in the process of change; finally, like most other parts of France, the region is covered by the cadastral survey of the early nineteenth century, and this enables complete reconstruction of land use and settlement patterns at a period prior to the impact of modern agricultural technology.[1]

The investigation consists essentially of fieldwork and documentary analysis, involving archaeologists, historians, soil scientists, geographers, and architectural and toponymic specialists. While the documentary work includes analysis of place-names as well as of ninth- to nineteenth-century documentation, the fieldwork involves a survey of standing buildings, environmental analysis and small selective excavation as well as a five-year programme of fieldwalking. Clearly each aspect of the programme makes its own specific contribution to the whole, but in addition interaction between the different stages and different methods of enquiry is crucial to the process of investigation. So, for example, information from the cadastral survey suggests areas for intensive environmental work (by indicating, especially, regions uncultivated in the early nineteenth century—the *landes*) and is critical in the interpretation of surface scatters and in determining areas for 'total' collection. Information from place-names is crucial in suggesting the early functions of settlements and fields, while a survey of standing buildings gives precision to the chronology of *recent* settlement history.

The greatest part of the fieldwork is the programme of fieldwalking, by which the four communes will get systematic coverage, organized in stages of increasingly intensive investigation. All available ploughed fields within the core are being walked at 50-m. intervals, with collection units of 100 m., and in this fashion at least 20 per cent of the core's surface areas should be covered in five seasons. Walking is organized within transects 2 km. wide, and weather conditions, the state of the crop, surface features and a plan are recorded on standardized recording forms for each field, in addition to the collection (and subsequent analysis) of material from the surface. In the two seasons so far completed, it is clear that there are considerable variations in the concentration of surface material, which consists, overwhelmingly, of pottery of the thirteenth century and later. The following conventions are used to distinguish between greater and lesser concentrations and to provide a means of reference to them: fields in which more than two neighbouring units each produced five or more sherds of the same period, or building material, are termed 'sites'; fields in which one unit produced five or more sherds or building material, and two or more neighbouring units produced one to four sherds, *or* two neighbouring units produced five or more sherds each, are termed 'probable sites'; fields in which there were irregular concentrations of material not covered by the above categories—for example, one unit with five or more sherds or building material—are termed 'possible sites'. The minimum number of finds necessary to qualify a concentration for comment has been *deliberately* fixed at a low level in order to secure a wide range of possibilities for future testing, although in many cases numbers are far higher than the necessary minimum; it should be stressed, however, that the terms are merely conventions—they do not necessarily denote the position of former settlements.

The second stage of fieldwalking involves rewalking a selection of the concentrations identified in the first, gridding the areas in 5 m. squares and walking to achieve 'total' collection. The selection is made so that all types of concentration—'site', 'probable', 'possible'—in all types of situation—near and far from present settlements, on cadastral arable, meadow, pasture, *landes*, etc.—can be investigated. Hence, types of concentration are defined not merely with reference to transect-walking but with reference to other sorts of input— cadastral, ninth-century, environmental, toponymic. In association with the 'total' collection, soil samples are taken from each 5 m. square for phosphate analysis and a soil magnetic susceptibility survey carried out. Depending on results, some of the fields will subsequently be subject to geophysical survey and some of those to small exploratory excavation. Where appropriate, particularly where there are buried soils beneath banks and lynchets in the neighbourhood of concentrations, environmental work will be undertaken in association with the site-based investigations.

Of equal importance for the ultimate objectives of the project is environmental work which is *not* specifically geared to the interpretation of concentrations of surface material. This involves detailed attention to soils, present and buried, in all parts of the four communes and particular attention to the areas classified as *landes* in the early nineteenth century—it is already clear, from simple augering, that some of the latter have no previous history of cultivation while others, although apparently marginal, do. It is also already clear that the pollen-bearing podsols on the ridges and peaty deposits in the flood plains do offer opportunities for useful environmental work in this area.

It is too early in the programme to finalize results, but initial indications are suggestive. In 1982 and 1983, respectively, 442 and 350 fields were walked at 50-m. intervals, in seven transects, generating over 100 kg. of pottery and man-made building material and locating seventy-nine 'possible sites', fifty 'probable sites' and thirty-two 'sites' (see fig. 26); 4 per cent of the pottery is Roman, 67 per cent medieval and 29 per cent post-medieval, but, although there are a few flints, no prehistoric pottery has yet been recovered. The relationship of concentrations of surface material to the cadastral pattern of land use is sometimes surprising; in 1983, for example, nearly half of concentrations of all types (42·4 per cent) lay within 100 m. of cadastral settlements and 27 per cent within 50 m., but 10 per cent lay more than 400 m. away. As might be expected, surface material tends to be found within areas of nineteenth-century arable— especially in *bandes* (arable divided into tenant strips)—but it is also found in areas of nineteenth-century meadow and/or pasture, in marginal *landes* and in areas of mixed land-use. In some parts, cadastral land-use, naming and road-patterns are in themselves strongly suggestive of former settlement sites, and these suggestions sometimes coincide with concentrations of collected material, as at G60/61 and E89. Such coincidences invite closer investigation, as

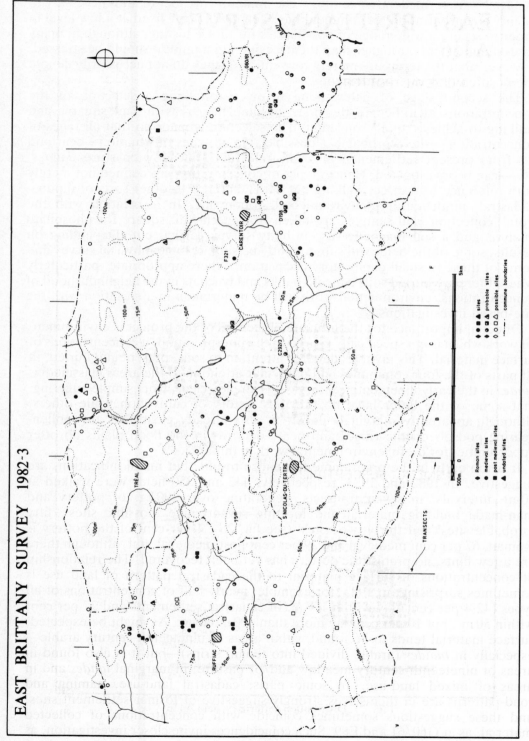

FIG. 26. Sites located in 1982–3

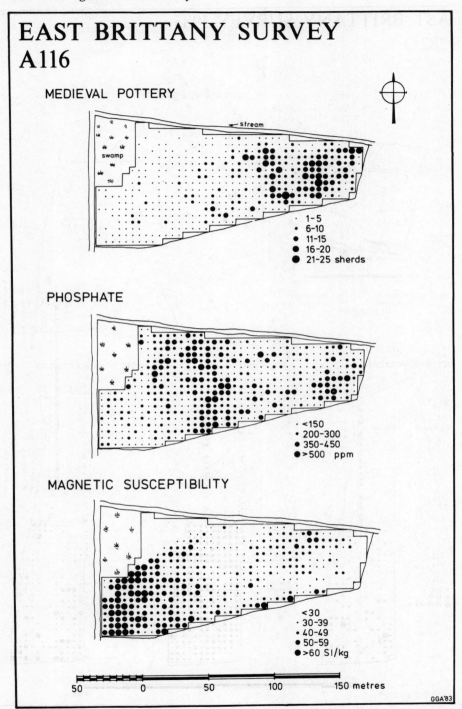

FIG. 27. Distribution patterns on field A116

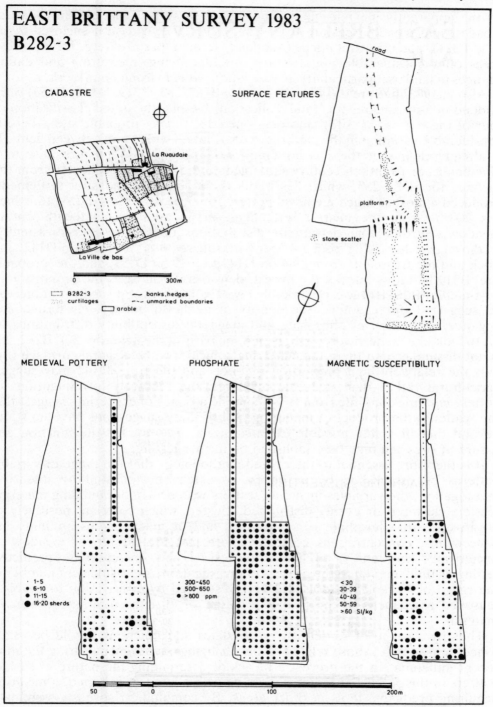

FIG. 28. Distribution patterns on fields B282–283

do the apparently inexplicable concentrations of surface material in cadastral meadow and meadow/pasture (e.g. E89, C292/293), cadastral enclosed *lande* (e.g. F321), and cadastral unenclosed *lande* termed 'pasture' (e.g. D198): these areas offer considerable opportunities for identifying, measuring and dating changes in land use, particularly in association with environmental work.

Also in 1983, five areas (fields A116/124, B282/283, B319, D142, D153) were gridded in 5-m. squares for 'total' collection. Despite the initial classification of four of these areas as 'sites' and only one (B319) as a 'probable site', there is considerable variation in the patterns of distribution within and between fields. It is already clear that there is no simple relationship between proximity to a nineteenth- or twentieth-century settlement and the amount collected from the surface, for B282/283, which lies beside a modern and cadastral settlement, produced almost as much medieval pottery from the surface as did A116, which lies 200 m. from the nearest settlement, in an area of nineteenth-century meadow. Further, the density of distributions does not vary consistently, medieval sherds varying from 4·47 per 5-m. square on A116 to 0·8 on D142, and brick and tile fragments from 3·84 on D142 to 0·29 on D153; and the 'probable site' B319 had low, but not the lowest, densities. In all cases the proportion of post-medieval pottery was remarkably low. Explanations for such variations can be suggested: for example, the density of medieval pottery, clustering, and negative correlation of phosphate and magnetic susceptibility distributions on A116 look like domestic occupation on some parts of the field (fig. 27). B282/283 is not dissimilar, and there the clustering coincides with cadastral curtilage (fig. 28); the relatively high proportion of brick and tile from D142 may suggest agricultural rather than domestic buildings; the relatively low quantities of pottery *and* brick and tile from B319, and the absence of clustering, suggest that the scatter is the product of manuring. All of these suggestions have no status beyond that of viable possible explanations at present, for the function and nature of sites can only be established by further testing.

It is therefore essential to the overall methodology that the range of variable patterns be established by a process of extensive, followed by intensive, investigation, the variables including scatters with or without building material, scatters clustered or evenly distributed, clusters which correlate positively or negatively with phosphate concentrations and/or magnetic susceptibility enhancements, concentrations coincident with cadastral arable or meadow or uncultivated land, and so on. Thereafter testing, and—increasingly—predictive testing, is fundamental to the process of investigation, and a sufficient number of the range of variable patterns will be investigated by exacavation to enable a reasoned assessment of the probable nature of all concentrations of surface material.

Thereby a range of settlement types, dates and functions should be established, and some of those related to the changing environment during the most recent millennia. In the process a means of determining the nature of surface scatters in this particular region should be devised and, it is hoped, a means of acquiring predictive tools in other areas. By combining rigorously systematic fieldwork with full exploitation of all available types of information, it should ultimately be possible to make some statement about the changing complex of spatial relationships, and the effect of environmental and human determinants upon the changes, within the relatively narrow time band of the two historic millennia.[2]

NOTES

[1] See further G. G. Astill and W. Davies, 'Fieldwalking in East Brittany, 1982', *Cambridge Medieval Celtic Studies*, iv (1982), pp. 19–31; *id.*, 'Un nouveau programme de recherche sur le terrain dans l'est de la Bretagne', *Archéologie en Bretagne*, xxxv (1982), pp. 29–42, and *ibid.*, xxxix (1984), pp. 13–23.

[2] Since this paper was sent to press the 1984 fieldwork season has been undertaken: 458 fields were walked at 50 m. intervals (transects J, H, K), indicating a further nine 'sites', sixteen 'probable sites' and fifty-three 'possible sites'; proportions of pottery were 0·06 per cent Roman, 47·6 per cent medieval and 51·7 per cent post-medieval. 'Total' collection was also made for four further fields, G60/61, A91, D282, B236.

The South-West Var Field Survey Project

Fiona Cameron

This field survey project is intended to form the basis of post-graduate research into the Roman settlement patterns in a large area of plain, known as the Permian Depression, of the Provence region of southern France. This plain forms one of the most extensive areas of cultivable land in the region and runs north and east from Toulon to Fréjus (fig. 29). Although a good deal of work has already been done in the area by the Director and staff of the Centre de Documentation Archéologique du Var at Toulon, neither the time nor the money has ever been available to enable them to embark upon a programme of intensive, systematic field survey. Most of the fieldwalking done in the area so far has been related to one of the several major excavations which they have undertaken there.

Because the Permian Depression was part of the first Roman province outside the Italian peninsula, it is of great historical importance, but its proximity to the resorts of the Mediterranean coast means that the construction of modern villas poses a very real threat to the ancient landscape. Thus, when the financial resources became available through grants from the Institute of Archaeology in London and from the Society for the Promotion of Roman Studies, a programme of systematic field survey was undertaken in order to investigate this area while it is still possible. It should be noted, however, that this is a modest operation, and that, up until now, the fieldwalking has been carried out virtually single-handed, so that the rate of coverage is inevitably slow. Nor does the programme enjoy the advantages of some projects, with their back-up teams of specialists. Nevertheless, the results so far have been encouraging, and with less than half the area covered, a considerable number of unknown sites have come to light. It is hoped, however, that after this seasons's work, this time with the help of a small team, most of the fieldwork will be completed.

The Permian Depression, so-called because of its geological origins, runs from coast to coast between the crystalline massif of Les Maures to the east and the limestone plateaux to the west, and shares some of the characteristics of both regions. Topographically it is divided into three well-defined zones: firstly, the

110

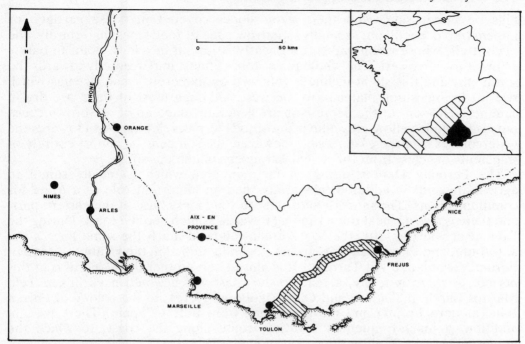

FIG. 29. South-West Var Survey: location of survey area and (inset) Gallia Narbonensis (hatched), Narbonensis Secunda (filled in)

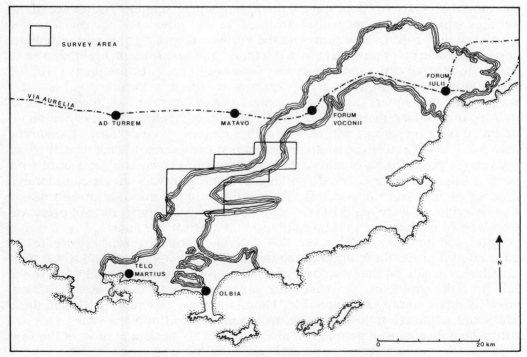

FIG. 30. The Permian Depression in the Roman period

hills on either side, with their steep slopes covered in dense garrigue or impenetrable woodland; secondly, a narrow zone of footslopes; and thirdly, the plain itself, whose width varies from nearly 20 km. at its widest point to barely 1 km. at its narrowest. The whole plain slopes almost imperceptibly towards the south-east and this slight incline is followed by numerous small streams which rise in the limestone plateaux to the west, although most of them are dry in summer. The soils of the depression are generally made up of red-brown clays, but also include yellow-grey alluvia and gravel terraces sloping down towards the watercourses. On the eastern side, however, the soil consists almost entirely of fragments of schist from the neighbouring crystalline massif.

The Permian Depression is, in fact, an area which is ideally suited to agriculture and, in addition, has always had an important role as a route for communications. The modern autoroute to Italy makes use of the eastern part, and there is also an axial route running towards Toulon and the coast. During the Roman period (fig. 30), the Via Aurelia followed much the same line as the autoroute, and three road-stations have been identified in the vicinity—Matavo, Forum Voconii and Ad Turrem.[1] It is almost certain that there was also in this period, as there is today, a road to the coast which would have linked Telo Martius (modern Toulon) and Olbia (modern Hyères) to the colony of Forum Iulii (modern Fréjus) and the great road from Italy to Spain. There was, in addition, a much-frequented maritime route along the coast, to which the numerous wrecks of all periods bear eloquent witness.

When embarking on a field survey of this kind in a geographical unit of this size, it is rarely possible to cover the entire area systematically, and it was therefore necessary to adopt some kind of sampling technique. The choice of the strategy which will be best suited to the area will obviously be crucial to the success of the project. In dealing with the Permian Depression, where systematic survey had been a hitherto unknown discipline, the best solution seemed to be to start with a 20 per cent random sample of one section of it. Consequently, for the first season, an area of about 60 sq. km. was chosen as a starting point and this was divided into squares with 500-m. sides. The squares were then numbered in two separate series, in order to divide those of the hills from those of the plain, and a 20 per cent sample was chosen with a random number table. The survey area was laid out across the width of the depression in order to take in all three of the topographical zones of hill, footslope and plain. During the summer of 1981 some 10 sq. km. were covered, walking at 10-m. intervals, and a considerable number of sites were discovered. These sites were recorded on pro-formas so that descriptions were made of position, topography, soil type, state of preservation, size of pot-scatter, present land-use and a list of the finds.

After the first season's work, the different problems which were to be encountered in the three different zones had become apparent, and it was then possible to decide on the final form which the survey strategy should take. In the hill zone the problems of access were severe, owing to the dense woodland, which is often literally impenetrable. There are numerous hunting trails in these areas and, although following them may seem to be of dubious value, they are often the only means of access. It is also in these very areas that most of the Iron Age *oppida* and late Roman and early medieval villages are to be found.

In the footslope zone, the problems of access can also be considerable, but owe more to human intervention. The same modern villas which pose a threat to the archaeological remains are making their discovery increasingly difficult. These villas are particularly prevalent around the villages which are closest to Toulon itself or to the Mediterranean coast, and their fenced enclosures and guard dogs make access both difficult and, indeed, dangerous. It is also in this footslope area, however, that most of the known Roman villas have come to light, often as a direct result of all this building activity. Some of the archaeological discoveries made in this way are reported to the Centre at Toulon, but it seems reasonable to suppose that the vast majority disappear without trace. The south-facing slopes, in particular, possess all the qualities desirable for the siting of a Roman villa, and it is presumably for the same reasons that most of the modern holiday villas are being built here. Most of the villages which were founded after about the fifteenth century A.D. are also situated in the footslope zone, and those which are on the hilltops can usually be shown to have their origins in the early medieval period.

Most of the surface area of the Permian Depression actually comes into the plain zone, where problems of access are rare and it is often possible to walk 80, or even 90, per cent of the terrain. Almost all of the fields there are at present under vines, and in all but the most ill-tended vineyards the visibility on the ground is excellent. Out of the whole year, it is only during the three or four weeks of the grape harvest that access to this area is at all difficult. All the sites so far discovered in the plain are of the Roman period and include two major villas, but apart from rare instances of deep-ploughing, sites in this zone are only brought to light by systematic survey.

The viticulture which is so widespread in the Permian Depression does present certain particular problems, and it has been necessary to consider its effects on the land and thereby on the archaeological remains. Although vineyards are rarely ploughed, there are, nevertheless, numerous activities which take place almost all the year round and which affect the state of preservation of the surface finds. The tractors may pass up and down between the rows of vines several times a week, turning over the ground, pruning the vines, or spraying insecticides. The result of all this activity is that the artifacts are not only badly abraded, but seem to get dragged along the field, so that the pot-scatter may become elongated in the direction of the vine rows. It is often on the ridges where the vines actually grow, and which are therefore not touched by the machinery, that most of the pottery is to be found. The end result can be a pot-scatter which is not only abraded, but which may cover an area that is disproportionately large in relation to the importance of the site. It was therefore decided that any site hierarchy must depend on the quality of the finds for its main criterion, rather than the size of the scatter.

More recently, however, it seems to have become current practice to dig up the vineyards every fifteen or twenty years and to deep plough the fields before replanting them. A large plough is used, known as a 'balance', which may go down to a depth of 80 cm. The plough is followed by a lorry, and any large blocks of stone, which may of course include ancient architectural fragments, are taken away at once. This practice does tend to be confined to the larger estates, however, and there are still many vineyards where all the work is done by hand. The fact that sites are not ploughed regularly means that new material is not

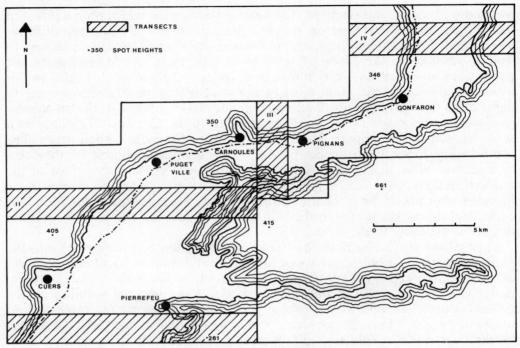

FIG. 31. Placement of transects

being brought to the surface, and if a site has been thoroughly sherded it can be very difficult to relocate. The widespread viticulture also means that the possibility of discovering new sites by aerial photography is not good.

When the different problems of the three zones had thus been assessed, it was decided that the survey should be done in a series of transects (fig. 31). Each of the transects is 1·5 km. wide and is laid out across the width of the depression, again taking in parts of each of the three zones. The transects were placed subjectively, in areas where access was likely to be at a maximum; had they been placed randomly, the possibility that they might include major population centres or otherwise inaccessible land, and thereby reduce the percentage of an already small sample, was considered to be too great a risk. Apart from these transects, a certain amount of time is devoted to a less intensive search of areas where previous work has shown that sites are likely to occur.

In conclusion, the following points seem to have emerged: firstly, this is not an easy area to work in because many parts are very overgrown or heavily built on, but it is an important part of the Roman world and there has been virtually no comparable work done hitherto in Provence. Secondly, it is clear that there are new and important sites to be found which are radically going to affect our understanding of the rural organization of this area, particularly in the classical period. Thirdly, there seems to be a conflict at this time between the team approach to field survey, which can mean blanket coverage, and the individual approach, which normally enforces a sampling strategy. In the case of the South-West Var Survey, sampling is obligatory, but cannot be entirely random, and must be adapted to what we know of the topography and geomorphology. It seems, moreover, that it is dangerous to extrapolate a general model of settlement patterns from a sample which, in this case, is of 15 per cent. Nevertheless, what these two seasons of work have shown is that field survey in this historically critical, threatened landscape is furnishing archaeological evidence of the utmost importance.

NOTE

[1] R. Boyer and P.-A. Février, 'Stations routières romaines de Provence', in *Revue d'études ligures*, xxvi (1959), pp. 162–85.

III. SPAIN

Settlement, Landscape and Survey Archaeology in Catalunya

R. F. J. Jones, F.S.A., T. F. C. Blagg, F.S.A.,
C. M. Devereux, D. W. Jordan
and M. Millett, F.S.A.

The particular problems of archaeological survey in Catalunya derive largely from the heavy use of the landscape over many centuries. It is a landscape which is still experiencing dynamic change. It shares with many other areas the effects of the introduction of modern farming practices, in particular the creation of ever bigger fields and deeper ploughing. It is also clear that the area has undergone very considerable geomorphological changes in historic times. Such areas have large parts obscured from survey archaeology as a result. Although deeper ploughing can be expected to bring to the surface traces of the sites it is destroying, it can be shown that in parts of this survey area all but the faintest traces of ancient sites have by now been removed. In these circumstances, it is necessary to consider carefully exactly what archaeological survey can achieve.

The work discussed here forms part of an Anglo–Catalan research project begun in 1979 and still in progress at the time of writing. It combines a survey programme in the area of Banyoles (provincia de Girona) with the excavation of the Roman and Visigothic villa of Vilauba.[1] Banyoles is situated in the south-western quarter of a lowland area, the Empordà, which extends some 40 km. from the Mediterranean coast south of the Pyrenees (figs. 32–3). The Empordà as a whole provides the main corridor for land routes around the western Mediterranean, but the Banyoles area itself lies to the west of the main routes, and is relatively isolated and rural in character. Although there are several sites of considerable interest, it cannot be claimed that in ancient times the region was of any special importance. In that respect it may be seen as a more useful indicator of the general patterns of ancient settlement than some areas influenced by extraordinary factors.

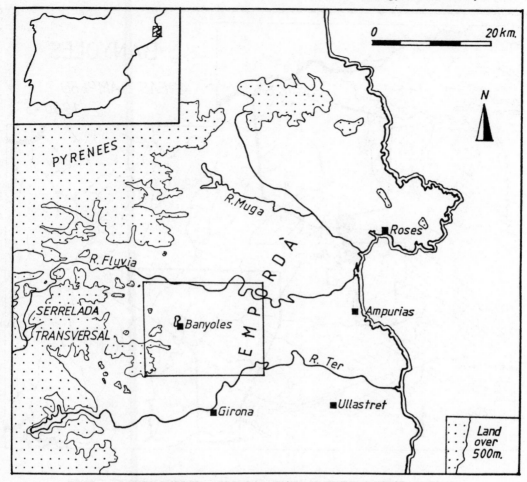

FIG. 32. Catalunya Survey: general location map

In our approaches to landscape and settlement we can define four levels of specificity. The most general is the geomorphological. Next comes the question of site location, which we can deal with both by intensive fieldwalking and by using existing references to discoveries and medieval documentation. Having located and defined sites, we have recorded them in detail, whether standing buildings by drawings and photographs, or buried sites by geophysical survey and gridded surface collection. The most specific technique of all is, of course, excavation, which has been virtually confined to Vilauba, but with some other limited exploratory work.

Geomorphological change has emerged as the first key to understanding the development of settlement in our area. Without an accurate assessment of its nature and extent it would be impossible to progress further. The Empordà is drained by two major rivers flowing eastwards. To the north the Rio Fluvia reaches the sea near the ancient city of Ampurias, and to the south the Rio Ter enters the Mediterranean near Estartit. Both rivers in their lower courses flow

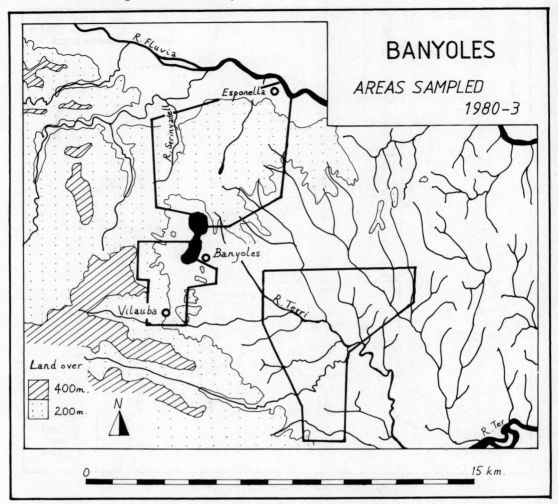

FIG. 33. The Banyoles region in north-east Catalunya

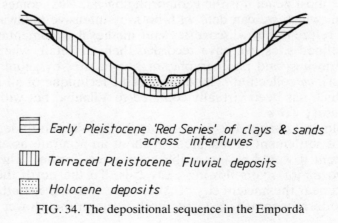

Early Pleistocene 'Red Series' of clays & sands
across interfluves

Terraced Pleistocene Fluvial deposits

Holocene deposits

FIG. 34. The depositional sequence in the Empordà

across wide flood plains, and in their upper reaches are incised into a landscape heavily dissected by current and earlier fluvial episodes. Within the region sedimentation has progressed on a large scale since the Pleistocene, interrupted on occasions by periods of erosion. The earliest clearly defined deposits are to be found near Cornellà de Terri, where bedded sands and clays occupy the valleys to the south-east of Banyoles, in some cases covering the interfluves between valleys. These were seen as Early Pleistocene 'Red Series' by Butzer,[2] but the deposits of the Pleistocene are those which have been reworked subsequently to produce major landscape changes not only in antiquity but also in more recent historical times (fig. 34).

High on the interfluves of many streams within the area, coarse deposits occur consisting of boulders and pebbles held in a matrix of sand and clay. In general, such deposits are cemented and appear a deep red in colour. Crude bedding is apparent in some of these sediments, but sedimentary structures are not clearly defined. A suite of terraces is found in most valleys which in the past have been attributed to various glaciations, by virtue of their height. As terraces are neither at accordant heights nor equal in number in the valleys throughout the region, it seems unwise to determine their age on the basis of a fourfold glacial sequence.[3] In north-eastern Spain valleys have been filled with sediments during the Pleistocene and Butzer has proposed a gradual fall in sea level and absence of tectonic activity to account for the dissected terraces on valley-sides.[4] Butzer is careful not to equate each terrace with pluvial aggradation phases of the established fourfold Alpine sequence.

Most of the available evidence for widespread alluvial sedimentation is to be found in the Holocene deposits that occupy the valley floors. These deposits were recognized several years ago by Vita-Finzi, and have also been identified in Greece by Bintliff.[5] In the Empordà region, valley floors are filled with historical deposits that range in depth from 10 m. to 1·50 m. and are to be found nesting in an earlier Pleistocene deposit. The stratigraphic sequence is characterized by a basal layer of subrounded gravels, pebbles and boulders, derived from earlier Pleistocene desposits, overlain by bedded sands and silts which grade into colluvial deposits. Figure 35 shows the generalized sequence of these deposits, for which the name Empordà Alluvium is proposed. It may be seen that this formation is divided into two discrete members, the lower Girona Gravels and the upper San Andreu Silts. In many cases the San Andreu Silts contain a lens of pebbles, indicated in fig. 35 as the La Bisbal Pebble Beds. A similar sequence of deposits has also been recognized in Mallorca and Portugal.[6] In the Empordà, pottery sherds of pre-medieval origin were found in the Banol valley at Avinyonet at a depth of 2·5 m. in the Girona Gravels. At San Andreu de Terri a piece of tegula was found at 3 m. below the modern ground surface, in the same sedimentary member. More pre-medieval pottery sherds were found at a depth of 3 m. in the Daro valley, 5 km. to the south of La Bisbal, again in the Girona Gravels. The upper San Andreu Silts have yielded medieval pottery: in the valley of the Torrente Junyet at Besalu a sherd less than 200 years old was found 1·4 m. below the surface.

Though a crude dating mechanism, such sherds still testify that the Empordà Alluvium belongs to relatively recent historical periods, but the dating needs to be confirmed by C14 dating. Elsewhere, in southern Portugal, a similar

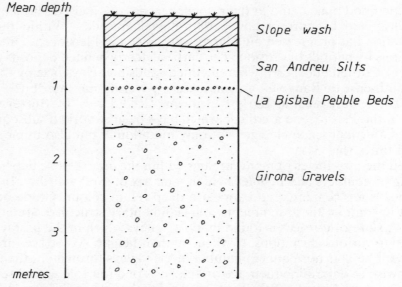

FIG. 35. The stratigraphic sequence of the Holocene deposits

depositional sequence has been dated from 1750 ± 90 B.P. at its base to 520 ± 60 B.P. near the surface, implying a period of deposition from Roman to medieval times.[7]

In archaeological terms much work needs to be done to explain the causes of such rapid sedimentation in recent times. Davidson and Tasker have outlined the difficulties involved in the interpretation of existing environmental evidence in their study of geomorphological evolution in Melos. Climatic explanations of erosion and sedimentation vie with those that see man as the main culprit.[8] Undoubtedly both are important, but studies seeking to throw some light on the matter in the New World have not been replicated in the Old.[9] However, evidence that climate can override the effects of man and lithology has been observed in southern Portugal, where sedimentation and erosion rates in recent decades have been closely allied to subtle climatic shifts.[10] It appears that major environmental changes have been caused by subtle rather than catastrophic events. By the same token, the Holocene valley fills of the Empordà could have been caused by similar mechanisms without involving large-scale interference by man.

Clearly the results of these geomorphological studies have considerable implications both at the level of the techniques of survey archaeology and at that of environmental and historical interpretation. It would be prudent to leave full discussion of the latter until the end of the project. However, at the technical level important problems are posed. A shortage of pre-classical period sites in the area, except in caves, had already been noted.[11] It can be more easily understood in terms of the extent of relatively recent landscape change. Our extensive surface collection has added only a tiny handful of waste flakes of flint to the knowledge of local prehistory. This is, of course, most unsatisfactory for any attempt to understand the overall development of settlement, but it seems effectively irremediable in this area. The large quantity of material from the classical period is partly to be expected simply from the greater durability of much of that period's pottery and building materials, compared with those from earlier and immediately later times. It is also the case that classical period ceramics are more easily recognized than local medieval material, and have been much more studied. Nevertheless, given these reservations, it is still worth stating clearly that the overwhelming majority of the discoveries from surface collection have been of classical date.

In selecting areas to be intensively surveyed it was necessary to bear the geomorphological evidence firmly in mind. There was no purpose in sending teams of fieldwalkers over areas which we had already proved to have been covered by deposits of relatively recent dates, certainly those that were post-Roman. Therefore the first terraces of river valleys were excluded. Also, little attempt has been made to penetrate the quite dense woodland which covers substantial parts of the area. It is normally the case that this woodland is unsuited for survey because of undergrowth and the more or less continuous ground cover of grass, leaf mould and pine needles. Given these limitations, our aim was to examine all fields that were available—recently ploughed and unplanted—over as large a part of the varying topography of the Banyoles area as possible. During our September field season, this normally means that about one in three arable fields are available. Another limitation has been the refusal of some farmers to give permission for survey, for a variety of reasons—including the suspicion that we might steal the farm's hams! More normal was the feeling that something worth money was involved, so that if permission was refused at first, some offer of payment would soon be forthcoming. It never was.

The total area examined has been about 70 sq. km. (fig. 33). In the full publication of the survey precise outlines of the areas covered will be given. The methods of intensive fieldwalking which we have used closely resemble what is becoming standard practice. Teams of up to nine or ten cross a field, spaced at intervals of about 10 m., collecting everything they think might be of archaeological interest. The method is clearly unlikely to recognize the smallest and sparsest scatters. It does, however, allow the relatively inexperienced labour which most surveys are obliged to use to yield a sample of surface material which can later be examined by pottery specialists to define what is diagnostic. The heavy reliance placed on what is termed 'diagnostic' must worry many archaeologists in the Mediterranean, where the common wares of so many periods remain virtually unstudied. Finally, this method of collection in transects that are widely spaced does mean that where some concentration of finds is deemed a site, the field surface should still have on it sufficient finds for more detailed surveys to record spatial distributions. We have also made use of local knowledge to identify sites already found. As in most parts of Catalunya, local antiquarian interest has a long and quite active history, and present activity. It is, however, disappointing that many early finds have only been recorded as 'somewhere near' a particular village. Nonetheless, these discoveries provide an essential background to modern work, and we have been grateful to take sites found through local amateur interests for more detailed study, including the Vilauba villa itself.

One of the most difficult problems encountered by virtually all surveys is that of site definition. What exactly constitutes a site? How dense does the evidence of occupation have to be? In several cases we have found only a handful of sherds of recognizably ancient types in a field—perhaps only two or three. There may also be sherds of less characteristic fabrics, which are probably ancient, but not yet demonstrably so. There may or may not be tile on Roman sites: we have found undisputed sites of that period with and without it. The difficulty remains of how to interpret the handful of undeniably ancient finds. It has been argued that the manuring of fields has left a thin scatter of ancient material across the whole landscape, so that occasional, isolated finds must be dismissed as 'noise'. However, our experience suggests that there is little such 'noise' in the Banyoles area. Certainly there is abundant evidence of post-medieval manuring of the fields, but where positively ancient material does occur in very small quantities, it is usually accompanied by rather more fragments of fabrics in the 'probably ancient' category. This seems to point to the surface material reflecting a genuine site of ancient activity. It therefore seems reasonable to plot on our distribution maps even very small groups of ancient finds, especially in view of the evident heavy damage suffered by many sites from erosion and ploughing. However, it is important that the exact nature of what has actually been found should always be made explicit and that the grounds on which sites are separated from occasional finds are made clear for every survey. Our own final judgement on where to set the line must await more work on the data recovered.

Where sites have been recognized, the system of detailed recording has been to collect all possible archaeological material in a grid, usually of 5 or sometimes of 10 m. squares. The grid is laid out to cover the estimated extents of the main concentrations of diagnostic material. The limits of the scatter are only fixed approximately before collection begins, but the grid can easily be extended if necessary. Total collection in this way has proved to be essential in order to retrieve the maximum amount of information. The proportion of datable pottery among the finds from Roman period sites in this area is so small that any strategy which reduced the amount collected would tend to leave too small a sample for any worthwhile conclusions to be drawn. This approach differs from that of many workers who have attempted various kinds of random sampling techniques on individual sites. Most of those techniques require the limits of the site to be defined before the sampling units can be identified. It is our experience that it is extremely difficult to make more than the crudest estimates of site limits using methods such as those proposed by Gallant and quoted by Cherry.[12] Of course, as Cherry states, the value of any method depends on what you want from it. For some purposes a very rough idea of the size of a site and its date is enough. We have tried to extract rather more, wanting to say something about the internal organization of the site as well. It is particularly worthwhile to maximize the information about these buried sites, because many will not survive modern ploughing for much longer and very few will ever be excavated. Part of our aims can be achieved by gridded surface collection and quantification of the finds. The other main source of information on the layout of sites is geophysical survey, which can usually use the same grids as the collection.

The role of geophysical survey needs to be clearly understood. It is a very site-specific technique. Before it can be used effectively a decision has to be taken that there is something under the surface worth surveying. It is wasteful and frustrating to attempt speculative surveys, on the off-chance that there is something there. We have used geophysical survey both to give detailed information on sites that were to be excavated and to record sites which were unlikely to have any further work done on them. Both magnetometer and resistivity survey techniques have been used with some success in this project. Although it has sometimes been thought that geophysical work is too slow and cumbersome to be used in such circumstances, we have found that both techniques are cost-effective in terms of the information gathered for the effort expended. The rate of work required obviously varies according to the particular project and the number of sites needing to be surveyed. In our case, it normally proved best to maintain a small geophysical team of three independent of the other survey teams. These three could survey one small or medium-sized site in one day. A block of land of 40×20 m. could be conveniently surveyed in a single day with the instruments we have had available. This involved 800 readings, taken at 1-m. intervals. The conditions were not particularly favourable for resistivity survey, since we were usually working in recently ploughed fields, which slowed progress considerably. In flat meadows with short grass it has been possible to achieve up to 5,000 resistivity readings per day.[13] Furthermore, the increasing use of direct recording on a small computer is leading to quicker surveys and can give a very rapid display of results in graphic form in the field.

The results achieved have varied, with some surveys very clearly showing features and some showing none. The failures can probably be best explained partly by the destruction of the substantial archaeological features by ploughing and erosion and partly by the ground conditions when the surveys were done. Because most surveys were undertaken on fields where sites had been identified from scatters of archaeological material on the ploughed surface, there was a continuing problem in achieving good ground contacts for the resistivity measurements among the large lumps of soil turned up by deep ploughing. These difficulties generated a considerable background 'noise', which often reduced the sensitivity of the survey technique and which can obscure some of the, perhaps slight, features surviving in the subsoil of deeply ploughed sites. The quite poor results of resistivity survey on some smaller sites serve to underline again the problem of destruction. However, the example of Vilauba itself shows that it is sometimes possible to use geophysical survey to trace features which are all but destroyed by ploughing and which only survive as debris in the topsoil. The published resistivity survey of Vilauba shows some quite clear structures in the eastern part of the site, which also correspond with the concentrations of tile found on the surface.[14] However, excavation of limited parts of this area in 1982 and 1983 revealed few substantial features surviving. It seems most likely that the geophysical and surface surveys have together given an overall picture of the layout of the villa structures through recording the evidence that survives more in the ploughsoil than as intact features.

Despite the problems caused by the levels of destruction and erosion, recent work has enabled us to begin to reconstruct something of the classical period settlement pattern. Particularly satisfying results were achieved in a small valley occupying an area about $3 \times 1 \cdot 50$ km. in the north-west corner of the survey area. The Rio Serinyadell flows north into the Rio Ser, a tributary of the Rio Fluvia, and the valley also acts as a natural communications route between the Empordà and the area of Banyoles itself and the mountains, via the Fluvia valley. One major Roman villa was already known at Usall on the eastern side of the valley. To this we added five definite Roman sites and a further eight examples of concentrations of finds which might indicate the presence of a site (fig. 36). Most of the definite sites occupied small side-valleys. From their surface remains these sites can only have been modest concerns, but their discovery means that now, for the first time in this region, we have an indication of the nature of the dispersed settlement pattern and some idea of the hierarchy of settlement types. The Usall villa was clearly an important site, at least on the same scale as Vilauba, which occupies about a hectare. It has revealed evidence of mosaics and abundant *dolia*. Most of the other sites were much smaller, few exceeding 1,000 sq. m. One site yielded tile but little pottery, but several had virtually no tile.

Nowhere else have we discovered the same intensity of evidence for ancient settlement, although in most areas investigated we have been able to find some indications of ancient occupation. However, in two contrasting areas we found barely a sherd of ancient pottery. One was a flat plain with thin soil cover immediately to the east of the Serinyadell valley; the other, a part of the eastern sector of the overall survey area where the landscape is heavily dissected by river valleys. Further consideration, which must await our final report, is needed about whether these gaps in the distribution of ancient material reflect a genuine absence of sites, are the result of more recent landscape changes, or are a misleading accidental consequence of not being able to examine every field. Although every effort was made in defining the survey areas to take in as many landscape zones as possible, the differing conditions over small distances mean that it is hard to put forward too confidently any conclusions to apply to the area as a whole on the basis of the part surveyed. In these circumstances, although no attempt was made to work out statistically random survey units, it is hard to see how such a strategy could have been effective in practice. However, within the survey areas chosen, the choice of which fields to survey was at least haphazard according to availability, even if not statistically random.[15] What can be said with confidence now is that there is a high incidence of finds of Italian amphorae dating to the Republican period. Clearly the sites discovered were in occupation in the first century B.C. This is most significant new evidence for this part of the Mediterranean littoral. It has been more difficult to define how long the sites remained in occupation, and their exact dates of origin, but the Republican dating of many of the new sites corresponds well with the elucidation of a contemporary important structural phase at Vilauba, excavated in 1983.

As has already been outlined elsewhere,[16] a major interest of the project has been to examine the nature of the transition from the Roman to the medieval period. Vilauba has produced clear evidence of its continued occupation as a farm in the Roman tradition up to the seventh century A.D. The documentary record for the Banyoles area permits us to reconstruct the outline of the early medieval settlement pattern in about the tenth century. We have devoted some attention to the medieval topography of the region, examining the relationships between villages with medieval origins and post-Roman geomorphological changes. We have also made some attempt to consider standing buildings of medieval date in structure, or at least origin. The extent to which we can make

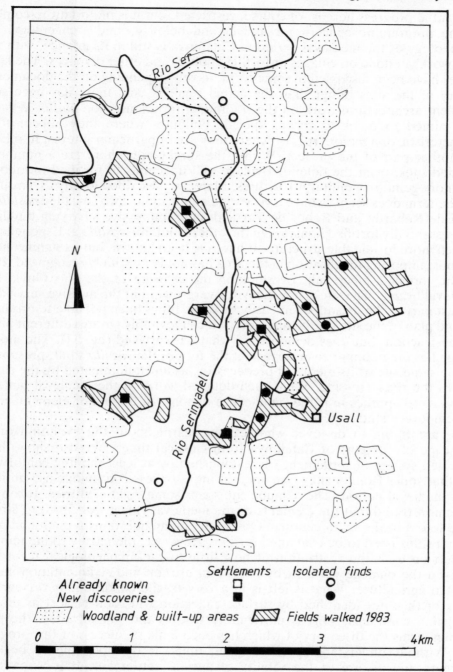

FIG. 36. The Serinyadell valley

substantial progress here is, of course, restricted, but it is important to combine in one programme concern for above- and below-ground archaeology. The archaeology of the medieval period in Catalunya is still in its infancy, with very little work yet done on villages or fortified houses and other defences. The larger castles have been discussed in some form, mostly depending on the documented history of the sites rather than the actual remains, and there has been some excellent architectural work on the traditional farmhouse, the *masia*. What we have aimed to do is to record specific buildings where they appear to be characteristic of a major type, or where they are of particular interest in relation to another part of the project. Within the survey area there are a number of fortified sites, from the defended village of Vilademuls to fortified farmhouses and more genuinely military structures. Many are described locally as 'castillos', but the term does seem to have a very wide application. Two so-called *castillos* at Palol de Rebardit and Rabos de Terri, despite impressive surviving buildings, were essentially fortified houses. On the other hand, the *castillo* at Esponella was a much more formidable structure. It has long been known, but its significance as the most imposing fortification in the area has not been widely recognized. It lies on the top of a steep hill, overlooking the crossing of the Rio Fluvia by a medieval bridge. The site is now heavily overgrown, but the massive survivals of at least part of the masonry can easily be seen. It has been possible to produce a ground plan of the site for the first time, which inevitably ignores different phases of construction, but does demonstrate what has survived (fig. 37). The modern village lies on an upper river terrace at the foot of the *castillo*'s hill, presumably on the same site as its medieval predecessor, as much dominated by the *castillo* as was the river crossing. What such detailed work on the medieval buildings allows us to appreciate is the significance of some of the major elements in the contemporary landscape.

We are trying to discover what can be learnt about the evolution of the landscape of our part of Catalunya from classical times. We can show that a dispersed system of settlement was established by at least the first century B.C. and that some Roman sites remained in more or less continuous use until the early medieval period. The Vilauba site spans some eight centuries. It can also be demonstrated that the elements of the medieval village system were already to be found in the tenth century. Obviously, many questions remain and many relationships need to be examined further. However, the most striking impression left on us is the realization of how little of the archaeological record has survived the damage wrought by long-term erosion and sedimentation and by modern agriculture. What is left is in a very fragile condition. It is clear that many of the sites identified by surface collection will soon be lost as modern ploughing continues. This is particularly true of the smaller sites, the small Roman farms the discovery of which has been a major success of this programme. Without understanding those small units, it is impossible to begin to re-create any picture of the totality of ancient settlement. It is a matter of urgency to continue surface prospection before all traces of such sites are lost. That, however, is really a task best achieved by local workers, who are in a position to examine the landscape as it passes through its annual farming cycle. What our kind of intensive survey can best achieve is a demonstration of what is possible.

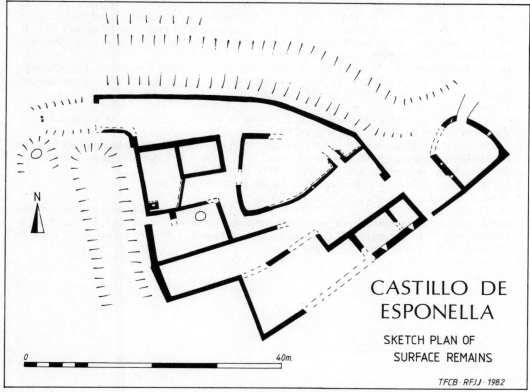

CASTILLO DE
ESPONELLA

SKETCH PLAN OF
SURFACE REMAINS

TFCB·RFJJ·1982

0   40m.

FIG. 37. The Castillo de Esponella

NOTES

[1] For the first report on the project, see R. F. J. Jones, S. J. Keay, J. M. Nolla and J. Tarrús, 'The late Roman villa of Vilauba and its context', *Antiq. J.* lxii (1982), pp. 245–82. The work has received generous support from many bodies: the British Academy, the Society of Antiquaries, the Universities of Bradford and Durham, the Museu Arqueologic Comarcal and the Ajuntament de Banyoles, the Diputació Provincial de Girona, the Generalitat de Catalunya, and the Spanish Government. We are very grateful to all of them, to our Catalan colleagues for their help, and to all the farmers who let us walk on their land.

[2] K. W. Butzer, 'Pleistocene geomorphology and stratigraphy of the Costa Brava region (Catalonia)', *Abhandlungen Akademie der Wissenschaften und der Literatur* (Mathematik und Naturwissenschaft), Mainz, i (1964), pp. 1–51.

[3] C. Vita-Finzi, 'Mediterranean monoglacialism?', *Nature*, ccxxiv (1969), p. 173.

[4] Butzer, *op. cit.* (n. 2).

[5] C. Vita-Finzi, *The Mediterranean Valleys: Geological Changes in Historical Times* (Cambridge, 1969); J. L. Bintliff, 'Mediterranean alluviation: new evidence from archaeology', *PPS,* xli (1975), pp. 78–84; *id., Natural Environment and Human Settlement in Prehistoric Greece*, BAR S28 (Oxford, 1977).

[6] C. M. Devereux, 'Recent Erosion and Sedimentation in Southern Portugal', unpubl. Ph.D. thesis, University College London, 1983.

[7] *Ibid.* C14 dates: Australian National University 2815 and University of Miami 1332.

[8] D. Davidson and C. Tasker, 'Geomorphological evolution during the late Holocene', in C. Renfrew and M. Wagstaff (eds.), *An Island Polity. The Archaeology of Exploitation in Melos* (Cambridge, 1982), pp. 95–105; C. Vita-Finzi, 'Diachronism in Old World alluvial sequences',

Nature, cclxiii (1976), pp. 218–19; G. W. Dimbleby, 'The impact of early man on his environment', in P. R. Cox and J. Peel (eds.), *Population and Pollution* (London, 1972), pp. 163 ff.; K. W. Butzer, 'Accelerated soil erosion: a problem of man-land relations', in I. R. Manners and M. W. Mikesell (eds.), *Perspectives on Environment*, Assoc. of American Geographers (Washington, 1974), pp. 57–77.

[9] R. U. Cooke and R. W. Reeves, *Arroyos and Environmental Change in the American South-West* (Oxford, 1976); L. B. Leopold, 'Reversal of erosion cycle and climatic change', *Quaternary Research*, vi (1976), pp. 557–62.

[10] Devereux, *op. cit.* (n. 6).

[11] J. M. Corominas and J. Marqués, *La Comarca de Bañolas*, Catálogo Monumental de la Provincia de Girona, Fasc. 1 (Girona, 1975).

[12] J. F. Cherry, 'Frogs around the pond: perspectives on current archaeological survey projects in the Mediterranean region', in D. R. Keller and D. W. Rupp (eds.), *Archaeological Survey in the Mediterranean Area*, BAR S155 (Oxford, 1983), pp. 375–416.

[13] D. W. Jordan, fieldwork in Greece 1983. Report forthcoming.

[14] Jones *et al.*, *op. cit.* (n. 1), figs. 9–11, pp. 260–2.

[15] cf. Cherry, *op. cit.* (n.12); J. F. Cherry and S. J. Shennan, 'Sampling cultural systems: perspectives on the application of probabilistic regional survey in Britain', in J. F. Cherry, C. S. Gamble and S. J. Shennan (eds.), *Sampling in Contemporary British Archaeology*, BAR 50 (Oxford, 1978), pp. 17–48.

[16] Jones *et al.*, *op. cit.* (n. 1).

IV. ITALY

The San Vincenzo Survey, Molise

Peter Hayes

This survey forms part of a much larger project directed by Dr. Richard Hodges of the University of Sheffield. From the outset, in 1980, the San Vincenzo Project was intended to integrate historical research (by Dr. Christopher Wickham of the University of Birmingham), excavations (directed by Dr. Hodges), and the survey outlined in this paper. Integration was seen as a dynamic process, an interaction between the different approaches while the archaeological fieldwork was in progress. This differs from the commonly adopted alternative, in which work is carried on more or less independently by various specialists, whose conclusions are brought together and synthesized in the final report.

The subject of the project is the eighth–twelfth-century Benedictine monastery of San Vincenzo al Volturno and its *terra*. The historical sources are particularly rich, and include a number of charters and leases as well as the *Chronicon Vulternese*, a twelfth-century history of the monastery. These sources show that the monastery was founded early in the eighth century, grew to a considerable size, was sacked by the Arabs in 881, and was rebuilt early in the tenth century. There followed a period of establishment of *castelli* (hilltop villages) in the *terra*, involving the granting of leases which contain valuable information about pre-existing settlements. This period was one of increasing difficulty for the monastery, which was faced by both military and political threats. Unlike its great rival at Monte Cassino, the monastery proved unable to maintain its wealth and importance and declined into relative obscurity.

The monastery of San Vincenzo and its *terra* were therefore seen as offering the opportunity to study the development of a major, well-documented, centre of economic activity in the Dark Ages and the early medieval period. The *terra* formed a clearly defined region situated on the edge of the high Abruzzi mountains in central Italy (fig. 38). In the Middle Ages the region was politically, as well as ecologically and geographically, marginal, since it lay on the border between the Carolingian empire and the minor kingdom of Benevento.

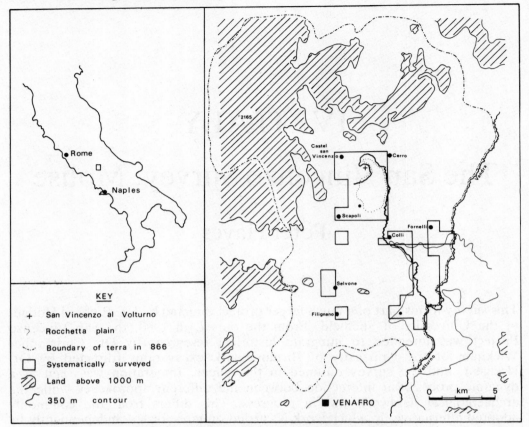

FIG. 38. The San Vincenzo Survey: location maps

It seemed likely that this marginality would make settlement in the *terra* a sensitive indicator of economic change in the region.

Methods

Dr. Wickham used the historical evidence to prepare a map of the *terra* showing the known or likely locations of settlements and *castelli* recorded before 1040, before 1150, and those not recorded before 1150. From the historical sources it was predicted that up to the tenth century settlement in the *terra* was dispersed and followed the late Roman pattern. Nucleation, and the foundation of the *castelli*, took place from the tenth century, mainly in response to political and military threats. Only rarely did the *castelli* seem primarily concerned with the clearance of previously uncultivated land, but two such examples were given. The survey was thus able to start with the aim of testing specific predictions in named localities within a defined study area.

Despite the restricted period of research interest, and the need to examine the named locations, the survey was organized using standardized survey units (a grid of kilometre squares). These units were systematically surveyed, with the aim of covering, so far as was practicable, the whole of each square, recording archaeologically relevant information relating to all periods. Notes were also made on the present-day topography, vegetation and soils. Records were made in the field, using copies of maps and standard recording sheets, numbered serially. The presence of all artifacts was recorded, including 'non-site' material, i.e. general scatters of material with no apparent nucleus or other indication of the former existence of a burial, settlement or other area of localized activity. All artifacts were generally collected, but in the case of large scatters of Roman and medieval material, and always in the case of post-medieval, an attempt was made to bring back a representative sample of fabrics, together with all rims, bases or decorated sherds. The sherding policy was far from ideal, but it must be borne in mind that the material collected had to be carried by the team for a long period, sometimes all day, in hilly country under the Italian sun.

The survey was carried out by teams of three or four people, mainly experienced fieldwalkers, some of whom had previous survey experience in Molise. Two teams took part in the first season and one in the second. Each team covered one kilometre square each day, except very occasionally when the square was less extensively cultivated than usual. Generally, about half to three-quarters of each square was sufficiently open to allow systematic walking.

The first aim was to establish the Roman settlement pattern, and to see whether there was evidence of Dark Age continuity. Even small Roman sites were relatively easy to find using the methods described. Their tile scatters even made it possible to locate them in weedy stubble fields. Had the survey been aimed primarily at, for instance, the recovery of flint scatters, different methods would have been necessary. Another factor to be considered in deciding upon survey strategy and methods was the nature of the settlement pattern and the size of settlement we were likely to encounter. The historical sources describe the area around the monastery in the early eighth century as a depopulated wilderness, a place of dense woodland, the haunt of thieves and wild beasts. Even allowing for a degree of exaggeration on the part of the monks, we were likely to be looking for small numbers of sites in difficult, highly variable, terrain. To the west of San Vincenzo the land rises impressively in a series of steep ridges, soon reaching a height of over 2,000 m. These mountains were excluded from the survey. Nevertheless, determined volunteers eventually scaled them. Above the tree-line they found not only present-day transhumant shepherds, living in seasonal huts and guarding a considerable number and variety of animals, but also evidence of Bronze Age and Roman structures and artifacts. Transhumance clearly has a long history in the region, but our survey could not study it without prejudicing the attainment of our primary objectives.

The survey strategy therefore had to take into account the logistical constraints imposed by the terrain, the demands of the main research aims, the likelihood that sites would be few in number (and might be totally missed by some sampling methods), the specific nature of the predictions to be tested, and the small area of land available for conventional survey. It was accordingly decided in the first season to survey the whole of the main block of arable land—the Rocchetta plain—which lies near the monastic complex, and to sample by means of a single square and a line of squares two other arable areas where dispersed settlement was predicted. In addition, Dr. Hodges, Dr. Wickham, and a survey team visited and searched hilltops to find, with a high success rate, the sites of lost villages which Dr. Wickham had identified and approximately located in the course of his researches.

Results of the first season

Agricultural machinery capable of ploughing deeply is only just being introduced into the area, and its use is revealing, and destroying, prehistoric and Roman sites which have previously been only slightly damaged. The cutting or widening of numerous small tracks up hillsides and through abandoned terraces is leaving exposed sections which often contain both archaeological material and evidence of colluviation. Around 100 record sheets were completed in each of the two seasons, and this detailed information is being used to prepare a gazetteer for publication. In this paper, therefore, the results will be described more generally, as part of a discussion of the methods used. However, two particularly notable prehistoric discoveries deserve a mention. The first is what has turned out to be a substantial scatter of apparently Palaeolithic flints across a low spur projecting into the Rocchetta plain, a former lake basin. The site is only a few hundred metres south of the monastic complex. The second notable discovery was of a large hilltop settlement, probably defended, which seems to be of Late Bronze Age–Early Iron Age date. It extends along the top of a prominent hill which overlooks the confluence of the rivers Vandra and Volturno, near Macchia d'Isernia.

Turning to the main aims of the survey, dispersed Roman settlements were found in those areas in which they had been predicted. It was found that small zones of red or brown soils exist within or adjacent to the present-day arable land, but that the modern arable area extends onto yellow or grey clay soils which show no evidence of pre-medieval artifacts. The zones of red and brown soils, in contrast, were found to contain both prehistoric and Roman material, often in large quantities. An area of red soil would characteristically contain perhaps five Samnite and earlier Roman sites, and one (rarely more) later Roman site marked by a large spread of pottery, tile and building debris. The proportion of fine wares was, however, always low, and no tesserae, coins or metal objects were found. There was no sign of seventh- to tenth-century material on the Roman sites, or indeed anywhere covered by the systematic survey.

In other words, the survey results did not support the prediction from the historical sources that there would be a continuity of dispersed settlement into the Dark Ages. The results did, however, strongly support the suggestion that the village of Scapoli had been established to clear and develop previously uninhabited forest. The village is a *castello* surrounded by steep slopes of the yellow clay soils, which were found to contain no artifacts or other evidence of earlier settlement. The other suggested example of a primarily clearance *castello*, Cerro, was not fully included in the survey area.

The excavations at the monastic site produced important, and to some extent unexpected, results, but these will be discussed only in so far as they concern the survey. Large quantities of late Roman (fifth–sixth-century) and Dark Age to early medieval (eighth–twelfth-century) pottery were discovered. An exceptionally large number of fresco fragments dating to the early years of the monastery also came to light, and later work has revealed frescoes *in situ* on the lower parts of walls. As far as the survey is concerned, the stratified sequence of ceramics ranging from the fifth to the twelfth centuries (excluding the seventh) was a crucial discovery. This sequence includes both wheel-made, red-painted wares and dark, hand-made coarse pottery, which was presumably made locally. Both these groups are sufficiently durable and visible for us to be confident that they would have been picked up by the survey if encountered. Indeed, both groups were found at Colle Castellano when the hilltop was visited by a survey team in order to confirm the location of an abandoned village presumed to have been called Olivella. The pottery was sufficiently visible to be noticed in dry grass in a small clearing in the woodland. A trial excavation subsequently confirmed the discovery.

Results of the second season

The first part of this season was devoted to completing the survey of the main areas in which dispersed Roman and Dark Age settlement had been predicted. The results conformed to the pattern of the first season. It could still be argued that there had been dispersed farms run by aceramic slaves belonging to estates managed from somewhere outside the *terra*, and thus invisible or at least undatable by means of survey. Nevertheless, the visible changes in the pattern of settlement during the Roman period, the relationship between archaeological evidence and the different soil classes, and the large quantity of Dark Age material found at the excavation site, suggested an alternative explanation. Instead of continuity of dispersed settlement from the late Roman period into the Dark Ages, a process of centralization, and probably of contraction, of settlement might have started in the late Roman period and developed in the succeeding period into a move into nucleated or loosely aggregated settlements. Instead of being situated on the present-day arable land, these hamlets might have been built on low hills or promontories rising out of the larger areas of red soil. This was deduced by assuming that a severe decline, or virtual collapse, of the Roman market economy took place. This would completely alter the relative importance of different types of land in the *terra*. Without a demand and outlet for agricultural surpluses, such as the products of olive trees or vines, and with the need to provide, out of local resources, food, shelter and security, priorities would change. The extensive tracts of steep hillsides would become relatively less important. It takes a great deal of labour to build and maintain terraces, cultivate vines and olives, and process their products. The purely local demand for these can be satisfied by the produce of a small area of land. The prime arable land, on the other hand, would become relatively much more important. This land is scarce in the *terra*, and consists of a few zones of deep, well-structured, red calcareous soil. The best mixture of resources for a primarily subsistence economy would be a sufficiently large area of prime arable land to provide the vegetable, especially cereal, needs of the people involved, together with a small area of forested hillside, to provide wood and, perhaps, pannage. Living in a hamlet on a low hill would have both social and defensive advantages.

This is a very simple model, and others are possible, but it enabled us to move to a second stage or level of survey. Using the model and the information gathered by the first stage survey, we predicted the likely location of a Dark Age settlement. Ideally, one would use a mechanical or objective technique to simulate the settlement patterns predicted by more than one model. These simulations could then be tested by survey, looking for both the presence and the absence of sites, by means of samples sufficiently large to allow the use of statistical significance tests. This is far from easy to achieve in practice, and in any event we did not have enough time to attempt it. Instead, we chose the nearest suitable hill, at Vacchereccia, at the southern end of the Rocchetta plain.

Vacchereccia presented a daunting prospect for a survey. Like nearly all the hills in the area, it was covered by woodland and dense scrub, and we are indebted to Dr. Eric Hansen of the University of Buffalo, New York State, for the methodological innovation which enabled us to meet the challenge. He organized a systematic survey along the top and down one side of the hill. The side which was chosen sloped down to a broad terrace of red calcareous soil. The remainder of the hill was surrounded by the yellow clay soils in which we had found no artifacts pre-dating the later medieval period. The new technique, dubbed 'shovel testing', involved the use of a grid of test pits. The soil from each pit was riddled to recover all artifacts. Vacchereccia was the most obvious hill on which to test the new settlement predictions, but at the time we were under the impression that we were flying in the face of the historical evidence. In the first season the survey had found a deserted medieval village on the summit of the hill, but we thought that it was one of the later foundations, not recorded in the historical sources until after 1150. It was therefore a relief not only to find the elusive eighth–tenth-century pottery just below the summit, but also to learn at a later date that the settlement had been given the status of *castello* by a charter of 985. Limited excavations at Vacchereccia in the following season resulted in the recovery of extremely large quantities of pottery from the hillside, dating possibly to the seventh century and certainly from the eighth–tenth centuries. The village on the summit seems to have replaced the hillslope settlement because the test pits and a trial excavation on top of the hill produced only post-tenth-century pottery.

A second prediction was made, tested, and found to yield similar results. This was at Filignano, where Peter Herring of the University of Sheffield dug a series of test pits up a long and steep hillside, again with a deserted medieval village on the summit. The hill rises out of an old lake basin filled with prime arable soil, and very rich in Roman and earlier settlement evidence. Eighth–tenth-century pottery was again found just below the crest of the hill.

Conclusions

The results of the surveys and excavations, and their implications, will be presented in various forthcoming publications arising out of the San Vincenzo Project as it nears its conclusion. This article is concerned with survey aims and methods at a more general level. Archaeological surveys usually set out to gather together a body of information from which conclusions and explanations are derived by inference and logical argument. In some circumstances, however, a different approach may be more effective. This alternative approach is essentially a cycle of suggested explanation, prediction and testing. The San Vincenzo

Survey itself is only an imperfect example. It is not put forward as a model, but it does illustrate the possibilities. While some general data-collection is usually necessary, the use of specific predictions makes it possible to evaluate alternative explanations while the survey is still in progress. Where appropriate, the form or intensity of survey may be changed, provided this is done by stating the explanation to be tested, the assumptions on which it rests, and the testable predictions which follow from it. This encourages flexibility and efficiency by focusing thought and effort on key questions and avoiding having to waste time and labour in gathering duplicate or redundant information. In the San Vincenzo survey the change from the first-level survey to a more intensive level compelled us to adopt a new survey technique ('shovel testing'), which we would not otherwise have used. That innovation enabled us to find small, loosely nucleated settlement in secondary woodland or scrub: an impossibility using conventional survey methods.

The kind of approach which is being suggested does undoubtedly carry with it dangers of simplistic reasoning, unacceptably partial, or even biased, survey, or of circular arguments. A critical attitude is needed, but it should be positive rather than negative or simply dismissive. On the positive side, the approach makes it possible, or even essential, to use new methods. For instance, we need more precise and rather less subjective methods for the generation of the testable predictions which follow from an explanation which is to be evaluated. One solution would be to use simulation models. These exist, but their value is limited if they are used after a survey has been completed. Simulations of, for instance, settlement patterns would fit very well into a multi-stage survey based on a cycle of predictions and tests. While more general, fact-gathering surveys remain essential, we need to develop our survey methods in order to tackle questions and terrain for which our existing techniques are inadequate.

Acknowledgements

I would like to thank Dr. Richard Hodges for the opportunity to take part in his San Vincenzo Project, Dr. Christopher Wickham for his enthusiasm and his invaluable research in connection with the project, the Soprintendenza Archeologica del Molise for permitting the survey, the local farmers for their good-humoured tolerance of our wanderings, and the members of the survey teams, who worked so hard and expertly, including, but not exclusively, Alison Borthwick, Judy Cartledge, Peter Chowne, Eric Hansen, Peter Herring, Graeham Mounteney and Marijke van der Veen.

The Chronology of the Sites of the Roman Period around San Giovanni: Methods of Analysis and Conclusions

Claude Roberto, James A. Plambeck and Alastair M. Small, F.S.A.

This paper is concerned with the chronology of the sites located by surface survey in the vicinity of San Giovanni in central Lucania, and in particular with the problem of presenting the information in a form which will be useful to historians. The report is limited to sites of the Roman period. Three different procedures of analysis are tried and assessed for their effectiveness in determining trends in site occupation. The deficiencies of the first two procedures are largely overcome in the third. The conclusions which we reach in these analyses differ significantly from those obtained by surface surveys in other parts of Italy.

The area covered by the survey comprises approximately 113 sq. km. of upland country (figs. 39–41). The fieldwork, which was carried out between 1979 and 1983, is centred on the Roman villa of San Giovanni,[1] since the primary purpose of the survey has been to throw light on the environment of the villa in the Roman period. The survey was therefore intensive: that is, we aimed to explore the whole area contained within a 6 km. radius of San Giovanni. The modern town sites and denser woodlands had, however, to be excluded from the investigation, so that in practice only about 80 per cent of the 113 sq. km. were covered.

A total of ninety-seven findspots produced material in sufficient concentrations to be considered as sites (fig. 41), many of which can be dated by artifacts to the Roman period (defined for the purposes of this paper as *c.* 300 B.C. to A.D. 460). The most typical material found is roofing-tile, with pottery in second place. Some of the pottery cannot be dated, but all the sites under consideration here have produced sherds which can be dated within our time limits. The

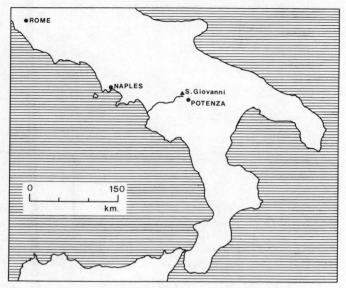

FIG. 39. San Giovanni di Ruoti: location map 1

strength of the evidence varies: some sites have produced only a single datable piece; others have produced more than forty.

The procedure for dating sites most commonly followed in reports of surface surveys in Italy is to classify them by periods defined by the accepted dates of the major classes of pottery wares found on them. In the South Etruria survey, to give a familiar example, sites of the Roman period were at first assigned to a 'black glaze', 'terra sigillata' or 'red polished' (i.e. African red slip) period. Subsequently, as knowledge of late Roman pottery improved, the red polished period was subdivided into three parts, and other categories were introduced,[2] but the principle remained essentially the same. This procedure makes it possible to detect changes in settlement pattern between these broad periods, but its usefulness to a historian is limited by the impossibility of detecting changes which took place in periods of historical interest differently defined. And there are other problems inherent in the method: the periods represented by these wares are of unequal length, so that one has to exercise great care in comparing settlement densities between them; and in the case of the black glaze period it is difficult, if not impossible, to assign a date at which black glaze came into use. Certainly it varied in different parts of Italy.

We may illustrate these points from the San Giovanni survey. Of the sites located in our survey area, forty-one can be dated to the black glaze period, thirteen to the Italian terra sigillata period and thirty-four to the African red slip period.[3] At first sight these figures suggest that the number of sites occupied must have reached its greatest height in the black glaze period, fallen to its lowest in the early Roman Empire and risen again in the middle or later Roman empire. But when we take the time factor into account all certainty vanishes, for whereas the Italian terra sigillata period lasts for little more than 100 years (*c.* 30 B.C. to A.D. 75), the black glaze period may extend for as much as 400 years, from its ill-defined beginning perhaps in the late fifth century to the late first century B.C.,

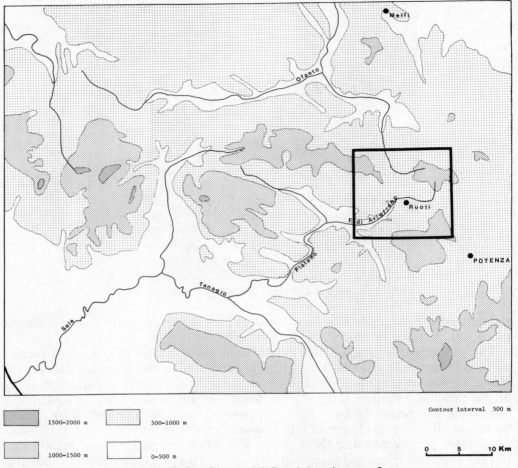

FIG. 40. San Giovanni di Ruoti: location map 2

and the African red slip period must extend for at least 450 years from the late first century A.D. to the early sixth or even later. Since we can have no idea of the average duration of a site, it is impossible to tell from this evidence how many sites are likely to have been occupied at any point in time. Common sense tells us that we can expect more sites to be attested in the longer periods, but we cannot estimate how many more we may expect, nor can we be confident that the trends which we detected at first sight have any validity.

Clearly, we need to define the period of occupation of each of our sites much more precisely, but still in a way that allows conclusions to be drawn objectively rather than impressionistically from the evidence. Most of the material collected on the San Giovanni survey consists of plain and coarse ware fragments and wall sherds of fine wares, many of which cannot be dated any more precisely than within the broad periods already discussed. These will not help us in this case. There are, however, 137 fragments of fine wares which can be identified by form (and frequently by fabric). Since these pieces can be dated by the known chronology of fine ware forms, they provide much more precise evidence for the

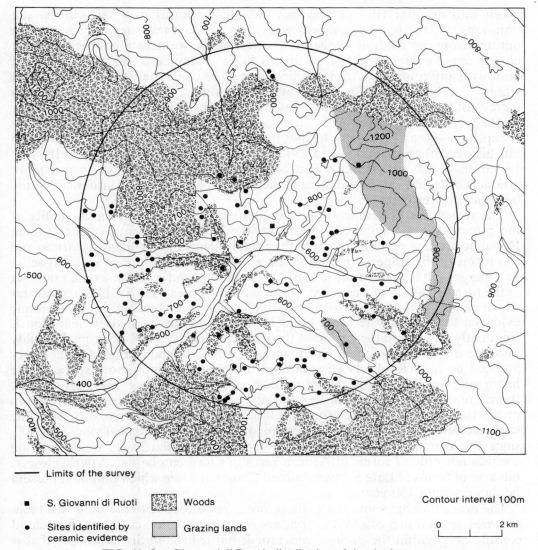

Limits of the survey

■ S. Giovanni di Ruoti   Woods

● Sites identified by ceramic evidence   Grazing lands

Contour interval 100m

0   2 km

FIG. 41. San Giovanni di Ruoti: distribution of sites in the survey area

dates of our sites. The quality of the evidence varies to some extent, since some forms can be dated much more precisely than others (and we may note at this point that black glaze forms are generally less closely dated than forms in Italian terra sigillata or African red slip), so that some sites will still be more closely dated by such pieces than others; but in general we may hope to obtain a much greater degree of precision by using this evidence alone. In our second procedure, therefore, which we may term the *procedure by the maximum duration of pottery forms*, we have dated each of our sites by the time-range of the fine ware forms and any other closely datable artifacts[4] found in it. We cannot hope by this procedure to establish the real number of sites occupied at any point of time, since on some sites some of the pieces which we have not taken into account (the pottery not datable by form) may fall outside the time-range of the fine ware sherds with form, while a few sites have had to be omitted from our analysis altogether. Nevertheless, we may hope that this more closely dated evidence will reveal *trends* in site occupation which we could not infer with any confidence from our first procedure by the periods of the principal wares. The histogram (fig. 42) shows the results of this analysis. It reveals a pattern of four peaks with intervening troughs. The first two peaks, which occur in the period of the Republic, are sharply defined: the first, which begins abruptly in 400 B.C. (though this lies outside our period and so is not shown in our histogram) ends suddenly in 250 B.C.;[5] the second lasts from 200 to 100 B.C. By contrast, the two peaks which occur in the Imperial period have a more gradual configuration, culminating in the middle of the second century and at the beginning of the fifth.

The reason for the contrasting configurations lies largely in the datability of the pottery types concerned. In general the black glaze forms of the Roman Republic are less precisely datable than the Italian terra sigillata or African red slip forms of the Imperial period. Many of the black glaze forms are assigned a date range of 100 years or more, with the beginning and end of the date range set at the turn or middle of a century. There is therefore a strong likelihood that sites which came to an end over a period of 100 years will appear from the ceramic evidence to finish at the same point in time. By contrast, better definition is frequently possible in the period of the Empire. This factor of differing datability must have a distorting effect on the trend revealed by the histogram, since sites attested by less closely dated forms will frequently occupy more space in the histogram than sites attested by more closely dated pieces. We may expect, therefore, that the sites of the Republican period may have been rather fewer in proportion to those of the Roman Empire than our histogram suggests. The same factor has led to some exaggeration of the height of the peak of *c.* A.D. 400, since the ceramic evidence which we have used to date sites of this period consists not only of forms of African red slip which can be dated fairly closely, but also of forms of Late Roman Painted Common Ware which cannot at present be dated within 150 years.

The procedure has some value, therefore, as a corrective to the simplistic table of wares, since it suggests that the pattern of site occupation must have fluctuated considerably within the periods concerned; but it has the disadvantages that it involves excluding a large body of evidence, and that we cannot accept the trends which it reveals as altogether accurate, since it tends to exaggerate the number of sites in periods when the pottery is less well dated.

The third procedure which we have tested in the San Giovanni survey enables us to overcome these defects, at least in part, by making some arbitrary, but not implausible, assumptions. We may call this the *procedure by means and standard deviations*. In it we assume for statistical purposes that a piece of pottery is most likely to have been deposited on a site at the mid-point of its date-range, and with decreasing probability on either side of it. Where several pieces of datable pottery have been found on the same site a statistical method has been employed to calculate the most probable period of occupation. This has been done by using a computer programme[6] to calculate the mean and standard deviation of each site by the method of least squares from the dated pottery found there. We at

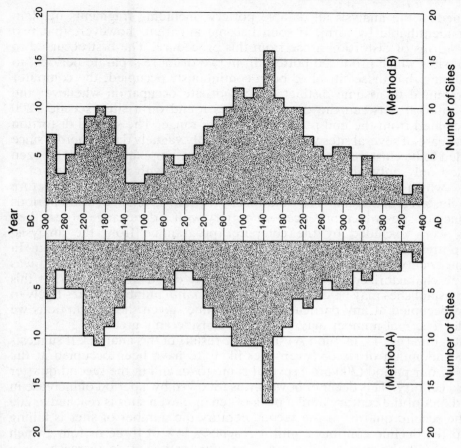

FIG. 43. Histogram showing the most probable number of sites occupied at 20-year intervals between 300 B.C. and A.D. 460 using the procedure by means and standard deviations. A site is included within a bar if its standard deviation extends into any part of the 20-year interval. For discussion of method, see text

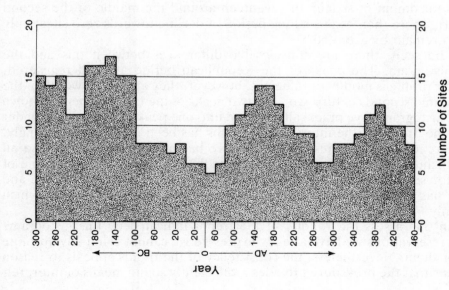

FIG. 42. Histogram showing the maximum number of sites occupied at 20-year intervals between 300 B.C. and A.D. 460 on the procedure by maximum duration of pottery forms

first included in the analysis all datable pottery, including fragments of plain wares not identifiable by form. It soon became apparent, however, that two systematic forms of distortion arose from this procedure. The first occurred in the case of sites which produced pottery from two or more separate periods: to avoid assuming that these sites had been continuously occupied, the computer was programmed to assume distinct periods of site occupation whenever the minimum interval between the dates of pieces found on a site exceeded 200 years, calculated from the mid-point of their date range. The second distortion arose in the case of several sites which contained only vaguely dated sherds, since these tended to be clustered at specific points of time. For example, half a dozen sites yielded only untypable fragments of black glaze with a date range of *c.* 400–0 B.C., which were assigned the mid-range date of 200 B.C., and therefore appeared clustered at 200 B.C. To avoid this distortion, sites or separate periods of occupancy of sites which produced *no* pottery with a date range of less then 200 years were excluded by the computer programme from the analysis, although pottery not datable within 200 years was not otherwise excluded. In each of the twenty exclusion cases the site or period of a site so excluded was found to be characterized by only *one* such poorly dated fragment. What this procedure establishes may be described as the *minimum* number of sites likely to have been occupied at any particular point of time, given the assumptions we have made. The real number may have been considerably greater.

The histogram (fig. 43, method A) shows the results of this analysis. It suggests that of the minimum of six or seven sites likely to have been occupied at the beginning of our period (300 B.C.) several came to an end in the second quarter of the third century. This decline, however, is followed by a period of increase in the second half of the century until a peak of ten or eleven sites is reached *c.* 200 B.C. By the second quarter of the second century the number of sites is falling again, and the decline continues until it reaches a low of three or four, which lasts for most of the first century B.C. The number begins to increase again shortly before the beginning of the Christian era, and continues to rise until it reaches its maximum of sixteen or seventeen around the middle of the second century A.D. There then begins a long period of decline towards zero sites; only one or two remain by A.D. 460.

As can be seen, there are considerable differences between this and the previous histogram. The peaks of the Republican period are still registered, though their profile is modified. In height, however, they are now lower than the peak of the mid second century A.D. The two peaks of the Imperial period shown in our first histogram have practically merged into one peak with a much broader base, and the profile of the intervening troughs has been modified accordingly. These differences arise because the procedure has made it possible to use all material, including wall sherds, datable within 200 years so that the volume of evidence for settlement during the Roman Empire has greatly increased, and because it has reduced the significance of the less closely dated pieces, which occur mainly in the period of the Republic and late Roman Empire.

How can one assess the validity of the trends indicated by this histogram? Given the reservations we have already expressed we cannot claim any absolute validity for them. Nevertheless, the consistency of the trends appeals to reason and suggests that the procedure provides a sufficiently sound means of interpreting the development of the site pattern in our area. We offer it here as a *ballon d'essai*.

One might also logically attempt a weighting procedure based upon the datability of each individual pottery type. We have carried out such an analysis (fig. 43, method B) using the same criteria of duration breaking and exclusion as before. No significant differences appear between the two histograms.

The tentative conclusions which we have drawn about these trends in site occupation and their place in time invite us to put them in their broad historical context. The first point to emerge is that the Roman conquest of south Italy, which culminated in the Pyrrhic war of 280–75, was followed in our area by the abandonment of some of the Late Iron Age sites. A significant number of new sites were, however, established during the second half of the third century, and these appear to continue, practically unaffected by the Hannibalic war, into the second quarter of the second century, when their number begins to drop rapidly. This decline is consistent with the view that the decrease in the rural population was one of the factors which provoked the Gracchan land reforms of 133 and 123 B.C. This low level of site occupation continued until the time of Augustus, when the gradual upward trend began, reflecting, presumably, the return to social stability brought by the Principate after a century of disorder. This upward trend continued until the time of Marcus Aurelius, when we reach another turning point. The subsequent decline, which seems to have been sudden at first, levels off during the Severan period, and then continues throughout the rest of the third century, which was a long period of political and social turmoil. The restoration of more stable conditions under Diocletian and Constantine is marked by some revival, but this is followed by further decline which continues until the end of our period.

In reaching these conclusions we have emphasized the trends rather than the numbers involved, for two reasons. Firstly, the distortions inherent in our three procedures of analysis provide a warning that the estimates of numbers involved are unlikely to be accurate. Secondly, we do not wish to claim that our survey has detected all the sites that existed in our area, or that the dates of the sites that we have detected are fully indicated by the pottery we have found on them. But although the numbers involved cannot be ascertained with certainty, we believe that the data which we have taken into account are sufficient for us to be confident that the trends which we have inferred from them are generally valid.

How do these trends compare with those which have been recognized in other parts of Italy? The lack of any agreed procedure for publishing the results of surface surveys makes close comparisons impossible. Nevertheless, some broad comparisons can be made on the basis of the published evidence, even if not consistently for the whole of our time period. The marked downward trend in the number of sites occupied in the second and first centuries B.C. which we have found in our survey area can be observed in some parts of Magna Graecia,[7] even if it was not general in the whole of south Italy.[8] In central Italy, by contrast, this seems to have been a time of rapid increase in site numbers,[9] although it must be said that the detailed chronological evidence for this, which depends on the typology of black glaze pottery, has not yet been adequately presented in the published surveys. Regional differences continue to be pronounced in the first and second centuries A.D. In our area the number of sites increased until the middle of the century. In south Etruria the number increased dramatically in the first century A.D. until it reached its peak, apparently at the turn of the century.[10] In the Liri valley the number of sites seems to have remained more or less static until the second century A.D., when there was a marked increased in the area around Interamna.[11] In the Basentello valley between Gravina and Venosa, however, this was a period of pronounced decline,[12] as it was also, apparently, in the Biferno valley in the Molise.[13] In the *Ager Cosanus*, too, decline set in early in the Imperial period.[14] Except perhaps in the Liri valley, rural settlement seems to have declined in all surveyed areas in the third century, and in most parts of Italy the decline continues into the fourth century and later. At San Giovanni, however, the decline seems to have been more gradual than elsewhere: as we have seen, it is probable that there were some moments of revival to slow the decline, and the area appears to be unique among those surveyed to date in showing more sites occupied in the period of Constantine than had been under Augustus.

Wightman has already pointed out that the results obtained from different surveys show that there were marked regional variations in the settlement pattern in Roman Italy.[15] The San Giovanni survey, which has produced results which are more out of line than most, confirms this impression. The economic and social factors which conditioned settlement in Lucania were quite different from those pertaining to Etruria, Latium or Campania, and they had different consequences.

NOTES

[1] The surface survey and excavation were financed by the Social Sciences and Humanities Research Council of Canada. For preliminary reports of the excavation, which was completed in 1983, see M. Gualtieri, M. Salvatore and A. Small (eds.), *Lo scavo di S. Giovanni di Ruoti ed il periodo tardoantico in Basilicata* (Bari, 1983) (hereafter cited as *Lo scavo di S. Giovanni*); A. Small, 'San Giovanni di Ruoti: some problems in the interpretation of the structures', in K. Painter (ed.), *Roman Villas in Italy, Recent Excavations and Research* (British Museum, 1980), pp. 91–109; and reports by A. M. Small, R. J. Buck, *et al.* in *Echos du monde classique*, annually since 1978.

[2] Summarized in T. W. Potter, *The Changing Landscape of South Etruria* (London, 1979), pp. 15–18.

[3] These figures do not include the site of San Giovanni itself, which has also been omitted from our histograms. San Giovanni was occupied from about the beginning of the first century A.D. to the second quarter of the sixth, with a period of disoccupation in the third century A.D. More precise dates will be given in the final publication.

[4] The fine ware sherds with form include sixty-nine pieces of black glaze, six of Italian terra sigillata and sixty-two of African red slip. We have also included sixteen fragments of Late Roman Painted Common Ware with form (on which see J. Freed, *Lo scavo di S. Giovanni*, pp. 99–100). The material comes from forty-two sites. Details will be given in our final publication.

It may be objected that the use of fine wares in the area around San Giovanni may have fluctuated, and that this would invalidate any conclusions about trends in site occupation that can be drawn from them. There is, however, no proof that there was any serious interruption in the use of such wares in our area until the middle of the fifth century A.D., when the proportion of fine wares in the area dropped noticeably (*ibid.*, p. 103), and we can to a large extent compensate for the shortage of fine wares in this period by taking the Late Roman Painted Common Ware into account. This pottery is abundant at San Giovanni in contexts of the late fourth, fifth and early sixth centuries. The stratigraphic sequences at San Giovanni give no indication that there was any other interruption in the use of fine wares during the occupation of the site. The decline in the proportion of fine wares in use in the middle of the fifth century was probably a widespread phenomenon brought about because the *supply* of African red slip was interrupted by the Vandal invasion of North Africa (J. Freed, 'Late Roman Pottery from San Giovanni di Ruoti and its Implications', unpublished D.Phil. thesis, University of Alberta, 1982, pp. 312–19) and not by any change in *demand*. There is no good reason to suppose that there was not always a demand for fine wares in our area, or that the supply was interrupted at any other time during our period.

[5] This appears as 240 in our histogram, since each bar covers a period of 20 years. Increases which occur within any part of a period covered by a bar are shown in that bar.

[6] Copies available on request to the authors. Weighting factor, where used, was (100 years/date range of pottery type). A single standard deviation was used as the date range of a site in calculating the histogram, fig. 42. The use of two standard deviations rather than one reveals little difference in the trends of site occupancy over time.

[7] Notably in the territory of Siris/Heracleia: L. Quilici, *Siris-Heracleia*, Forma Italiae, reg. III, vol. I (1967), pp. 226–9, and of Metapontum: see *The Territory of Metaponto 1981–1982* (The University of Texas at Austin, 1983). The team from the University of Texas at Austin has identified at least 227 sites of the Greek period in the surveyed area, and only forty-nine of the Roman period [see now this volume, pp. 146–57].

[8] S. P. Vinson notes only a very small decrease in the number of sites occupied in the Basentello valley between Gravina and Venosa: Peter Vinson, 'Ancient roads between Venosa and Gravina', *Pap. Brit. School at Rome*, xl (1972), p. 89.

[9] As in south Etruria, where there was an impressive increase in the number of sites occupied in the last three centuries B.C.: Potter, *op. cit.* (n. 2), p. 125; the Liri valley, where the black glaze pottery belongs overwhelmingly to the second and first centuries B.C.: E. M. Wightman, 'The Lower Liri Valley: trends and peculiarities', in G. Barker and R. Hodges (eds.), *Archaeology and Italian Society*, Papers in Italian Archaeology II, BAR S102 (Oxford, 1981), p. 281; and probably in the Biferno valley: G. Barker, J. Lloyd and D. Webley, 'A classical landscape in Molise', *Pap. Brit. School at Rome*, xlvi (1978), p. 42.

[10] Potter, *op. cit.* (n. 2), pp. 132–3. The trend varied locally, however, and the details are not altogether clear, since Potter's 'Period VII sites [second century A.D.] include all sites with Red Slip wares although some of these could well be much later in the Roman period'.

[11] Wightman, *op. cit.* (n. 9), p. 284.

[12] Vinson, *loc. cit.* (n. 8).

[13] *Pap. Brit. School at Rome*, xlvi (1978), p. 42.

[14] Dyson dates the beginning of the decline to the transition from Republic to early Empire: S. L. Dyson, 'Settlement patterns in the Ager Cosanus', *J. Field Arch.* v (1978), p. 260; but it may not have set in until the Flavian period: I. Attolini *et al.*, 'Ricognizione archeologica nell'Ager Cosanus e nella valle dell'Albegna. Rapporto preliminare 1981', *Archeologia Medievale*, ix (1982), p. 371. The differing interpretations produced by the various surveys carried out in the *Ager Cosanus* illustrate the need for a more objective method of assessing the trends of site occupation.

[15] Wightman, *op. cit.* (n. 9), p. 286.

Metaponto and Croton

Joseph Coleman Carter, F.S.A., and Cesare D'Annibale

The two surveys described here have a common orientation. They are part of a multidisciplinary approach to the problem of the rural population in Magna Graecia (southern Italy) in the Greek and Roman periods. Even more specifically, they aim to reveal the *chora*, or territory, immediately surrounding two ancient cities on the Ionian coast, two cities which had a comparable origin (founded by Achaean Greeks in the great age of colonization), fame (renowned for their wealth and power), and fate (domination by the Romans and decline).

On another level, they are both the products of a spirit of open and forward-looking international collaboration fostered by the Archaeological Superintendencies of Basilicata and Calabria over the years. We are particularly grateful to Professor Dinu Adamesteanu, Dr. Elena Lattanzi and Dr. Angelo Bottini for their initial welcome and constant, active support of these projects.

The territory of Metaponto has been an object of study for a considerable time (Carter 1980a, pp. 167 ff.). Surveys have been carried out by various groups from 1965 to the present, but it was not until 1981 (D'Annibale 1983a) that systematic and intensive survey of large areas began to reveal the true density and complexity of rural settlement between the Bradano and Basento (fig. 44, and see location map on fig. 48). The Croton survey was undertaken in 1983 in what is, by contrast, archaeological *terra incognita*, to provide a basis for comparison and for generalization about rural settlement in Magna Graecia. For the interpretation of its results the Metaponto survey benefits from a variety of related research: excavation at numerous sites in the territory, which have clarified the chronology of the major phases of the settlement of the territory, and special studies of geomorphology and palaeoenvironment, with particular emphasis on the question of agricultural production at various phases in its long and illustrious history (Carter 1984, forthcoming). For the time being, at least, knowledge of the territory of Croton is largely limited to the still very preliminary results of the first survey campaign (Carter and D'Annibale 1983, forthcoming).

146

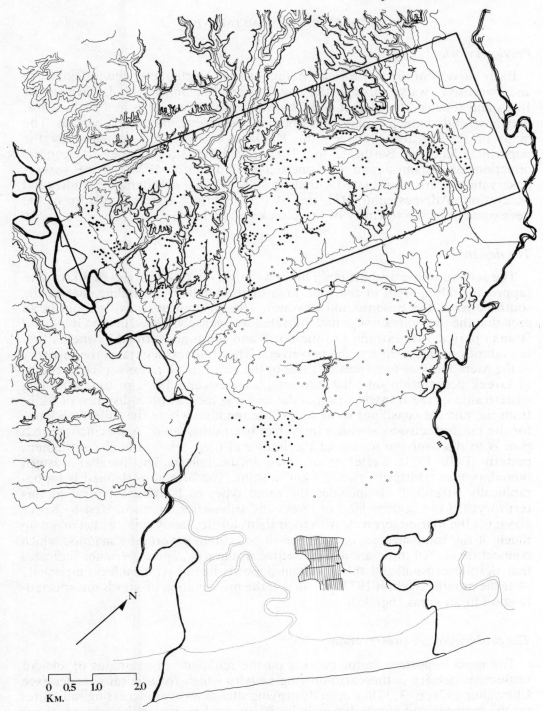

FIG. 44. Territory of Metaponto, between the R. Bradano (to the north) and the
R. Basento, as in autumn 1982. The area of the transect is indicated by a rectangle.
Open circles = sites previously known to the Superintendency of Antiquities of
Basilicata; solid dots = sites surveyed by the University of Texas since 1981. See
also general location map on fig. 48

THE TERRITORY OF METAPONTO

Previous work

Early surveys of the territory of Metaponto can be characterized as 'extensive and purposive' walks through the countryside. Beginning with Lacava in the 1880s and renewed by Uggeri and Chevallier in the late 1960s and early 1970s, they have added much valuable information about settlement in all periods. The maps of the territory between the Bradano and Basento prepared by the Superintendency of Basilicata in 1976 showed 109 sites. Under the general direction of Adamesteanu (Adamesteanu and Vatin 1976), these various observations were coordinated with the results of aerial photographic studies and excavation (Adamesteanu 1973, pp. 51 ff.) to form a coherent picture of the development of the territory of the Greek colonial city.

The design

The second writer and his team limited the survey to a transect of 40 sq. km. (approximately a sixth of the total area of the territory, including that to the south between the Basento and Cavone). This was 'purposively' laid out in an area that the previous surveys had indicated was densely settled in the Greek and Roman periods. Its extremes to the north and south are formed by the natural boundaries of the territory, the two rivers. The Bradano separates the territory of the Metapontines from that of Taras to the north. Both rivers served as routes of Greek penetration into the interior (Adamesteanu 1973, p. 61). The long eastern side of the transect towards the city was located (at a distance of 6 km. from the ancient coastline) so as to include the area where the fullest evidence for the much discussed 'division lines' had been discovered. A specific research goal is to discover the nature of the lines and their relation to the settlement pattern (Folk 1981; Carter *et al.* 1984 forthcoming). The parallel western boundary was arbitrarily placed 4 km. distant. The area thus defined is topographically 'stratified'. It includes the three types of landscape typical of this territory: (1) the bottom land of rivers and tributaries, characterized by heavy clays; (2) the marine terraces, with their light, fertile, sandy soils, which make up much of the total surface; and (3) the slopes (often covered by maquis) which connect these. All three areas were settled in the past, and experience indicates that despite erosion and thick alluvial deposits in the river valleys, especially near the mouths (Neboit 1977, pp. 48 ff.), the preservation of sites is unexpectedly good in all areas (fig. 45).

The problem of site preservation

The most important factor bearing on the reliability of estimates of ancient settlement density is the earth-moving activity which for several decades (see Chevallier 1971, p. 313) has been destroying sites at an ever increasing rate. Sites on the terraces and slopes typically lie 30 cm. to 1 m. under the surface; those along the river bottoms are sometimes deeper (Carter 1980b, pp. 29 ff.). Resurvey after a ten-year interval bears eloquent testimony to the thoroughness

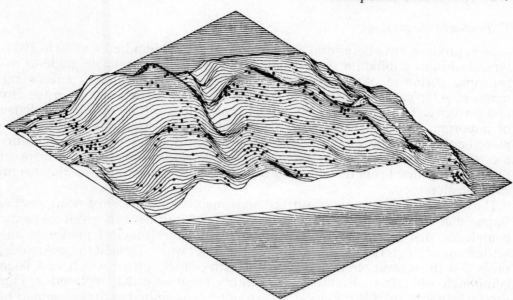

FIG. 45. Territory of Metaponto: contour relief map of the transect with total number of sites surveyed, as in autumn 1982

with which the past can be obliterated: at just 3 km. from the city, locations of sites formerly considered very large now have to be reclassified as non-sites. This wide-scale destruction, particularly of sites close to the ancient city and the coast, was a major consideration in the location chosen for intensive survey.

Some areas within the transect have been bulldozed for fruit orchards and vineyards, but on the whole the fields, divided among small-holders, have been largely given over to grain, and cultivated with light ploughs. All this is, of course, changing. The north-western section of the transect was fortunately surveyed the same year that deep ploughing and irrigation were introduced there.

Method

The survey was carried out by a team of four to five people, walking at intervals of from 3 to 10 m. apart, depending on surface visibility. Thus, recovery of even the smallest sites (e.g. tombs, with a scatter diameter of 5–10 m.) should be complete. The sites are recorded on 1:10,000 scale maps. At each site, the size and density of scatter is measured, and an estimate made of the structure's size. Its proximity to water and other resources and the present land use are all regularly observed. All visible pottery is collected, and samples are taken of the various types of tiles and of slag and kiln by-products for eventual analysis. Features, such as loose building stones, exposed walls and drainage channels, are noted. Both the site and its surroundings are documented photographically.

Estimates of chronology

Sites produce anywhere from a few sherds to several hundred, but 50 to 100 is typical of most habitation sites. These numbers provide a reliable guide to the principal period(s) of occupation. For the Greek and Roman periods the material is typical of that found in stratified contexts in excavations in the city and territory. Though it is hoped that current studies will refine our knowledge of important classes of ceramic evidence, such as the locally produced black-glazed pottery, for the crucial period from the sixth century to the third century B.C. the fine wares from the survey can be dated with a margin of error of twenty-five years. From the third century B.C. to the first century A.D. the margin must be increased.

Dating sites on the basis of surface finds involves a number of assumptions. Experience has taught us to be cautious, and testing has given us some confidence that in the aggregate we can define the principal phases of the settlement of the territory. One site, for example, which seemed to be Archaic, proved with excavation to have had a sixth-century phase which had been completely obliterated by the fourth-century farmhouse that replaced it. Our survey 'window' on this site, located on a slope, was limited to the oldest part of the site. A large site on fairly level ground, by contrast, had major phases corresponding to all of those indicated by surface finds (D'Annibale 1983b). We conclude that it is clearly valuable, when possible, to resurvey sites, as recent changes in land use may bring new evidence for dating to light.

The changing pattern of settlement

After three campaigns and nearly 500 man-days, our objective, 100 per cent coverage of the transect, has nearly been achieved. Less than 10 per cent remains to be walked. 463 sites had been put on the map by the autumn of 1983. That is a density of over twelve sites per square kilometre, which compares favourably with recent surveys elsewhere in the Mediterranean (Cherry 1983, p. 410).

Though the focus of the survey is the Greek and Roman territory, the team was prepared to deal with sites of all periods (and eventually had the opportunity at Croton). Prehistoric sites here, however, are concentrated in a few areas; for example, at San Marco for the Bronze Age. Post-Roman sites are hardly more numerous, the medieval remains at Pietra San Giovanni being the principal example. The mixture of periods and functions corresponds very closely to that revealed by the various excavations of rural sites over the years (Carter 1980a, 1980b).

The fundamental contribution of the survey is the clarity with which it reveals massive changes in the settlement pattern, over relatively short spans of time. The results can, perhaps, best be appreciated in graphic form. Figure 46 represents the total site density for the period 450–275 B.C. The majority of these sites belong to the seventy-five years from 350–275 B.C. Comparison with fig. 47, on which appear sites datable to the Hellenistic–Roman and Imperial periods (second to fourth centuries A.D.), demonstrates the sudden, rapid drop in population after the third century B.C. Recent environmental studies, especially pollen analysis, suggest that the reasons are complex. It is not enough, any

FIG. 46. Territory of Metaponto: map of the transect with sites dating from 450 to 275 B.C. (solid dots), as in summer 1983. Open circles = sites of other periods

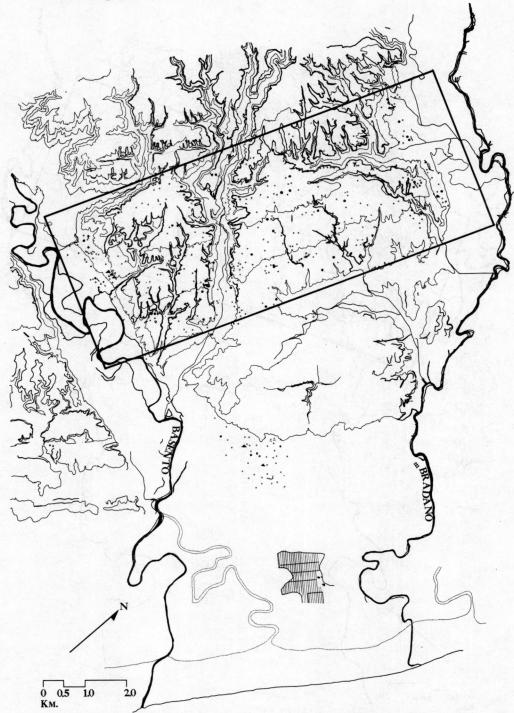

FIG. 47. Territory of Metaponto, with sites dating from the second century B.C. to the fourth century A.D. (solid dots), as in summer 1983. Open circles = sites of other periods; triangles = sites continuously occupied from the fourth century B.C. to the late Roman period

longer, simply to invoke the Lucanians or Romans as the sole agents of destruction (Carter *et al.* 1984, forthcoming).

Roughly 20 per cent of the 463 sites are tombs or clusters of tombs belonging to family burial grounds (originally associated with rural habitation sites). The second writer has identified a number of kiln sites spaced out along the Basento. A small percentage of sites, on the evidence of abundant votive material, are rural cult places, likewise fairly uniformly distributed along the river valley (Carter 1980b, p. 27). The majority of sites, however, are farmhouses, isolated from one another in the countryside. They vary from modest to very extensive. Excavated examples range from 200 to 1,000 sq. m. in area. These 'homesteads' are found in all three topographical zones. They cluster along the slopes of valleys and are located often, as Folk (1981) has shown, at the interface between the sand and gravel of the marine terraces and the underlying pliocene clays. Availability of fresh water was a major determinant in site location.

Studies now in progress are examining the randomness of the settlement pattern in various periods (point-pattern analysis) and statistical relationships between variables such as site size, topographical situation, distance from the city, distance from water, and date. There is, for example, a significant difference between the size and date, and size and elevation, of a farmhouse for the Greek and Hellenistic–Roman periods in the area of the survey. These results are tentative and may well need to be revised as the data are refined. Taken together with evidence from excavations and palaeoenvironmental studies, the survey results are a powerful instrument for the study of this rural population. We intend to extend their range of applicability to the whole territory by sampling other areas.

THE CROTON SURVEY

The survey area lies primarily in the municipal lands of the towns of Cutro and Isola Capo Rizzuto, and covers approximately 270 sq. km. The boundaries are formed by a line at a distance of 5 km. from Croton on the northern side, the river Tacina on the west, and the Ionian Sea to the south and east (fig. 48).

The terrain within this area is marked by steep coastal bluffs and a series of coastal terraces. In some areas these terraces reach inland as far as 6 km. Such is the case in the vicinity of Isola Capo Rizzuto. The interior of the territory is predominantly plateau, with an elevation range of 150–200 m. above sea level. This plateau, however, is extensively dissected by steep river gullies, making it very irregular and creating narrow ridges. Only near the Croton airport does the plateau consist of uniform flat stretches.

The main objective of the survey here, as at Metaponto, is to identify the distribution pattern for Greek and Roman farm sites within the territory of ancient Croton. Since the proposed survey area is quite extensive and archaeologically almost unknown, a random sampling technique was, and will continue to be, employed. From the northern boundary southwards, the survey area was divided into five 3-km. wide transects, running east–west. Each of these transects included an area of approximately 55 sq. km., from which seven 1-km. units or quadrats have been randomly selected. Following this method, a 7 per cent

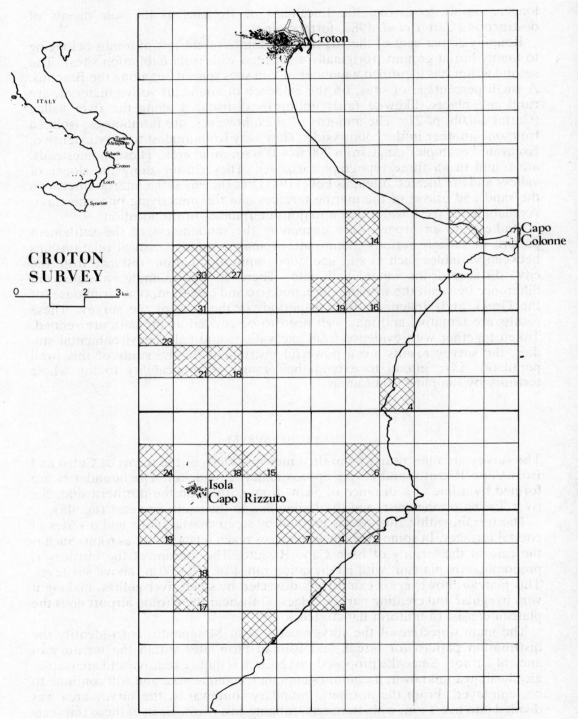

FIG. 48. Partial schematic map of the territory of Croton, with transects and quadrats of the random sampling design. The town of Cutro lies to the west of Capo Colonne

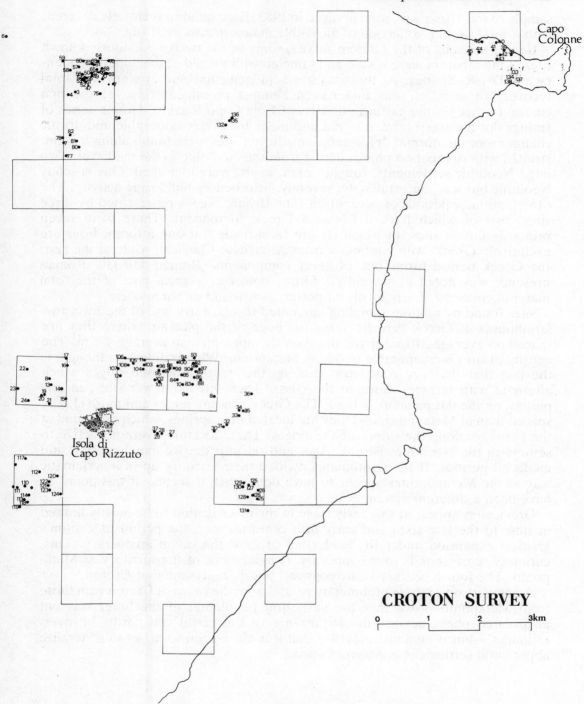

FIG. 49. Territory of Croton with sites surveyed, as in autumn 1983

sample of the 270 sq. km. was surveyed in 1983. Each quadrat is entirely covered, with a total surface collection of all visible diagnostic material (fig. 49).

Before the start of the random survey, some of the twelve previously known sites in the territory were visited and sampled with the aid of the Superintendency and Dr. R. Spadea. At this time some 'judgemental' survey work with total recovery of artifacts, was undertaken along a prominent ridge of the first coastal terrace on the eastern outskirts of Isola Capo Rizzuto. Here a series of springs dot the steep terrace slopes and make for a very noticeable and drastic change from the normal dry vegetation. Eleven sites were found along a 2-km. stretch, with occupation phases dating from the Neolithic to the medieval. Two large Neolithic settlements, roughly 2 km. apart, were identified. One is solely Neolithic but was, unfortunately, severely disturbed by bulldozing activity. The other had later periods of occupation. The Bronze Age is represented by three sites, two of which have a Classical Greek component. There were seven primarily Greek sites, of which six are farmsteads and one a tomb. Four are exclusively Greek, with continuity from Archaic to Classical, while at the rest, the Greek period forms one of many components. Roman and late Roman presence was noted at several. It forms, however, a small part of the total material collected. Early medieval pottery was found on three sites.

Sites found by random sampling amounted to 122; forty-one of the forty-two farmhouses of Greek date lie along the edge of the plateau, where they are spaced on average 210 m. apart; those on the open plateau average 475 m. The density of sites is comparable to that at Metaponto. What is different, though, is the fact that they are concentrated along the steep, limestone ridges which alternate with terraces down to the coast. There are far fewer sites, in any period, on the flat plateaux behind. The Greek sites are larger and more closely spaced than at Metaponto, and they are located near springs, which are found at the bases or along the slopes of the ridges. These locations were attractive to settlers in the Neolithic, Bronze Age, and on into the Roman Imperial, and medieval periods. If the Crotoniates divided their territory up in a systematic way as the Metapontines appear to have done, then it seems, at this point, to have been a different system.

Greek sites appear at this early stage in the investigation to be mostly limited in time to the late sixth and early fifth centuries B.C., the period of Croton's greatest expansion under the leadership of its Pythagorean aristocracy. This, curiously, corresponds to a temporary abandonment of the territory at Metaponto. The fourth century is, by contrast, poorly represented at Croton.

A comparison of these preliminary results from the *chora* of Croton with those from Metaponto prove that the vast rural population of the latter was not an isolated phenomenon—the importance of this result can hardly be overestimated—but it demonstrates also that it is clearly too soon yet to generalize about rural settlement in Magna Graecia.

BIBLIOGRAPHY

Adamesteanu, D. 1973. 'Le suddivisioni di terra nel metapontino', in Finley, M. I. (ed.), *Problèmes de la terre en Grèce ancienne*, Paris, pp. 50–61.

Adamesteanu, D. and Vatin, C. 1976. 'L'arrière-pays de Metaponte', *Compte rendu de l'Académie des Inscriptions*, pp. 110–23.

Carter, J. C. 1980a. 'Rural settlement at Metaponto', in Barker, G. and Hodges, R. (eds.), *Archaeology and Italian Society*, BAR S102, Oxford, pp. 167–77.

— 1980b. 'A classical landscape. Rural archaeology at Metaponto', in *Archaeology*, xxxiii, pp. 23–32.

Carter, J. and D'Annibale, C. 1983 forthcoming. 'Crotone e Metaponto', *Atti del 22° Convegno di studi sulla Magna Grecia*, Taranto (Naples).

Carter *et al.* 1984 forthcoming. 'Population and agricultural production: Magna Grecia in the fourth century B.C.', *Third Conference of Italian Archaeology*.

Cherry, J. 1983. 'Frogs around the pond: perspectives on current archaeological survey projects in the Mediterranean region', in Keller and Rupp 1983, pp. 375–416.

Chevallier, R. 1971. Mission archéologique de la Faculté des Lettres de Tours à Metaponte', *Révue arch.*, pp. 309–26.

D'Annibale, C. 1983a. 'Field survey of the *chora* of Metaponto', in Keller and Rupp 1983, pp. 191–3.

— 1983b. In *The Territory of Metaponto 1981–1982, University of Texas at Austin*, University Publications, Austin, Texas.

Folk, R. 1981. In *Excavations in the Territory of Metaponto, 1980. University of Texas at Austin*, University Publications, Austin, Texas, pp. 5–6.

Keller, D. and Rupp, D. (eds.). 1983. *Archaeological Survey in the Mediterranean Area*, BAR S155, Oxford.

Neboit, R. 1977. 'Un exemple de morphogenèse accélérée dans l'antiquité: les vallées du Basento et du Cavone en Lucanie (Italie)', *Méditerranée*, iv, pp. 39–50.

V. YUGOSLAVIA

The 'Neothermal Dalmatia' Project

Š. Batović and J. C. Chapman

NEOTHERMAL RESEARCH IN THE EASTERN ADRIATIC

Fieldwork

As in most of the Balkans, the development of archaeological fieldwork in the eastern Adriatic mirrors the history of archaeological institutions and the proliferation of museum collections. Despite the discovery of prehistoric cave occupations as early as 1774 (Marović 1979), the emphasis in excavation and fieldwork on the classical period was almost total until the late nineteenth century. From the 1870s, the location of prehistoric sites began and continued at a steady rate, as exemplified by the rate of discovery of Neolithic sites (table 1).

Whilst increasing marginally after World War Two, site discovery rates in Dalmatia lack the dramatic exponential increase of the 1940s–1950s noted in Serbia, eastern Hungary and Wallachia. Two factors are relevant: first, the absence of extensive or systematic survey in Dalmatia until the 1970s (one exception is Batović's survey of the Zadar archipelago (Batović 1973)); second, and more important, the pattern of environmental change has led to the burial of many, if not most, lowland prehistoric sites beneath hillwash (Chapman 1981). Anthropogenic removal of the forest cover in the coastal zone and the Dinaric mountains began in the Late Iron Age and Roman periods (Beug 1961; Brande 1973) and culminated at the time of the Venetian domination (Jedlowski 1975). One of the results of deforestation was rapid erosion of the thin karstic soils subsequently deposited in the lowland zone as hillwash. This late Roman and post-Roman phenomenon was responsible for the burial of large areas of the prehistoric landscape; an instance is the discovery of Neolithic sites near Dubrovnik through well-digging at a depth of 2 m. (pers. comm. S. Petrak). Hence the distribution of Neolithic settlements in Dalmatia, as recorded by Batović (1963, 1966) is one of the few instances in south-east Europe where site recovery is biased in favour of upland (cave) settlement. This interpretation is

158

TABLE 1. Rate of discovery of Neolithic sites in Dalmatia (source: Batović 1966)

Period	No. of new Neolithic sites	Mean no. of sites per annum
1876–99	45	1·9
1900–14	30	2·0
1919–39	39	1·9
1946–66	50	2·5
1967–80	30	2·1

one reason for the rarity of prehistoric remains in Batović's (1973) systematic survey of the Zadar archipelago and for their widespread absence from the fertile lowland basins (*polja*). Other factors concern island ecology and the rate of colonization of small islands (Cherry 1981).

If this interpretation is correct, two conclusions are apparent: first, lowland sites are likely to be found only in those areas of broad coastal plain or wide river valley where there is likely to be greater geomorphological stability; and second, in most other areas, it is unlikely that an unbiased sample of lowland sites will ever be recovered.

Excavation

Recent excavations in the eastern Adriatic have focused on five classes of prehistoric sites: (1) Palaeolithic and Mesolithic caves; (2) Neolithic caves; (3) Neolithic open settlements; (4) Bronze Age–Iron Age tumuli; and (5) Bronze–Iron Age gradina sites (i.e. hilltop enclosed sites). Excluding burial sites, large-scale investigations have been mounted at only five sites (table 2).

TABLE 2

Site	Type of site	Period	Area excavated	% of total site size
Odmut	Cave	Mesolithic–Bronze Age	—	100%
Smilčić	Open	Neolithic	1,280 m.^{2}	4%
Danilo	Open	Neolithic	2,400 m.^{2}	—
Grapčeva Spilja	Cave	Neolithic–Eneolithic	—	80%
Markova Spilja	Cave	Neolithic–Iron Age	—	80%

In addition, test trenching has been carried out at between thirty and forty Mesolithic and Neolithic sites (Batović 1979), and a total of some ten gradina sites (Batović 1977). An important result of excavation is the relative chronological attribution of approximately forty Neolithic sites from a total of over 200 known in Dalmatia, and an additional ten to fifteen in the eastern Adriatic zone. The uncertain chronology of the remaining 'Neolithic' surface sites is illustrated by the site of Kopačina. On the basis of surface finds of chipped stone, a Neolithic date for Kopačina was proposed (Vrsalović 1960); recent excavations indicate early Mesolithic and Bronze Age occupation with a hiatus in the Neolithic period (pers. comm. B. Čečuk).

This review of excavations makes it clear that, for a number of historical and socio-economic reasons, prehistoric sites in Dalmatia have remained largely unexplored, even in the post-war period. It was clear that the intensive excavation programmes on many classical sites and colonies (e.g. Zadar, Split–Narona, Nin, Vis, etc.) had left a backlog of rural settlement work for the future.

Artifactual and environmental analyses

With relatively few exceptions, analysis of prehistoric data from the eastern Adriatic has focused on typological studies of material culture, usually stone tools and pottery (Basler 1979; Batović 1965a and b; Malez 1975, 1979; Novak 1959–1982). On the basis of these studies, a relative chronological framework has been constructed for the region (see p. 191). This scheme is partially supported by radiocarbon dates from the Odmut cave (Marković 1974; Srejović 1974) and the Gudnja cave (Chapman and Mook forthcoming); however, C14 dates from Istria, central Bosnia, upland Montenegro and eastern Italy broaden the spatial context within which Dalmatian cultures may be examined.

Characterization analyses in Dalmatia have so far been limited to prehistoric pottery. Clay analysis of pottery found on Middle Neolithic sites and postulated to have originated in Italy indicated no similarity with the clays of either local Neolithic wares or Italian Neolithic fine wares (Korošec 1956). Analysis of the red material comprising crusted decoration revealed the use of iron oxide (e.g. Smilčić: Batović 1963a), and cinnabar (e.g. Markova Spilja: Novak 1955), for which there are three major sources on the east Adriatic coast (Chapman 1981). Although non-local flint and axe materials have been recognized in museum collections, their sources remain unidentified.

Analysis of the remains of prehistoric subsistence patterns have remained on the qualitative level (Batović 1980; Chapman 1981). A valuable source of economic information remains to be tapped in the faunal samples from Dalmatian prehistoric sites still preserved in local museums.

The east Adriatic prehistoric environment can be partially extrapolated from pollen diagrams in Istria, the Neretva valley, Mljet and the Adriatic Sea itself (Beug 1961, 1977; Brande 1973), as well as through marine sedimentological studies (Van Straaten 1965, 1970). Whilst studies of modern soil conditions are available, the data latent in soils buried under earthworks remain to be exploited.

Conclusions

In comparison with other regions in Yugoslavia and other parts of the Mediterranean basin, it is clear that the archaeological and environmental potential of prehistoric Dalmatia has scarcely been realized.

For a number of theoretical and practical reasons (see below) the most effective method of gaining new insights into Dalmatian prehistory is the development of a regional research design. Selection of a suitable region is, in effect, simplified by the unfavourable geomorphological conditions of much of the coastal lowland, where loss of sites through erosion is compounded by the burial of many prehistoric sites under hillwash. The only suitable regions not affected by such deposition are broad coastal plains and wide river valleys. The rarity of both types of landscape unit in the coastal zone further constrains choice, so that the selection of the largest coastal plain, the Ravni Kotari, or plain of Zadar, if not entirely automatic, is highly predictable on logical grounds. As will become apparent, there are other archaeological, environmental and organizational reasons for the suitability of the Ravni Kotari as a study region for the elucidation of culture process in Dalmatian prehistory.

THE 'NEOTHERMAL DALMATIA' PROJECT

Settlement and environment

The environmental backcloth to the project can be sketched at a high level of generality. These hypotheses concern the whole east Adriatic area and are presented notwithstanding any regional variations to be found in the ecological data for the Zadar lowlands. There are two essential parts: first, the fragility of the karstland environment, and, secondly, the long-term decline in biological productivity of the east Adriatic zone from the early Neothermal (*c.* 10,000 bc) onwards. The karstlands are environments on a knife-edge: typified by small quantities of groundwater and very slow pedogenetic processes, karstic soils requiring millennia to develop can be eroded within a decade; all karstlands are unstable ecosystems and any disturbance tends towards degeneration (Simpozij 1971). Within the long-term reduction in consumable energy (biomass), four major peaks of environmental stress can be identified (Chapman 1981): (1) the rise in Adriatic sea-level between 8000 and 6500 bc flooded fertile lowlands and adversely affected the hydrology of coastal rivers; (2) partial replacement of the coastal deciduous oak forests by evergreen oakwoods in the late seventh to fifth millennia bc reduced plant species variability and grazing potential; (3) major deforestation phases in Dalmatia dated to the Late Iron Age–Roman and the Venetian periods resulted in large areas of secondary vegetation (maquis, garrigue and šibljak); (4) soil erosion of karstland soils buried more fertile lowland soils under hillwash, with severe results for hydrology (reduction of the karst's water-retention capacities; creation of seasonally flooded upland polja; choking of lowland watercourses).

The ecological 'climax' of the Altithermal period (Nandris 1978) had a very different effect in Dalmatia than in temperate south-east Europe. In the latter, higher mean temperature and precipitation and rapid increases in plant diversity and overall biological productivity typified the sixth millennium bc. These coincided with the extensive adoption of farming, and preceded the consolidation marked by the 'climax' societies of the fifth and fourth millennia bc. By contrast, in Dalmatia, the period of rapid vegetation diversification (ninth to eighth millennia bc) precedes the origins of farming, owing to the earlier onset of temperature thresholds for recolonization of thermophilous plants and forest herbivores. The 'climax' vegetation of the coastal zone—the eu-Mediterranean forest—is characterized not only by stability, but also by lower biological productivity than in the preceding deciduous forests. Later, in the second to first millennia bc, the first signs of anthropogenic effect on Dalmatian coastal vegetation can be seen (Beug 1977; Brande 1973), whilst the more serious consequences of soil erosion and hillwash deposition on Late Iron Age and Roman agriculture have yet to be documented in detail.

It remains for much of this general scenario of Dalmatian environmental change to be tested against local and regional information. Juxtaposed with the ecological sequence are processes of cultural change normally associated with the 'Big Questions' of prehistory—the origins of food production, the socio-cultural differentiation of later farmers and the development of enclosed and, later still, defended sites. Evaluation of the competing models purporting to explain these major trends in settlement and economy depends heavily on the collection of new, quantified data and, wherever possible, the restudy of existing material. Hence the main goals of the Neothermal Dalmatia project are closely related to 'Big Questions' as well as to problems of more strictly regional concern.

Cherry and Shennan have stressed that selection of the archaeological problems for investigation is inevitable and should be made explicit. Amongst the many thousands of archaeological goals, they stress four basic questions to which survey can provide at any rate partial answers (Cherry and Shennan 1978, esp. p. 22):

1. The number of sites in the area.
2. The number of sites by period and function.
3. The relationship between archaeological sites and environmental variables.
4. The interrelationships between archaeological sites.

In effect, the questions form sub-sets of information on the overall regional settlement pattern of the Zadar lowlands. Hence the primary aim of the Neothermal Dalmatia project is the definition and explanation of long-term changes in settlement, society and economy in the study region. In the following section, the selection of a study region and the approach to survey strategy will be outlined.

Methodology

In his classic paper on archaeological research strategies, Binford (1964) defined the region as the essential unit of research into culture systems. The logic of this proposal relates primarily to the spatial integration of sites within a region, i.e. the region should be large enough to permit study of all the seasonal movements and exchanges of goods and services that are essential to the culture system in question. Hence regional analysis provides a perspective not only on period-by-period site distribution, but also on the variability of human behaviour across different ecological zones within the region.

The modern topography of the east Adriatic seabord is such that there are but few lowland areas large enough not to be entirely masked by hillwash deposited in the Iron Age or later periods. The largest of these areas is the Ravni Kotari, near Zadar (fig. 50). Definition of a suitable lowland area, however, is not necessarily coincident with the boundaries of a viable study region. Since some form of summer transhumance cannot be excluded *a priori*, an upland component in the study region is necessary; in addition, data are required from the third element in the physical geography of Dalmatia—the offshore islands. Not

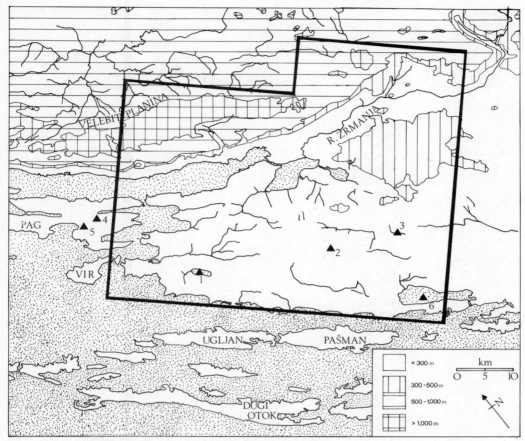

FIG. 50. Dalmatia Survey, topography of the study area and environs. Sites of scientific importance: 1. Bokanjačko Blato; 2. Nadinsko Blato; 3. Podlug; 4. Velo Blato; 5. Malo Blato; 6. Vranjsko Jezero

the least advantage of selecting the plain of Zadar and its hinterland for study is the fact that a relatively intensive survey of the Zadar archipelago has already been completed (Batović 1973).

The boundaries of the study area are indicated above (fig. 50). The location of the boundaries has been selected for the following reasons:

1. Coverage of the full altitudinal range of environmental variation, from sea-level to the eastern peaks of the Velebit range: (a) ecology (climate, soils, geomorphology, geology, vegetation, hydrology); (b) landforms (basins, hilly terrain, mountains, coastline, bays and inlets, inland seas, lakes, etc.).
2. Inclusion of part of the only major river system in northern Dalmatia (the Zrmanja valley).
3. The distribution of currently known surface sites, which indicates exploitation of a broad range of environments from sea-level to at least 600 m. above sea-level (fig. 51).

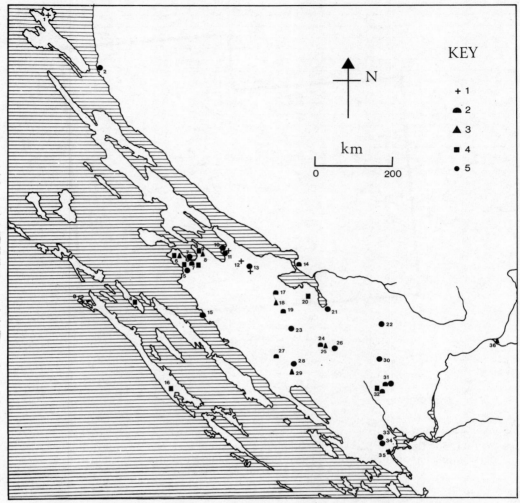

FIG. 51. Map of important known sites in the Zadar lowlands: 1. Palaeolithic; 2.
Neolithic; 3. Eneolithic; 4. Bronze Age; 5. Iron Age

1 Lopar on the isle Rab (P)
2 Jablanac (IA)
3 Veli Rat on the isle Dugi otok (P)
4 Sestrunj (BA)
5 Zaton ninski (BA) (IA)
6 Privlaka (E) (BA)
7 Nin (Aenona) (N) (BA) (IA)
8 Vrsi (Mulo) (E)
9 Vrsi (Jamine) (BA)
10 Rtina (Venac) (IA)
11 Ljubač-Rtina (P) (IA)
12 Ražanac-Podvršje (P)
13 Radovin (Beretinova gradina)
    (P) (IA)
14 Jesenice (Pećina) (N)

15 Zadar (Iader) (IA)
16 Sali (Dugo polje) on the isle Dugi
    otok (BA)
17 Islam Grčki (N)
18 Kašić (E)
19 Smilčić (N)
20 Pridraga (BA)
21 Karin (Corinium) (IA)
22 Medvida (Hadra) (IA)
23 Nadin (Nedinum) (IA)
24 Benkovac (N)
25 Buković (E)
26 Lisičić (Asseria) (IA)
27 Tinj (N)
28 Jagodnja Gornja (IA)

4. The occurrence of excavated and/or dated sites located in sharply contrasting environments (fig. 51)
5. The occurrence of several important scientific sites of potential value for environmental reconstruction (fig. 50).
6. Administrative factors (the line of the northern boundary coincides with the border of the modern province of Dalmatia, and the edge of jurisdiction of the Arheološki Muzej, Zadar).

The study region is dominated by limestone geology. In the north-east, the limestone massif of Velebit remains a constant barrier to inland movement, not least because its minimal supplies of surface water have always discouraged more than short-term settlement. South of the long inlet of Velebitski Kanal, catenae of exposed limestone alternating with flysch are characteristic of much of the lowland zone. The limestone itself varies from gently undulating areas where soil and vegetation cover is still present to zones of pure karst areas of bare rock, so deeply fissured that no surface water survives to support soil and plant growth. Smoother, more rounded topography is found where the limestone is overlain by more recent deposits—Quaternary clays and conglomerates, Holocene marsh and lake sediments. The hydrology of the study area is characteristically varied, with no available surface water on most of the Velebit range and the lowland karst, a number of spring-lines closely associated with limestone-flysch interface and occasional excesses of groundwater, as in the marshes of the lowland zone, which were seasonally flooded until post-war drainage works (e.g. Nadinsko Blato, Bokanjačko Blato).

It is thus clear that the biological potential for human settlement of the study area is immensely variable, with some areas providing no life support whatsoever, other areas perhaps offering possibilities of rough grazing, whilst yet others appear to offer wider scope for mixed farming. Around the coastlines and in the two inland seas—Novigradsko More and Karinsko More—the potential for fishing and shell-collecting must have been high. It is also significant that the landscape is divided into these natural geological areas along a north-west—south-east axis, providing a ready opportunity for transect sampling across the grain of the country as well as systematic survey in locations of high settlement potential.

Research strategy: survey

The research strategy for archaeological survey in the Zadar lowlands has been, and will continue to be, determined by two invariable factors: first, the size

29 Jagodnja Donja (E)
30 Dobropoljci (IA)
31 Bribir (Varvaria) (N) (IA)
32 Krković (N) (BA)
33 Dragišić (IA)
34 Zaton šibenski (Velika Mrdakovica) (IA)
35 Zaton šibenski (cave Tradanj) (E)
36 Knin (Ninia) (E)

P = Palaeolithic
N = Neolithic
E = Eneolithic
BA = Bronze Age
IA = Iron Age

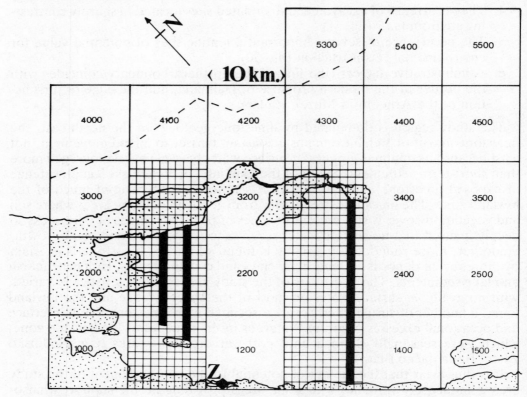

FIG. 52. The study area: solid bars = transects (1982 season, squares 1100–3100; 1983 season, squares 1300–3300); dotted lines mark the boundary of the modern province of Dalmatia; Z = Zadar

of the study area, viz. 2,200 sq. km., and, secondly, the high cost and slow speed of intensive survey (e.g. coverage of 1 sq. km. requiring from 4 to 30 person-days' labour). The initial target of a sampling fraction of 10 per cent of the study area (costing *c.* 1,000 person-days) is still attainable, given modified survey organization and increased funding levels.

Whilst information on each of the four principal questions defined above (p. 162) is clearly a requirement for explaining regional settlement change, it is equally clear that any single survey will produce information of more relevance to some of the questions. In his recent review of Mediterranean surveys, Cherry (1983) points out that settlement-pattern information giving data on the spatial relationship between sites is best provided by coverage of large blocks of land, whilst scattered land blocks are more appropriate for the unbiased estimation of overall site characteristics. Indeed, the obvious dilemma is that no single survey is likely to provide both types of information. Which was the most valid approach for the Neothermal Dalmatia survey?

A multi-stage strategy including survey, test and area excavation, and environmental analysis appeared most appropriate to the problem. Whilst the Arheološki Muzej, Zadar, and institutions in the Croatian capital of Zagreb, as well as Split, have collected surface material from sites within the study area and have recovered much valuable information, it was regarded as axiomatic that the 'purposive' selection of survey areas solely on the basis of past knowledge accumulated by 'judgemental sampling' was not sufficiently objective for the purposes of the project. Hence the survey strategy for the first two seasons was to examine transects 1 km. in width across the grain of the landscape. In the first (1982) season, two parallel transects were located north of Zadar and covered the area between the northern coast (the southern shore of Velebitski Kanal) inland as far as the edge of a former lake and site of environmental importance— Bokanjačko Blato.

In the second (1983) season, a single, longer transect was selected to run from the Adriatic coast near Krmčine to the southern shores of one of the two inland seas, Karinsko More, thus providing coverage of the zone south of Zadar. The transects (fig. 52) in fact represent a compromise between pure quadrats (usually 0·5 km. or 1 km. wide) and pure transects (maximum width often no greater than 300 m.), primarily as a control over environmental variations within the sampled area and as a means of maximizing settlement-pattern data from initial survey runs. The goal of the initial transect, then, was to establish the relative density of settlement in each landscape unit by medium-intensity coverage of as many different units as possible. Once a preliminary idea of site densities was established, further seasons could provide more intensive coverage of areas of particular interest and importance, to correct potential procedural bias (e.g. differential recovery rates of hilltop versus lowland sites, large centres versus small seasonal sites, etc.). This second-stage, more intensive work would concentrate on survey along the grain of the landscape, covering larger blocks of land to provide settlement-pattern data.

Research design: excavation

Whilst anything more than an outline strategy for excavation was, by definition, hard to provide at the outset of a multi-stage project, after two seasons' work a clear excavation strategy is beginning to emerge. In each of the survey transects, there emerged areas of higher-density land use, in some cases (e.g. the Mataci area) with archaeological site types not previously recorded in the survey area. To complement the higher intensity survey planned for future seasons in these areas, it seemed appropriate to attempt to establish the character of rare site-types by test excavation. Excavation here was designed to answer specific, limited questions. Such questions include: definition and absolute dating of site occupation; the composition of refuse deposits, both qualitative and quantitative; and the nature of the site environment. It is recognized that, at the test excavation stage, relatively small artifactual, faunal and botanical samples will be of limited reliability, although any opportunity to collect such material will be exploited. In the light of the results of second-stage survey and test excavations, larger-scale excavation will be mounted at one or two nodal sites, where good artifactual and ecofactual preservation has already been proved. Before this final project stage is reached, a series of multiple working hypotheses are anticipated which can be tested only by intensive, area excavation. Conversely, the value of probabilistic sampling at the survey stage will be confirmed when hypotheses arising out of area excavations can be satisfactorily tested against the survey data. The deductive–inductive interplay inherent in this strategy is arguably the most effective epistemology for behavioural explanations.

Environmental reconstruction

Above (p. 161), current hypotheses were advanced for a generalized reconstruction of the east Adriatic Neothermal environment. Since regional variations in that record are not unlikely, an obvious priority is to test the general hypotheses against new data for the Zadar area. Three classes of analysis are proposed initially: pollen analysis; analysis of sea-level changes; and soil and geomorphological analyses.

Pollen analysis. Five potential sites exist, all in the coastal plain, but there is the possibility, documented elsewhere in the Dinaric Alps, of high-level bog formation in the Velebit mountain range. The known sites are as follows (see fig. 50): *Bokanjačko Blato*—a former lake in a Tertiary basin, now under agriculture. Cored in the late 1960s by a team from Göttingen University, the lake pollen is moderately preserved and radiocarbon dates indicate deposition from *c.* 2000 bc to Roman times; *Nadinsko Blato*—a slightly smaller former marsh in a Tertiary basin: as yet unexplored; *marsh near Podlug*—a small marsh in the south-central part of the Benkovac trough: as yet unexplored; *Velo Blato and Malo Blato*—two adjacent marshes near the southern end of the island of Pag: as yet unexplored.

Sea-level changes. One of the largest 'lakes' in Dalmatia, Vransko Jezero, lies at or slightly below current sea level. Whilst a Miocene ridge *c.* 71 m. above sea-level separates the sea from the lake along most of its length, at the south-east end deposits of less than 3 m. separate salt-water from fresh. Hence relatively minor fluctuations in sea-level would have produced an alternation of coastal embayments and freshwater deposits. According to Serčelj, some of the Vransko Jezero sediments are black non-polleniferous muds (pers. comm. Professor H.-J. Beug).

In addition to its significance as a potential indicator of sea-level changes, Vransko Jezero may yield sediments appropriate to a mineralogical analysis of the type Mackereth (1966) performed in the English Lake District. Any indication of the sequence of erosion and deposition from limestone hills would be most valuable for studies of man-environment relationships.

Soil and geomorphology. In the absence of detailed soil and geomorphological mapping of the study area, a site-based survey of these variables would provide information on land-use potential at various stages of the Neothermal. Published sections from the coastal plains site of Smilčić (Batović 1966) indicate potential for interpretation of soil changes as pioneered in the Balkans by Weide (1974) at Anzabegovo.

Whilst the potential of the sites of known scientific importance for environmental study is considerable, there is an equally obvious bias in site location towards the coastal plain. A priority during preliminary reconnaissance of the hill-country and the mountain zone is the location of such sites to redress the balance.

Conclusions

The methodology of the multi-stage Neothermal Dalmatia project is based on a long-term cumulative and controlled increase in the intensity of investigation. The first stage of intensification marks the introduction of medium-intensity transect survey into an area previously studied by extensive and 'judgemental' techniques. In the next stage, trial excavation of key or rare site-types is juxtaposed with a higher-intensity survey of blocks of land in which high-density land use is predicted from the results of the transect survey. In the final stage, larger-scale excavation of a nodal site within the survey areas is expected. At any given time, further survey work of varying intensities may be required to answer questions posed by excavation. In this way, maximum advantage is gained of new thoughts into the settlement pattern of past societies in the Zadar lowlands.

THE FIRST (1982) SEASON

The first season's fieldwork was completed in August–September 1982. Two parallel transects, each of a width of 1 km., were located in the lowlands north of Zadar; the transects stretched between a site of known scientific importance, the drained lake of Bokanjačko Blato, and the southern shore of the Velebitski Kanal, between Ražanac and Jovići. The eastern transect, of 14·5 km. in length, was completed in nine days, whilst 11·8 km. (or 80 per cent) of the western transect was finished in the remaining nine days at a rate of 6·8 person-days per sq. km.

Intensity of survey has been measured in two ways: distance between fieldwalkers and the amount of person-days needed to cover a unit area of, say, 1 sq. km. (Plog 1976). In the case of the two 1982 transects, spacing between walkers (each of whom followed a fixed bearing across the terrain) ranged from 25 m. to 50 m., with 25-m. intervals being used on almost one-half of the western transect (fig. 53). Analysis of both findspots and single finds recognized confirms the evident value of 25-m. spacing in areas rich in finds, whilst a relatively small percentage increase in single finds and sites occurs with 25-m. spacing in areas of apparently little human activity. It is recognized, however, that it is not possible to state categorically that, on the basis of such spacings, sites or single finds do *not* occur in areas of supposedly low biological potential. This negative conclusion would have required more intensive coverage than was considered practicable for an initial across-the-grain reconnaissance. In addition, it is questionable whether the labour required to cover several square kilometres of limestone karst (fig. 54) would have been considered an efficient use of scarce resources.

Rather than the recording and collection of any visible monuments or artifacts at regular intervals along the transect, each fieldwalker collected material as and when discovered. After the edge of the findspot was discovered and plotted, collection of all artifacts within randomly placed 5 × 5 m. quadrats was completed. The number of quadrats depended on the size of the artifact distribution (one quadrat for distributions up to 20 × 20 m., two for 40 × 40 m., etc.). Future analysis will identify any significant differences in the densities of surface material and attempt to identify possible functional connotations. On the basis of

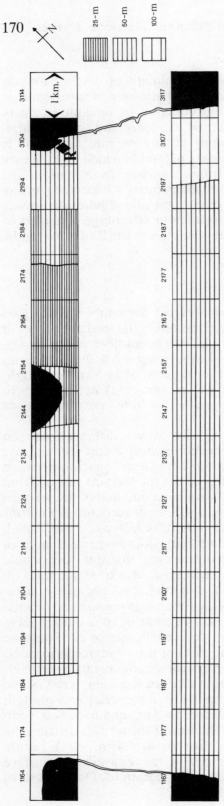

FIG. 53. 1982 survey transects: survey spacing. The diamond (R) represents the village of Ražanac

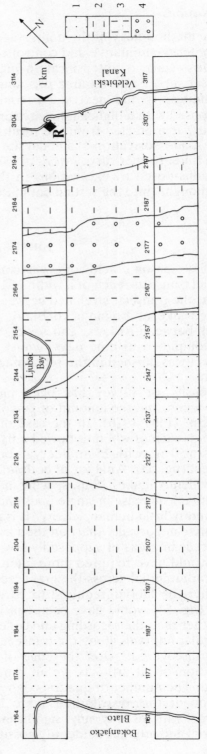

FIG. 54. 1982 survey transects: geology. 1. Limestone karst; 2. Dry Pleistocene sands and sandy clay; 3. Flint-bearing Eocene gravels and marls; 4. Non-flint-bearing Eocene marls and conglomerates. The diamond (R) represents the village of Ražanac

immediate (i.e. on-site) analysis, archaeological remains were divided into three categories: (a) standing monuments (tumuli, cist graves, enclosed settlements, hillforts, deserted medieval villages, etc.); (b) findspots (defined by the presence of a minimum of four artifacts within a 5×5 m. collection quadrat); (c) single finds (defined arbitrarily by the presence of one to three artifacts within a 5×5 m. collection quadrat). At each instance of categories (a) and (b), fieldwalkers filled in a bilingual recording form (Croatian and English) by which standard locational information, environmental information and data on the context of collection were gathered (figs. 56–7, pp. 192–3).

The location of single finds was recorded, but no site form was filled in. The terms 'monument', 'findspot' and 'single find' merit clarification, in view of the difficulties of defining and using terms such as 'site' (Thomas 1975; Doelle 1977; Keller and Rupp 1983), and because of the ubiquitous artifactual 'background noise' found in Mediterranean lands (Cherry 1983; Gallant 1982). The term 'monument' refers to those sites which are defined by upstanding remains or ditches, whether or not their function is apparent. The terms 'findspot' and 'single find' are preliminary categories for areas where discard from some as yet unspecified form of human activity took place.

The significance of individual 'findspots' and 'single finds' varies according to the accuracy with which their function can be determined. For generalized clusters of abraded pottery it is hard to assign a definite function; for chipped stone remains, microwear may be more useful. Hence there will always be a residue of 'findspots' with chronological attribution but no functional information. These finds are best assessed not at individual 'findspot' level but at the level of overall density of finds in each ecological unit per period (see below). A similar principle applies to 'background noise', viz. the random discard of small quantities of material produced by human occupation. If it is assumed that greater quantities of 'noise' will derive from heavier occupations of a landscape, then 'background noise' can be informative.

In gross terms, the following totals of archaeological remains were discovered:

TABLE 3. Summary of archaeological finds, 1982 season

	Western quadrat	Eastern quadrat	Total
Monuments	44	29	73
Findspots	144	64	208
Single finds	>28	>50	>78

Single finds totals should be regarded as only a fraction of the total number of single finds discovered, since exhaustive analysis of this find category is incomplete.

Monuments

By far the largest proportion of standing monuments were stone tumuli (pl. I*a*). Whilst dating evidence from excavated examples indicates a time-span of two millennia (Early Bronze Age–Late Iron Age, 2000 bc–200 B.C.), most of the surface material from survey tumuli was attributable to the Iron Age. In several cases (e.g. sites 2174/0037: 2164/0031) chipped stone of Neolithic or Bronze Age date was found on the slopes of tumuli. The essential problem is whether the flint tools were discarded during burial rites or present in the soil/rocks later used to construct the tumulus.

In two cases (2174/0019 and 2174/0093), tumuli were associated with enclosed settlements dating to the Middle to Late Bronze Age (*c.* 1600–900 bc). In the first, a large tumulus was set inside, and symmetrically opposite, the entrance to a site enclosed by a stone wall (pl. I*b* and fig. 55). In the second, one end of the perimeter stone wall of an enclosed site ran over the lower slopes of a tumulus. In the case of 2174/0019, large quantities of Bronze Age pottery were visible on the surface of the site, and even greater quantities had been washed from the eastern edge of the site into a deep gully. By contrast, low densities of material characterized the second enclosed site (2174/0093).

Findspots

Two principal types of materials were recovered—pottery and chipped stone. Diagnostic pottery from the Neolithic and Bronze Age was easily recognizable (pl. VI); however, continuity in local coarse ware production from the Iron Age to the present day made chronological attribution hazardous. Chipped stone material from the Palaeolithic (pls. III–IV) was distinguishable from later stone material (i.e. Mesolithic–Bronze Age (pl. V) by size of artifacts and raw material; the later industries were in any case defined by a low ratio of distinct tool types (*sensu* F. Bordes) and tool blanks to debitage.

On the 208 recorded findspots, 324 occupations of varying dates were recovered (table 4).

TABLE 4. Summary of classes and dates of archaeological finds, 1982 season

	Western transect	Eastern transect	Total
Chipped stone			
Palaeolithic	18	17	35
Later	133	58	191
Pottery			
Neolithic	0	1	1
Bronze Age	44	6	50
Iron Age	8	7	15
Roman	2	3	5
Medieval and later	19	8	27

Single finds

Large numbers of single finds were located within certain geological formations of the transects. Preliminary analysis of this class of data suggests that later chipped stone represents the largest finds category, with Neolithic, Bronze Age and Iron Age pottery conspicuous by its absence.

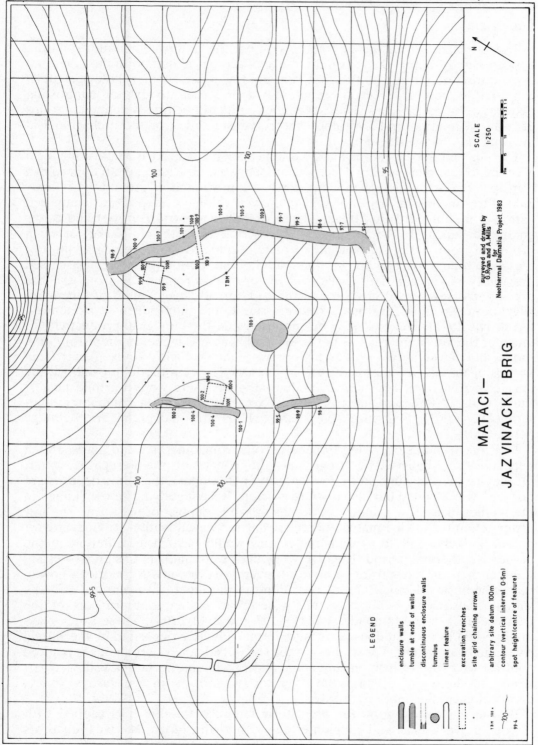

FIG. 55. Plan of the enclosed site at Mataci-Jazvinački brig

Landscape studies

The principal advantage of transects across the grain of the country is the opportunity to sample the maximum range of ecological units with the minimum expenditure of effort. In the first season, the main geomorphological units common to both transects were identified and seen to exhibit contrasting patterns of human activity. These ecological units will be briefly defined in terms of soils, vegetation and hydrology before consideration of the archaeological material (fig. 54: geology).

The inhospitable limestone karst has long been recognized as a landscape form with the lowest biological productivity in Dalmatia. Gračanin (1960) defines two principal characteristics of modern karst: a low volume of groundwater (300–3,000 litres in 100 cm. depth of soil, in a given volume of deposit, as compared with 3–4 million litres in 100 cm. depth of soil in Central Europe) and a low volume of earth (100 kg. of karst yields 0·5 kg. of earth, cf. 100 kg. of earth produced from 100 kg. of volcanic or metamorphic rocks). The degradation of the limestone environment in the Neothermal period has been discussed previously (Chapman 1981); removal of forest cover since the Iron Age has precipitated severe soil erosion and the widespread development of secondary vegetation—maquis, garrigue, dry grassland and unproductive stonebrash (Andrović 1971). Hence it may be supposed that the biological productivity of much of the limestone regions in the lowland zone was higher in prehistory than today, but never necessarily as high as in other ecological units. Apart from groups of tumuli (a linear cemetery in quadrat 2197, on the hilltops above the village of Jovići (pl. I*a*)), and individual mounds, there were four findspots or single finds earlier than the Iron Age. Exceptions include a Palaeolithic findspot (2127/0002), a Bronze Age sherd (2117/0001) and prehistoric debitage (2147/0001).

Pleistocene sands overlying Eocene gravels, conglomerates and marls stretch between the Skulići–Jovići ridge and the course of the Jaruga N. river. Displaying marked changes in gradient (up to 15° slopes), the sandy deposits are not only well drained but also open to erosion. Recent gullying below Skulići, in the hamlet of Ražanac, indicates depths of sandy deposit of over 3 m. The low water-retention of this matrix has restricted recent cultivation to vineyards: it seems unlikely that the soil characteristics would have been different in the earlier Neothermal period. Relatively few finds were made in this area—despite the fact that, on this hillside, a hoard of twenty-six *Spondylus* bracelets, now in the Arheološki Muzej, Zagreb, was found in the nineteenth century. Broadly similar Pleistocene sandy clays are widespread in the southern part of the transects (e.g. notably quadrats 2117–1197 and 2114–2104). These sandy clays are overlain in restricted areas by Neothermal alluvium deposited by the Jaruga river and by diluvium. The dryness of the soil outside the valley stands in marked contrast to a strip of lush pasture some 500 m. wide in the Jaruga valley. Apart from the discovery of an isolated group of barrows in the Jaruga valley, archaeological findspots were rare.

By far the richest zone for prehistoric land-use was the hills capped with Eocene gravels, marl and conglomerate south of the Jaruga N. river (quadrats 2174–2164 and 2187–2177). This was the only unit encountered in the survey

PLATE I

a. Iron Age tumulus near Jovići (quadrat 2197)

b. View of the enclosed site at Mataci-Jazvinački brig, from the south-west showing
enclosure rampart

PLATE II

a. The Iron Age hillfort of Venac-Rtina from the south, with Iron Age tumuli in the foreground

b. Pridraga cairnfield: view of lines of tumuli along natural grassy terraces

PLATE III

Middle Palaeolithic flintwork from Podvršje-Ražanac-Rtina (Matakov brig—Ljubačka kosa): *a*, *c*. Site 2175/0012; *b*. Site 2174/0015; *d*. Site 2174/0031; *e*. Site 2174/0059 ($\frac{1}{2}$)

PLATE IV

Later Palaeolithic flintwork from Podvršje-Ljubać (Matakov brig—Ljubačka kosa): *a–b*. Site 2174/0020; *c–d*, *g–h*. Site 2175/0012; *e*. Site 2174/0031; *f*. Site 2174/0061 ($\frac{1}{2}$)

PLATE V

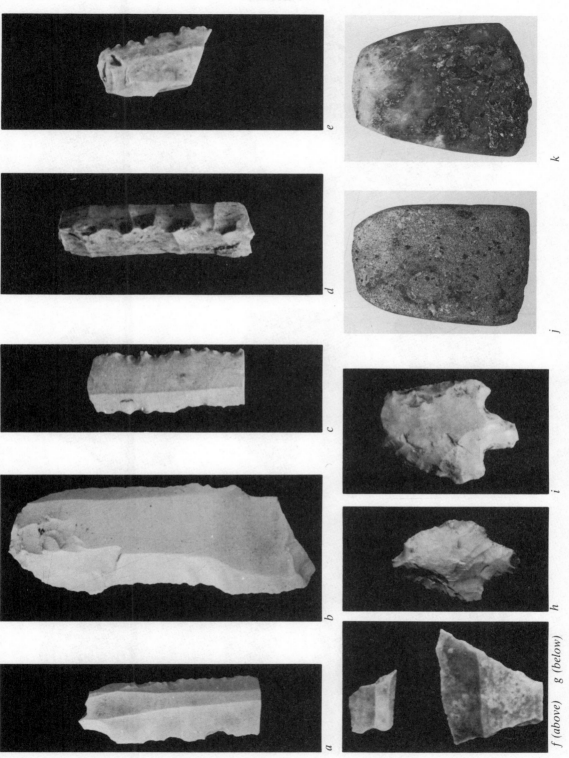

Neolithic and Eneolithic stone tools: *a–g, j–k.* Tinj-Podlivade (Early Neolithic); *h.* Site 2174/0064 (Rtina-Ljubačka kosa, Eneolithic); *i.* Site 1388/0002 (Lisane Tinjske, Eneolithic) (*a–i*, ½; *j–k*, ⅓)

PLATE VI

a

b

c

d

e

f

g

Early Neolithic Impressed Ware from Tinj-Podlivade (⅓)

transects in which low-quality but usable pebble flint and chert was available for prehistoric exploitation. Not surprisingly, therefore, a large number of findspots consisting of chipped stone-working debitage were located, both eroding out of gulleys in the fine marl and within extensive scatters of gravel pebbles. In quadrats 2187–2177, a higher proportion of Palaeolithic material was found, including sites where discard of worked-out cores implies flint-knapping *in situ* (e.g. 2187/0019, 2177/0028). Relatively few findspots in the eastern transect contained Bronze Age pottery in association with flintwork.

By contrast, in quadrat 2174, a Bronze Age landscape including enclosed sites, huts, flint scatters and tumuli was discovered eroding out of the fine marly soil. The principal monuments were two enclosed sites of the Middle Bronze Age, 2174/0019 and 2174/0093, each associated with a tumulus (pl. I*b*). Trial excavation of 2174/0019 is reported on below. Beside these foci, over forty chipping floors were associated with Middle Bronze Age pottery. In one case (2174/0037), an eroded surface of *c.* 100 × 70 m., with dense areas of chipping debris and Bronze Age pottery, was found next to a badly eroded tumulus. In addition, on a hill west of the enclosed site a group of four sub-rectangular depressions was found in an area of 40 × 30 m.; from their homogeneous shape, it is possible that these were houses of the prehistoric period (site 2174/0114). This area represents one of the rare examples outside Greece of a south-east European Bronze Age landscape lying outside the zone of agricultural destruction. Since the area is likely to remain as heathland in the future, the Bronze Age monuments are not at risk; however, active soil erosion is a form of uncontrolled excavation of flint-working sites.

A later development in this landscape was the creation of a linear tumulus cemetery on the Mataci–Stojići ridge, above the bay of Ljubač. This linear cemetery contains at least 150 tumuli, some of which have yielded Iron Age artifacts (Batović, pers. comm.). It continues east of Mataci village, as well as 3 km. west of the transect as far as the Ljubač peninsula. It culminates in a stone-walled (?funerary) enclosure enclosing sixteen large tumuli, which stands opposite the site of Venac—the most strongly fortified Iron Age hillfort in north Dalmatia (pl. II*a*). In addition to the visible Liburnian tumuli of the linear cemetery, there also exist an unknown number of flat graves with Hellenistic grave-goods, mostly clustering to the south of Venac. The contents of some of these graves were exposed by nineteenth-century excavation.

The Arheološki Muzej, Zadar, has initiated negotiations with republican and federal agencies to schedule the entire Iron Age landscape from Ljubljana to Mataci. The discovery of the hitherto unknown Middle Bronze Age landscape next to the highly organized and very visible Iron Age remains is perhaps the most significant of the first season, since it represents the first largely complete Bronze Age landscape located on the Dalmatian coast.

To the south of this rich zone of Eocene sediments lies the valley of the Jaruga S. river. The geological deposits are, again, Eocene marls and conglomerates, but nowhere in the transects were any major sources of chipped stone raw materials discovered. Along the northern edges of the valley, yellow-grey hillwash derived from the Podvršje–Stojići ridge has been deposited over Eocene marls to a depth of 1·5 m., diminishing further to the south. The current course of the Jaruga S. stream lies within a thin strip of alluvium; however, there is enough preliminary locational and geomorphological evidence to suggest that the river course may have fluctuated in the later Neothermal period. This hypothesis will be tested in future seasons; the current evidence is the restricted distribution of pre-Iron Age material in a narrow zone within the Ljubač depression, contrasting with purely Iron Age and later material on the upper slopes surrounding the depression. Of the prehistoric material, there is some evidence for Palaeolithic artifact scatters, including on-site tool production and core dispersal (e.g. 2144/0007). A dense scatter of Roman pot and tile south-west of Ljubački Stanovi may well indicate the site of a farmstead (2134/0002).

Because the greater part of the surface finds were collected within 5×5 m. quadrats, it is possible to make a broad comparison of artifact density and findspot frequency according to ecological unit. For the purposes of this comparison, four gross geomorphological units are used: limestone karst; dry Pleistocene sands and sandy clays; flint-bearing Eocene gravels and marls; and non-flint-bearing Eocene marls and conglomerates. Included in the artifact calculations are findspots and monuments with finds, but not single finds. For calculations of findspot density per square metre, findspots with more than one 5×5 m. collecting quadrat are treated as a single findspot; whereas in the calculations of mean artifact density per square metre of collecting quadrat, each separate collection quadrat is given equal weight (see table 5).

The results of these basic statistics suggest that, cultural and natural transformations being equal, there is a predominance of findspots on the flint-bearing Eocene deposits on the Mataci-Stojići ridge. The supposed low biological productivity of the limestone karst is amply reflected in the lowest findspot density for both transects, whilst the flint-free Eocene marls reach a medium level of findspot density. It should, of course, be recalled that relatively wide spacing of 25 and 50 m. was used by fieldwalkers to gather this data. What is less predictable, however, is the parity of the mean artifact densities for the different ecological units. Whilst the range of artifact densities on Eocene gravels is far greater than for other units, the overall artifact density, even in areas rich in useful stone resources, is remarkably low. Indeed, only thirty-eight findspots (thirty-four on Eocene gravels) reveal an artifact density higher than one artifact per square metre reached. Recalling Doelle's (1977) third criterion of an archaeological 'site'—'if no other criteria are present, an artifact density of $>5/m.^2$'—it is clear that 'siteless' or 'non-site' archaeology is here to stay in Neothermal Dalmatia. To underline the fact of very low discard rates, it should be noted that, even at the later Bronze Age enclosed site 2174/0019, maximum surface artifact densities reached just over 3 per square metre.

A further point of interpretation concerns the evidence for flint-knapping *in situ*, here inferred from the presence of discarded cores or core rejuvenation flakes. Although the absolute number of findspots with cores is greatest on the Mataci-Stojići ridge (thirty-eight out of forty-seven cases), there is clear evidence for transport of flint and chert into areas where these resources are not locally available for final tool production. In most cases, later prehistoric cores were discarded, but Palaeolithic tool-making is attested on one site on dry Pleistocene sands (2114/0001) and on another on the Eocene marls of the Ljubač depression (2144/0007).

TABLE 5. Artifact and site densities, 1982 transects

	Area (km.²)	No. of findspots	Mean density of findspots (km.²)	No. of quadrats	Mean artifact density (m.²)	% quadrats with artifact density of >1 per m.²	% quadrats with core rejects
East transect							
Limestone karst	8·2	1	0·12	1	0·64	0	0
Pleistocene sands and sandy clays	3·4	12	3·5	14	0·24	0	7
Eocene gravel	1·1	40	36·4	41	0·54	19	15
Eocene marls	1·2	13	10·1	13	0·42	15	15
West transect							
Limestone karst	3·6	4	1·1	4	0·59	0	0
Pleistocene sands and sandy clays	3·8	6	1·6	9	0·64	22	22
Eocene gravels	1·0	113	113·0	128	0·49	20	26
Eocene marls	1·8	33	18·3	36	0·42	5	8
Total							
Limestone karst	11·8	5	0·4	5	0·6	0	0
Pleistocene sands and sandy clay	7·2	18	2·5	23	0·4	9	13
Eocene gravels	2·1	153	72·8	169	0·5	20	23
Eocene marls	3·0	46	15·3	49	0·42	8	12

A final comment on the findspot and artifact densities is by way of comparison with other survey areas in the Mediterranean. It is clear that much of the past settlement in the Zadar lowlands is either less well preserved or less intensively attested for reasons of low discard rates than on the opposite side of the Adriatic Sea.

An example is Lloyd and Barker's (1981) categorization by size of Roman scatters in the Molise survey: A—very large debris scatters (500×500 m.), B—large debris scatters (50×50 m.—100×100 m.), C—medium debris scatters (20×20 m.—50×50 m.), D—small density scatters ($<20 \times 20$ m.), and E—cultural material with no nucleus of finds (scatters of comparable size have been found in Potter's (1976) survey of the Narce area and Dyson's (1978) work on the Ager Cosanus).

Nothing approaching the Molise category A has yet been found in the Zadar survey, whilst relatively few findspots of category B–C size have been surveyed. By and large, the findspots of the 1982 season fall within Molise classes D and E (categories Lloyd and Barker do not even deign to discuss: 1981, p. 296). One of the most pressing tasks of future studies in the Zadar lowlands is to determine, by experiment or by analogy, the range of cultural and natural transformations which have resulted in the survival of such low densities of material.

THE SECOND (1983) SEASON: A PRELIMINARY ASSESSMENT

The 1983 season comprised one week's study of the finds from the first season, a three-week survey period, and a week's excavation of a Middle Bronze Age enclosed site discovered in the 1982 survey.

The 1983 survey team covered a 1-km. wide transect in the lowlands east and south-east of Zadar, complementing the survey transects of the first season north of Zadar. The single transect was aligned across the grain of the countryside, beginning at the southern shore of the inland sea Karinsko More and ending on the Adriatic coast near the village of Krmčina. The transect was 24·3 km. long and was completed in about eleven days (4·5 person-days per square kilometre).

A survey strategy comparable to the 1982 design was used in the field, namely fieldwalkers at either 25- or 50-m. intervals following a fixed compass-bearing across the terrain. On geological units other than karst, a 25-m. spacing was considered essential, whilst the wider spacing was normally utilized on limestone areas. A similar classification of archaeological units—monument, findspot and single find—was used; minor modifications to the site record form and single finds labels were incorporated to improve the quality of locational information. The following gross totals of site categories were discovered in the survey transect:

TABLE 6. Comparison of archaeological finds, 1982 and 1983 seasons

	1983 (24·3 km.²)	1982 (both transects 26·3 km.²)
Monuments	99	73
Findspots	121	208
Single finds	133	>50

This year, the main bulk of the monuments, as well as many findspots and single finds, were clustered along landscape units to which the transect ran perpendicular. This was particularly true of two landscape units—the limestone karst immediately to the south of Karinsko More, and a range of rounded limestone hills north-east of Nadinsko Blato. Whilst human occupation was not altogether lacking in other parts of the transect (e.g. the coastal range of limestone hills), the monuments in these two zones merit particular attention.

The Pridraga cairnfield

South of Karinsko More, the smaller of the two inland seas in the study area, and in the village territory of Pridraga, lies an extensive cairnfield which includes some contemporary field boundaries (pl. II*b*). Unknown before this year, the cairnfield was bisected by the transect, and it was clear that the monuments were found both north and south of the quadrats. In the first two days of the survey, some forty-five cairns were discovered in quadrats 3348–3338. On the basis of these discoveries, Ms. G. Ryan and Mr. A. Mills were asked to prepare a detailed survey of the Pridraga cairns in the third week. The survey team covered an area of *c.* 4 sq. km. in an attempt to locate all the cairns in this extensive site. By the end of the third week, over 200 cairns had been plotted at 1:1,000 and an additional twenty-five others had been plotted on a base map of 1:15,000, making a total of *c.* 230. This total makes the Pridraga site one of the largest cairnfields in Dalmatia (cf. the Zaton cairnfield with 137: pers. comm. S. Batović; the sites near the source of the Cetinja river, or the Lika cairnfields: Drechsler-Bižić 1975, 1983; Marović 1976; Marović and Čović 1983). All the pottery recovered from the thirty or so cairns yielding surface material can be dated to the Bronze Age, broadly comparable to the Mataci material (see below). The size of the cairns rarely exceeds 10 m. in diameter and 0·75 m. in height; the largest mounds are often those higher up the slope towards Pridraga village. An interesting aspect of the Pridraga cairnfield is that the cairns were laid out in small groups on the natural grassy terraces in between karstic limestone outcrops. Such a use of natural topographic features is a rarity in prehistoric Dalmatia.

An additional and most important element of the Pridraga site was the presence of a dry-stone wall which ran in a straight line from the edge of the Pridraga outfield (defined by large recent stone walling), across the open limestone area where most of the cairns were concentrated almost as far as the shore of Karinsko More. The wall was rarely more than 0·4 m. high, regularly 1·5–2 m. wide, and was constructed with medium-sized limestone boulders, in a haphazard style utterly unlike modern dry-stone walling. The current interpretation is that the date of the wall can be determined by what appears to be a stratigraphic superposition of two tumuli, one containing surface finds of Bronze Age pottery, constructed on top of the wall. The apparent existence of a prehistoric wall some 850 m. in length is a rare occurrence in Balkan prehistory and may be interpreted, after well-known north-west European parallels (Coles and Harding 1979), as some form of territorial boundary, dividing the land later covered by the Pridraga cairnfield into two, unequal, parts.

The settlement component of the Pridraga cairnfield is unknown within the area surveyed, but two 'gradine' (enclosed hilltop sites) some 2·5 km. to the south-east near Karin, as well as two additional gradine at the northern end of the inland sea, near Novigrad, may well contain at least some Bronze Age occupation layers.

The Nadin area

Between the main Donje Biljane–Benkovac road and the former marsh Nadinsko Blato lies a range of rounded hills of Upper Cretaceous origin, composed of limestone karst and ranging in altitude from 168 to 266 m. above sea-level. The highest point of the 1983 transect, the Nadin hill, was one of the most important later prehistoric and classical sites in the Zadar lowlands. Named 'Nedinum' by the Romans, the hillfort of Nadin was first occupied in the later Bronze Age, later becoming the centre of a large Liburnian (Iron Age) territory, continuing its occupation in the Hellenistic and early Roman periods as well as the Croatian period (seventh to sixteenth centuries A.D.), and completing its settlement with a large Turkish fortification of the sixteenth to seventeenth centuries. In addition to Nedinum, gradine of the Bronze or Iron Ages were built on all the other peaks of this range of hills, a distance of 8 km. to the east (Grubica Glava, near Benkovac).

Whilst it is clear that the Nedinum site merits closer attention and a systematic tacheometric survey next season, in this season intensive surface collection in the hillfort and the 'urban' areas on its north and eastern flanks gave a preliminary indication of the settlement spread over different periods. Not surprisingly, surface artifact densities were higher in the neighbourhood of Nedinum than at almost any other point in the transect. One indication of a rural settlement interdependent with the Nadin centre was the discovery of a 'villa rustica' (2338/0002) some 1·8 km. north of the hillfort and complete with mosaic floors, painted wall-plaster, fragments of window-glass and a rich ceramic assemblage. Further Roman settlement is indicated by outliers above the northern edge of Nadinsko Blato. In addition, the transect crossed part of what is probably a group of small, low, stone tumuli, possibly associated with stone walls which traversed the lower southern slopes of the Nadin hill. In summary, there is great potential for intensification of the study of the Iron Age, Roman and Byzantine landscape in the centre of the 1983 transect.

Neolithic sites at Lišane and Tinj

As in the 1982 survey, Neolithic remains were rare in the second season. Nevertheless, one major focus of Early Neolithic remains was located 2 km. east of the transect, in the village territory of Tinj, whilst a second concentration of later Neolithic finds was found between the southern edge of Nadinsko Blato and the hamlet of Miljovići near Lišane. The Lišane finds comprise low-density scatters of small, often abraded, sherds with little characteristic decoration, but a clearly identifiable Neolithic paste and temper. At Tinj, however, intensive fieldwalking at spacings of 5–10 m. allowed the definition of the limits of an Early Neolithic Impressed Ware site, covering 250 × 50 m. (1·25 ha.). Artifact densities of as high as 10 per square metre were encountered in the central part of the settlement (pls. IV–V). Local informants gave us to believe that a late Neolithic focus is located in another part of the village. Further intensive collection is planned in the Tinj area in future seasons.

Trial excavation at Mataci–Jazvinački Brig

Limited excavations were carried out at the later Bronze Age enclosed site of Mataci–Jazvinački Brig (2174/0019). The main aims of the campaign were four-fold: to determine whether or not there was an intact culture-level remaining on the flattest parts of the site; to determine the conditions of preservation of artifactual and ecofactual material; to clarify the nature of the enclosure wall and to identify where possible, any trace of surviving prehistoric buried soil; and to obtain a more accurate dating of the site occupation.

Three trenches were opened in the single week of excavation; all of them were excavated to bedrock over at least part of their area. Trench 1 measured 5×5 m. and was located in the south-west part of the flat spine of the site. Trench 2, also 5×5 m., was placed on the north-east part of the spine. Trench 3 measured 10×1.5 m. and was laid across a well-preserved section of the northern part of the enclosure wall (fig. 55). The notion of excavating part of the tumulus inside the enclosure wall was discarded, since bedrock was showing over part of its area and erosion had badly affected the chances of uncovering a prehistoric buried soil.

The stratigraphic picture was consistent in each trench and comprised the following sequence:

(1) Basal Upper Cretaceous limestone with some sandstone and conglomerates: the 'natural' of the site, the limestone has at some time, possibly in the recent past, undergone karstification, with consequent chemical weathering and the creation of deep fissures.

(2) Decomposing limestone, sandstone and soil fill the fissures: basal fill is yellow marl mixed with limestone boulders; middle fill is decomposing lumps of sandstone mixed with limestone boulders; upper fill is light brown sandy loam. Bronze Age pottery is included in the fill of the fissures.

(3) The formation of a brownish-yellow silty soil from the Eocene marls as the prehistoric soil existing prior to the construction of the enclosure wall.

(4) The construction of a later Bronze Age stone enclosure wall, by creating a primary rampart 2.5 m. wide composed of large limestone blocks and heaping smaller stones on top of the primary rampart. It is assumed that the tumulus was laid out at the same time as the rampart.

(5) At some unidentified, presumably post-Bronze Age, time, tumble from the rampart fell outwards onto the same brownish-yellow silty soil.

(6) Formation of the modern topsoil, a brown silty loam, a matrix ubiquitous on site except under the primary rampart and rampart tumble.

As far as could be discerned, and with the possible exception of an oval area with some burning in Trench 1, there was no certain trace of an intact prehistoric culture level indicating occupation. Nevertheless, in the three trenches a total of almost 1,100 sherds of Middle Bronze Age date and some seventeen unretouched flint flakes indicates fairly intensive discard rates by local standards. At least three possibilities can be raised: that the rampart was built to enclose the tumulus, not to act as a boundary for human occupation, and the sherds represent ritual deposits; that the Bronze Age occupation was so short or seasonal that a genuine culture-level was not formed; or that a Bronze Age culture-level did exist at one time but was eroded following deforestation of the Mataci ridge. In support of this third hypothesis, it is clear that much of the enclosure wall is badly eroded; also, in 1982 a large quantity of Bronze Age pottery was found in a secondary position in an erosion gully to the east of the site.

In summary, no unequivocal traces of a culture-level were found at Mataci. Organic preservation at the site is poor: apart from flecks of charcoal in Trench 1, no organic finds were made (including bone). Hence, no dating of the site closer than the Middle Bronze Age (*c.* 1500–1200 bc) is possible. On the positive side, the method of rampart construction has been established and soil samples of Bronze Age buried soil—the first to be recognized in Dalmatia—have been collected. It is hoped that this trial season may shed light on processes of karstification in the Zadar lowlands.

DISCUSSION AND CONCLUSIONS

After two seasons of survey and one limited excavation, some general points about the Neothermal Dalmatia project should be made, first about the survey, then the natural environment and the archaeology. Much of what is offered in the way of comment on settlement patterns is necessarily both tentative and preliminary.

The initial transect surveys across the grain of the Dalmatian landscape have exposed the main geological units in the Zadar lowlands. Given financial limitations, it could be argued that a greater number of narrower transects would have led to increased efficiency, at the cost of losing settlement density information. Nevertheless, the fact that a limited quantity of settlement data has been recovered in addition to the broad ecological picture means that the compromise of a wide transect may be worth further consideration. Additionally, in both seasons the 1-km. width enabled a clear judgement of the importance of linear features running at right-angles to the transect in terms of overall archaeological landscapes.

A second question concerns the value of settlement data recovered from wide transects. In connection with the Conoco survey project, Doelle (1977) found problems in attempting to record both 'sites' and 'non-sites' simultaneously; he proposed an initial widely spaced reconnaissance to pick up very visible sites and a second phase of more intensive survey to identify non-sites. In the Zadar lowlands, the paucity of dense artifact scatters in any of the geological units surveyed so far exacerbates this problem. After an assessment of transect geomorphology it can be stated that, whilst there are certain areas in which existing scatters would have been covered by later deposition or eroded, there remain areas of relative geomorphological stability in which no such finds have been identified. The conclusion for future planning is that 'sites' would appear to be so clustered and yet so small in area that recovery of meaningful settlement-pattern data requires widespread systematic and intensive survey coverage, in areas of long-term ecological equilibrium.

The results of the site and artifact density analyses confirm preliminary suppositions about the relative settlement potential of different geological formations. Unless a large quantity of archaeological material has been eroded from broad swathes of limestone terrain, these areas were probably never densely settled, but rather existed as a seasonal resource, predominantly for rough grazing. Several areas of limestone hills devoid of monuments were, perhaps surprisingly, rich in grass and herb cover capable of supporting substantial herds of modern sheep (e.g. 1982—quadrats 2147–2137 north of Poljica; 1983 quadrats 2378–2368, north of Gornje Biljane). The extent of limestone terrain in the Zadar lowlands appears as much a limitation to population growth and settlement expansion as a stimulus to the pastoralist sector of prehistoric and later economies. By definition devoid of usable rocks and minerals, the limestone terrain is also a spur to inter-site exchange or resource procurement. The intervening geological formations provide richer settlement potential, sometimes in soil (the alluvial soils of the Ljubač depression, the well-watered soils of the Benkovac trough and the Nadinsko Blato valley), sometimes in stone resources (the Podvršje–Skulići ridge), sometimes in minerals (the salt-pans at Nin and on Pag), sometimes in marine resources (the inland seas of Novigrad and Karin, and the indented, island-dominated coastline), and sometimes in water (the many springlines at the junction of flysch and limestone, the isolated springs, as at Vrulje on Karinsko More, etc.). The relative 'pull' of these varying and unevenly distributed resources has yet to be estimated; on that basis it may be possible to model settlement patterns in the lowland zone.

With early prehistoric exceptions, important archaeological features in the landscape have been concentrated in specific environments, and have tended to be linear, along the grain of the countryside. From the Bronze Age onwards, the higher potential of certain areas for settlement was systematically exploited. The Pridraga cairnfield and the Mataci landscape are but two examples discovered in survey; other linear Bronze Age clusters include the cairnfield at Zaton (pers. comm. Š. Batović) and the probable early occupation at hillforts near Velim and Stankovci. The formalization of linear settlement in the Iron Age was partially related to the proclivity for hillfort settlement on the limestone, but also to richer agricultural areas of intervening flysch. By the Late Iron Age and early Roman period, political boundaries between territories had been determined and boundary disputes between Nadin (Nedinum) and Karin (Corinium) are reported (Wilkes 1969). In the first century A.D., large areas of the countryside around Zadar were enclosed in the centuriation system made famous by the aerial photography of John Bradford (Bradford 1957). As such, the later prehistoric and Roman populations appear to have been clustered into a relatively restricted range of environments, some of which (e.g. Mataci) were not densely settled, others (e.g. Nadin) having far denser occupations. As suggested above, overall intensity of rural settlement in the Zadar lowlands appears to be far lower than in many areas of lowland Greece or Italy. It should be noted that transect survey across the grain of essentially linear settlement patterns cannot be expected to yield high numbers of settlements, but rather to indicate likely areas of higher-density settlement.

For the earlier prehistoric periods, a similar pattern of clustered occupation appears to be the norm. Two main clusters of Palaeolithic findspots, at Skulići and in the Ljubač depression, are known from survey; in addition, there is the likelihood of Palaeolithic cave occupation in the Kličevica canyon to the east of the 1983 transect near Benkovac (pers. comm. M. Malez). It is highly probable that other caves in the southern slopes of the Velebit massif will yield further Palaeolithic material.

For the Neolithic material, the larger excavated sites of Smilčić and Nin (Batović 1965a, 1966) can be compared with forty scatters of later prehistoric chipped stone, some associated with Neolithic pottery. Although it is assumed that natural transformations have acted more strongly on Neolithic material than on later finds, the number of unequivocal Neolithic 'sites' in the Zadar lowlands is still remarkably low. The current pattern may be interpreted as low-density, dispersed settlement in small population groups.

These tentative comments on settlement pattern should be regarded more as hypotheses to be rigorously tested in future intensive survey than as final and fixed interpretations of a carefully investigated set of data. After two seasons of extensive survey, the Neothermal Dalmatia project has reached the point where it is possible to assess the settlement potential of a wide range of ecological zones. In future seasons, survey work will be intensified in selected areas of long-term geomorphological stability, with the aim of providing a wider selection of settlement-pattern data.

Acknowledgements

We are delighted to acknowledge the kind assistance of the local, republican and federal authorities in providing permits for the 1982 and 1983 fieldwork in the Zadar lowlands. Special thanks are due to the director of the Arheološki Muzej, Zadar, Dr. Zdenko Brusić, for his support of the project. The following institutions are warmly thanked for their financial contributions to the project: the British Academy, the Society of Antiquaries of London, and the University of Newcastle upon Tyne. We are grateful to Dr. Anthony Harding, F.S.A., Dr. Zdenko Brusić and Mrs. Branka Nedved for commenting upon earlier drafts of this paper, and to Professor J. D. Evans, F.S.A., Professor C. Renfrew, F.S.A. and Professor G. W. Dimbleby, F.S.A., for their constant encouragement.

Finally, none of this research would have been possible without the enthusiasm and expertise of the project staff: Mrs. B. Nedved, Ms. M. Kolega, Ms. Lj. Klarin, Dr. M. Jurić, Dr. I. Fadić, Ms. I. Anzulović, Ms. M. Zelinac, Ms. D. Djokić, Mr. S. Bilić, Mr. I. Batović; Mrs. M. Chapman, Dr. A. F. Harding, F.S.A., Ms. G. Ryan, Ms. B. Smith, Ms. H. Riley, Mr. C. Schwartz, Mr. H. Evans, Mr. A. Mills and Mr. T. Beverley; our grateful thanks to them all.

TABLE 7. Chronological Table

Absolute dating B.C.	Period	Cultures		Sites
−0				
−200			V	Jagodnja G.
−400	Iron Age	Liburnian	IV	Bribir
−500			III	Zadar
−600			II	Radovin
−800			I	Nin
−900				
		Late		Vrsi
−1,100				Nin
	Bronze Age	Middle		Pridraga
				Podvršje
−1,600		Early		Zaton
−2,000				
	Copper Age or Eneolithic			Knin
				Buković
				Vrsi
−2,500				
		Hvar I–III		Islam Grčki
−3,500				
		Danilo I–III		Bribir
−4,500	Neolithic			Smilčić
		Impressed		Tinj
		Ware I–III		Nin
−7,000				
	Mesolithic			
−10,000				
		Epigravettian		Lopar
−11,000				
		Gravettian		
−31,000	Palaeolithic			
		Aurignacian		Podvršje
−53,000				Ražanac
		Mousterian		Radovin
−100,000				Veli Rat

NEOTHERMAL DALMATIA SITE SURVEY

1. GRID SQUARE/SITE NO.   ⬚⬚⬚⬚╱⬚⬚⬚⬚   2. MAP REFERENCE   ⬚⬚⬚⬚╱⬚⬚⬚
1. BROJ KVADRATA/BROJ LOKALITETA _____   2. BROJ KVADRATA NA MAPI

3. VILLAGE/LOCALITY NAME _____   4. DATE RECORDED   DAY   MONTH   YEAR
4. MJESTO/POLOŽAJ _____ ,   4. DATUM NALAZA   ⬚⬚⬚⬚⬚ 1 9 8
                                                              DAN   MJESEC   GODINA
5. RECORDED BY _____   6. LOCAL INFORMANTS _____
5. IME PRONALAZAČA _____   6. OBAVIJEST DAO _____
_____

7. TYPE OF REMAINS   ISOLATED TOMB   ⬚ CEMETERY   ⬚ SINGLE FIND   ⬚ SCATTER   ⬚
7. VRST NALAZA   IZOLIRANI GROB   NEKROPOLA   IZOLIRANI NALAZ   GRUPA NALAZA

                  SETTLEMENT   ⬚ SETTLEMENT + CEMETERY ⬚ SANCTUARY/SHRINE ⬚ OTHER ⬚
                  NASELJE   NASELJE + NEKROPOLA   CRKVA   DRUGA VRSTA _____

8. PERIOD OF OCCUPATION   PALAEOLITHIC ⬚ MESOLITHIC ⬚ NEOLITHIC ⬚ BRONZE AGE ⬚
8. DOBA   PALEOLITIK   MEZOLITIK   NEOLITIK   BRONČANO DOBA

             IRON AGE   ⬚ ROMAN ⬚ MEDIAEVAL ⬚ UNKNOWN ⬚
             ŽELJEZNO DOBA   RIMSKO   SREDNI VIJEK   NEPOZNATO
_____

9. LOCATION (INCLUDING PERMANENT LANDMARKS) _____
9. SMJEŠTAJ NALAZIŠTA _____
_____

10. TOPOGRAPHY _____
10. TOPOGRAFIJA _____

11. SURFACE SLOPE   NONE ⬚ LIMITED ⬚ MODERATE ⬚ STEEP ⬚
11. NAGIB ZEMLJIŠTA   NEMA   MALO   VEĆI   STRM

12. AMOUNT OF EROSION   NONE ⬚ LIMITED ⬚ MODERATE ⬚ EXTENSIVE ⬚
12. PROCENAT EROZIJE   NEMA   MALO   VEĆI   JAKO

13. TERRACING   PRESENT ⬚ ABSENT ⬚ 14. OTHER DAMAGE _____
13. TERASE   IMA   NEMA   14. DRUGA VRSTA OŠTEĆENJA _____

15. FUTURE THREATS _____
15. KOJA VRSTA OPASNOSTI PRIJETI LOKALITETU ? _____

16. GEOLOGY _____
16. GEOLOGIJA _____

17. SOIL TYPE _____ MUNSELL COLOUR   ⬚⬚╱⬚⬚
17. PEDOLOŠKI TYP _____ MUNSELL BOJA

18. pH READING   SAMPLE 1 ⬚ 2 ⬚ 3 ⬚   19. HYDROLOGY _____
18. PEDOLOŠKA KISELINA KVADRAT 1 ⬚ 2 ⬚ 3 ⬚   19. HIDROLOGIA _____

20. WATER SOURCE (DISTANCE,SEASONALITY) _____
20. REZERVE VODE (KOLIKO DALEKO?,SEZONSKA UPOTREBA) _____

21. DIRECTION OF PREVAILING WIND   22. EXPOSURE TO WIND   SHELTERED ⬚ EXPOSED ⬚
21. VRSTA VJETRA _____   22. NA UDARU VJETRA   ZAKLONJEN   NEZAKLONJEN

23. VEGETATION   SCRUB/BRUSH ⬚ SCRUB & TREES ⬚ SCATTERED TREES ⬚ FOREST ⬚
23. VEGETACIJA   ŠIBLJE   NISKO I VIŠE RASLINJE   RIJETKO DRVEĆE   ŠUMA

          ORCHARD ⬚ VINEYARD ⬚ PASTURE ⬚ ARABLE ⬚ OTHER
          VOĆNJAK   VINOGRAD   TRAVA   OBRADIVA ZEMLJA   DRUGA VRSTA _____

24. CULTIVATION
24. OBRADA   FALLOW ⬚ CEREALS ⬚ FRUIT ⬚ OLIVES ⬚ CITRUS ⬚
            TRAVA   ŽITARICA   VOĆE   MASLINE   JUŽNO VOĆE

       TOBACCO   ⬚ ALMONDS ⬚ POTATOES ⬚ OTHER VEGETABLES ⬚ OTHER
       DUVAN   BADEMI   KRUMPIR   DRUGA VRSTA POVRĆA   DRUGA VRSTA _____
_____

25. REF. NO OF SAMPLE UNITS _____
25. BROJ KVADRATA ZA SKUPLJENJE _____

26. REF. NO. OF PHOTOGRAPHS   B & W _____   COLOUR _____
26. BROJ FOTOGRAFIJE   CRNO-BIJELA _____   U BOJI _____

27. % MATERIAL BROUGHT IN   ⬚⬚   28. % MATERIAL LEFT   ⬚⬚⬚
27. % MATERIJALA DONIJET   28. % MATERIJALA OSTAVLJEN

FIG. 56. Bilingual site record sheet

NEOTHERMAL DALMATIA FINDS RECORD CARD

1. GRID SQUARE/SITE NO.
1. BROJ KVADRATA/BROJ LOKALITETA

2. SAMPLE UNIT
2. BROJ KVADRATA
   ZA SKUPLJENJE

3. RECORDED BY
3. POPUNIO

4. CHIPPED STONE   TOTAL NO.   TOTAL WEIGHT (gms)
4. ORUDJE OD KAMENA UKUPAN BROJ   UKUPNA TEŽINA (gms)

NO. OF RETOUCHED PIECES   TOOL TYPES   BLADES   NO.   END-SCRAPERS
BROJ RETUŠIRANIH KOMADA   OBLIK RUKOTVORINE REZACI   STRUGACI NA VRHU
                                                        BROJ

SIDE-SCRAPERS   POINTS   BURINS   BORERS   MICROLITHS
STRUGALICE   ŠILJCI   UBADAČI   SVRDLA   MIKROLITI
(POSTRANE)

OTHER TYPES/DRUGE VRSTE _____

TECHNOLOGICAL TYPES   UNWORKED LUMPS   CORES   NO   CORE REJUVENATION   NO
TEHNOLOŠKI TIPOVI   NEOBRADJENI MATERIJAL JEZGRA   OTPADAK JEZGRE
                                                                                BROJ

BLADES   BLADE   FLAKES   PLUNGING FLAKES/
REZAČI   SEGMENTS   ODBITAK   BLADES
          DIO REZAČA   NEPRAVILAN REZAČ

RAW MATERIALS FOUND
GEOLOŠKA VRSTA _____

PIECES DRAWN   PIECES PHOTOGRAPHED
CRTANI KOMADI _____ FOTOGRAFIRANI KOMADI _____

5. POTTERY   TOTAL NO.   TOTAL WEIGHT (gms)   FEATURE SHERDS
5. KERAMIKA   UKUPAN BROJ UKUPNA TEŽINA (gms)   UKRAŠENA KERAMIKA

UNDECORATED BODY SHERDS   NO WT   DATABLE SHERDS
NEUKRAŠENA KERAMIKA   DETERMINIRANA KERAMIKA

PERIOD   NEOLITHIC   ENEOLITHIC   BRONZE AGE   IRON AGE
PERIOD   NEOLITIK   ENEOLITIK   BRONČANO DOBA   ŽELJEZNO DOBA

ROMAN   MEDIAEVAL   MODERN
RIMSKO   SREDNJI VIJEK   NOVIJI

SHERDS DRAWN   SHERDS PHOTOGRAPHED
KERAMIKA NACRTANA _____ KERAMIKA FOTOGRAFIRANA _____

6. OTHER STONE   SR REF NOS.
6. DRUGA VRSTA KAMENA SN BROJEVI _____

7. OTHER FIRED CLAY   BRICK   NO WT   TILE   DAUB
7. DRUGA VRSTA PEČENE GLINE CIGLA   TEGULA   KUĆNI LIJEP

OTHER   SF REF. NOS.
DRUGA VRSTA _____ SN BROJEVI _____

8. METAL SF REF. NOS.
8. METAL SN BROJEVI _____

9. BONE/ANTLER/SHELL   TOTAL NO.   NO. WORKED
9. KOSTI/ROGOVI/ŠKOLJKE   UKUPAN BROJ   BROJ OBRADJEN
                          B/K   A/R S/S   B/K   A/R S/S

SF REF. NOS.
SN BROJEVI
SPECIES REPRESENTED
VRSTA ŽIVOTINJE _____

FIG. 57. Bilingual finds record card

BIBLIOGRAPHY

Andrović, M. 1971. 'Zaštita šuma na kršu', in *Simpozij o 'Zaštitu prirode u našem kršu'*, Jugoslovenska Akademija Znanosti i Umjetnosti (=JAZU), Zagreb, pp. 93–107.

Basler, D. 1979. 'Paleolitske kulture u jadransko-mediteranskom području Jugoslavije', unpublished M.A. dissertation, University of Zadar.

Batović, Š. 1963a. 'Neolitsko nalazište Smilčić. Prethodni izveštaj iz iskapanja 1957–1959, godine', *Radovi Zadar*, x, pp. 89–138.

— 1963b. 'Razvoj istraživanja prapovijesti u Dalmaciji', *Radovi Fil. Fakulteta u Zadru*, ii, Zadar, pp. 37–73.

— 1965a. 'Neolitski ostaci iz Nina i njihov položaj u okviru neolita na Mediteranu', *Diadora*, iii, Zadar, pp. 5–44.

— 1965b. 'Prvi paleolitski nalazi u sjevernoj Dalmaciji', *Diadora*, iii, Zadar, pp. 205–10.

— 1966. *Stariji neolit u Dalmaciju*, Belgrade.

— 1973. 'Prapovijesni ostaci na zadarskom otočju', *Diadora*, vi, pp. 5–165.

— 1977. 'Caractéristiques des agglomérations fortifiées dans la région des Liburniens', *Godišnjak*, xv (Centar za Balkanološka Ispitivanja knj, 13), pp. 201–25.

— 1978. 'Origines du néolithique à l'Adriatique et les rapports avec la Mediterranée occidentale', *Godišnjak*, xvi (Centar za Balkanološka Ispitivanja knj, 14), pp. 45–60.

— 1979. 'Jadranska zona', *Praistorija jugoslavenskih zemalja*, II, *Neolit*, Sarajevo, pp. 473–634.

— 1980. 'L'economia sull'Adriatico nell'età del Neolitico, Abruzzo', *Rivista dell'Ist. di Studi Abruzzesi*, xix, 1–3, Rome, pp. 73–95.

Beug, H.-J. 1961. 'Beiträge zur postglazialen Floren- und Vegetationsgeschichte in Süddalmatien', *Flora*, cl, pp. 600–56.

— 1977. 'Vegetationsgeschichtliche Untersuchungen im Küstebereich von Istrien (Jugoslawien)', *Flora*, clxvi, pp. 357–81.

Binford, L. R. 1964. 'A consideration of archaeological research design', *Amer. Antiquity*, xxix, pp. 425–41.

Bradford, J. 1957. *Ancient Landscapes*, London.

Brande, A. 1973. 'Untersuchungen zur postglazialen Vegetationsgeschichte im Gebiet der Neretva-Niederung (Dalmatien, Herzegowina)', *Flora*, clxii, pp. 1–44.

Chapman, J. C. 1981. 'The value of Dalmatian museum collections to Dalmatian settlement studies', in Cantwell, A.-M., Griffin, J. B. and Rothschild, N. A. (eds.), *The Research Potential of Anthropological Museum Collections*, Annals of New York Academy of Sciences, 376, New York, pp. 529–55.

Chapman, J. C. and Batović, Š. 1983. 'The Neothermal Dalmatia Project—preliminary report on the first season', *Universities of Durham and Newcastle upon Tyne Arch. Reports for 1982*, pp. 7–12.

— in press. 'The Neothermal Dalmatia Project—preliminary report on the second season'.

Chapman, J. C. and Mook, W. G. in press. 'Radiocarbon dating and the Dalmatian Neolithic'.

Cherry, J. F. 1981. 'Pattern and process in the earliest colonization of the Mediterranean islands', *PPS* xlvii, pp. 41–68.

— 1983. 'Frogs around the pond: perspectives on current archaeological survey projects in the Mediterranean region', in Keller and Rupp 1983, pp. 375–416.

Cherry, J. F. and Shennan, S. 1978. 'Sampling cultural systems: some perspectives on the application of probabilistic regional surveys in Britain', in Cherry, J. F., Gamble, C. and Shennan, S. J. (eds.), *Sampling in Contemporary British Archaeology*, BAR 50, Oxford, pp. 1–48.

Clarke, D. L. 1975. *Mesolithic Europe—the Economic Basis*, London.

Coles, J. M. and Harding, A. F. 1979. *The Bronze Age in Europe*, London.

Doelle, W. H. 1977. 'A multiple survey strategy for cultural resource management studies', in Schiffer, M. B. and Gumerman, G. J. (eds.), *Conservation Archaeology. A Guide to Cultural Resource Management Studies*, London, pp. 201–9.

Drechsler-Bižić, R. 1975. 'Istraživanje tumula ranog brončanog doba u Ličkom Osiku', *Vjesnik Arh. Muzeja u Zagrebu*, ix, pp. 1–22.

— 1983. 'Srednje brončano doba u Lici i Bosni', *Praistorija jug. zemalja*, IV, *Brončano doba*, Sarajevo, pp. 242–58.

Dyson, S. L. 1978. 'Settlement patterns in the Ager Cosanus: the Wesleyan University Survey 1974–1976', *J. Field Arch.* v, pp. 251–68.

Gallant, T. W. 1982. 'The Lefkas-Pronnoi Survey', unpublished Ph.D. thesis, Cambridge University.

Gračanin, M. 1960. 'Das dinarische Karstgebiet', *Bull. scientifique*, v, no. 4, p. 118.

Jedlowski, D. 1975. *Venecija i šumarstvo Dalmacije od 15. do 18. veka*, Split.

Judge, W. J., Ebert, J. I. and Hitchcock, R. K. 1975. 'Sampling in regional archaeological survey', in Mueller, J. W. (ed.), *Sampling in Archaeology*, Tucson, pp. 82–123.

Keller, D. R. and Rupp, D. W. (eds.). 1983. *Archaeological Survey in the Mediterranean area*, BAR S155, Oxford, pp. 82–123.

Korošec, J. 1956. 'Ceramica dipinta della Costa Dalmata', *Bull. di Paletnologia Italia*, x, pp. 297–320.

— 1964. *Danilo in Danilska kultura*, Ljubljana.

Lloyd, J. and Barker, G. W. W. 1981. 'Rural settlement in Roman Molise: problems of archaeological survey', in Barker, G. W. W. and Hodges, R. A. (eds.), *Archaeology and Italian Society: Prehistoric, Roman and Medieval Studies*, BAR S102, Oxford, pp. 82–123.

Mackereth, F. J. H. 1966. 'Some chemical observations on post-glacial lake sediments', *Phil. Trans. Royal Soc.* (B) ccl, pp. 165–213.

Malez, M. 1975. 'Neki problemi paleolitika na istočnoj obali Jadrana', *Rad Jug. Akademije*, cclxxi, Zagreb, pp. 121–53.

— 1979. 'Paleolitsko i mezolitsko doba u Hrvatskoj', *Praistorija jug. zemalja*, I, *Paleolit*, Sarajevo, pp. 195–295.

Marković, C. 1974. 'The stratigraphy and chronology of the Odmut Cave', *Arch. Iugoslavica*, xv, Belgrade, pp. 7–12.

Marović, I. 1976. 'Rezultati dosadašnjih istraživanja gomila oko vrela rijeke Cetine u god. 1953, 1954, 1958, 1966, i 1968', *Materijali Saveza arh. društava Jug.* xii, Zadar, pp. 55–75.

— 1979. 'Rezultati arheološkog sondiranja u Gospodskoj Pećini kod vrela Cetine', *Vjesnik Arheologiju i Historiju Dalamacije*, lxxii–lxxiii, pp. 13–50.

Marović, I. and Čović, B. 1983. 'Cetinska kultura', *Praistorija jug. zemalja*, IV, *Brončano doba*, Sarajevo, pp. 191–231.

Nandris, J. 1978. 'Some features of Neolithic climax societies', *Studia Praehistorica (Sofia)*, i–ii, pp. 198–211.

Novak, G. 1955. *Prethistorijski Hvar*, JAZU, Zagreb.

— 1959–1982. 'Markova spilja na otoku Hvaru', *Arh. Radovi i Rasprave*, i–ix, Zagreb.

Plog, S. 1976. 'Relative efficiencies of sampling techniques for archaeological surveys', in Flannery, K. V. (ed.), *The Early Mesoamerican Village*, London, pp. 136–58.

Potter, T. W. 1976. *A Faliscan Town in South Etruria: Excavations at Narce 1966–1971*, British School at Rome, London.

Simpozij 1971. *Simpozij o 'Zaštitu prirode u našem kršu'*, JAZU, Zagreb.

Srejović, D. 1974. 'The Odmut Cave', *Arch. Iugoslavica*, xv, Belgrade, pp. 3–7.

Thomas, D. H. 1975. 'Non-site sampling in archaeology: up the creek without a site?', in Mueller, J. W. (ed.), *Sampling in Archaeology*, Tucson, pp. 61–81.

Tringham, R. 1971. *Hunters, Fishers and Farmers of Eastern Europe 6000–3000 B.C.*, London.

Van Straaten, L. M. J. U. 1965. 'Sedimentation in the northwestern part of the Adriatic Sea', *Colston Papers*, xvii, pp. 143–60.

— 1970. 'Holocene and late-Pleistocene sedimentation in the Adriatic Sea', *Geologische Rundschau*, lx, pp. 106–31.

Vrsalović, D. 1960. 'Pretpovijest i Stari Vijek', *Bračni Zbornik*, iv, pp. 31–110.

Weide, D. 1974. 'Stratigraphy' (pp. 11–28), 'Climatic Conditions' (pp. 283–6), 'Regional Setting and Geomorphic History', (pp. 418–40), in Gimbutas, M. (ed.), *Neolithic Macedonia*, Los Angeles.

Wilkes, J. J. 1969. *Dalmatia*, London.

VI. GREECE

The Boeotia Survey

John Bintliff[1]

As this and the other papers in the volume should demonstrate, regional study of settled landscapes is far more informative about the population history, economy and socio-political development of past societies than the excavation of any single site could be, and is very much more cost-effective.

It can very rarely, if ever, be claimed, that any geographical region is not only a natural enclosed unit for study, but has acted as a distinct cultural zone at all times in the past. However, it is desirable to attempt to isolate a region where natural boundaries do at least create a perceptible tendency towards cultural 'internalization', a great *Siedlungskammer* with a recurrent tradition of local ethnicity and/or political coherence. Such contexts add interpretative depth to the investigation of past cultures by allowing us to perceive the interaction of physical geography and human cultural phenomena.

The modern *nomos* (county) of Boeotia (fig. 58), immediately north of the region of Athens (Attica) in central mainland Greece, fulfils these requirements admirably. In the Graeco-Roman world its distinctiveness in historic tradition, dialect and political development was clear-cut, whilst in the Bronze Age and post-Roman times there is comparable evidence for regional particularism. On the other hand, we have archaeological and historic proof that within the region during most periods of the past there existed numerous political subdivisions (fig. 59), whose interplay with the larger 'ethnos' (tribal region) of Boeotia can shed significant light upon the processes of state formation and 'nationalism'.

Our own previous experience of earlier site survey work in Greece made it clear from the first that an area the size of Boeotia—2,580 sq. km. (about 1,000 sq. miles)—would require between 100 and 200 years of summer season exploration for a total, field-by-field coverage. We settled for a ten-year project and a number of sample areas which might form the basis for provisional extrapolation to the whole of Boeotia, together with the study of all sites discovered by previous scholarship.

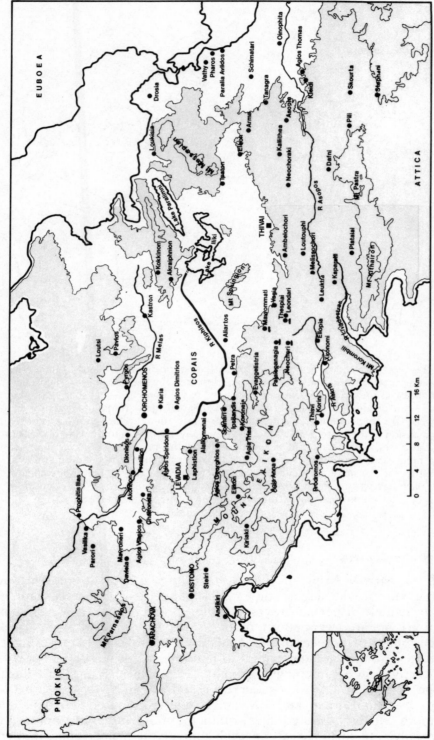

FIG. 58. The modern province of Boeotia, central Greece. Villages in the Project survey area, in the centre of the map, are underlined (Mavrommati, Palaiopanagia, Neochori, Thespiai)

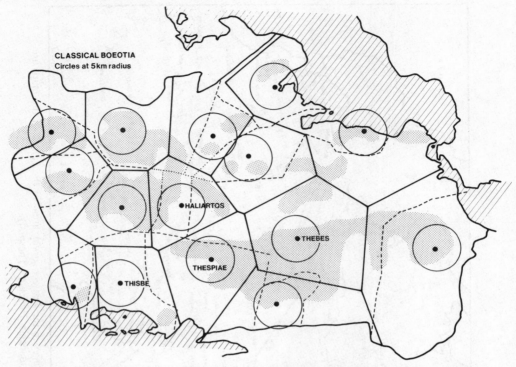

FIG. 59. The rival city states (15) of early historic Boeotia. Actual boundaries reconstructed from ancient sources represented by dashed lines. Theoretical boundaries created with Thiessen Polygons, based upon an equal sharing of land between neighbouring cities, represented by solid lines. Major divergences between the two boundary systems are primarily due to the known territorial expansion of the more powerful states (especially Thebes) onto the land of weaker neighbours. The 5-km. radius circles indicate the probable range of intensive farming carried out by city residents and the main human catchment of their role as district foci for surrounding farms and hamlets. We may suspect that the remainder of each cell was probably focused on one or more satellite towns. Shaded areas represent concentrations of prime-quality light arable soil

Selecting sample areas

Small or narrow strips, or boxes, laid or scattered at intervals over a landscape, may provide a reasonable sample of a settlement pattern composed of numerous, widely dispersed sites (such as farms and hamlets in a period of high population), but are a very poor tool for picking up a small number of nucleated sites in a phase of synoecism or population decline, and likewise are a very inadequate approach for detecting the minority of foci representing a higher level of activity in a settlement hierarchy. This point can easily be illustrated from the results of the Melos Survey (Renfrew and Wagstaff 1982). It is therefore essential to expand each sample unit so as to be confident that the rarer, more widely separated sites, often the more important politically and economically, are included within each unit of the survey zone. Experience

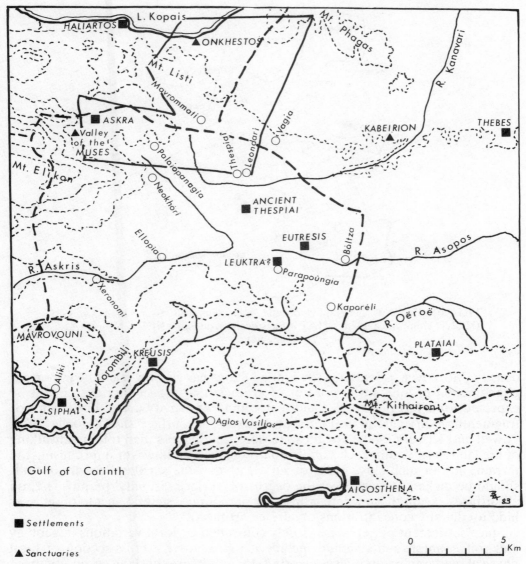

FIG. 60. Map of south-west Boeotia showing the major ancient sites and localities, and the approximate borders of the city states of Thebes, Thespiai, Thisbe and Haliartos. The solid outline indicates the general area within which the 1979–82 survey took place. North at top of page

discounts the view often quoted by proponents of discrete sampling, that large sites 'are obvious anyway'.

The number of sample areas that can be covered in the time allotted to the research programme is also conditioned by the intensity of fieldwalking and site analysis. Comparative analysis of site surveys in the United States (Plog, Plog and Wait 1978, fig. 10.1), demonstrates convincingly that survey intensity (i.e. time and manpower per given area) is directly correlated with detected site

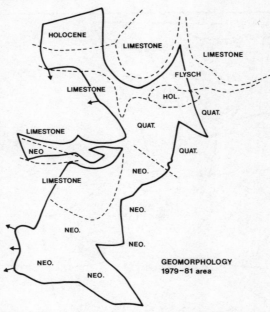

FIG. 61. Physical geography of the area surveyed from 1979 to 1981 (HOL = Holocene alluvia; QUAT = Pleistocene sediments; NEO = Noegene sediments)

density. Moreover, research in the United States has also revealed the important phenomenon of 'non-sites', scatters of artifacts that are smaller than might be expected for a farm or hamlet and may represent activity areas, burial sites or fragmentary survivals of formerly more extensive surface sites (Doelle 1977; Powell and Klesert 1980). For these reasons nothing less than total fieldwalking of the landscape within each sample unit is demanded, however unpromising the terrain, and in such close order of surveyors that the smallest scatters of finds should be picked out wherever the degree of 'surface visibility' permits (i.e. on all surfaces except those where crop cover or natural vegetation act to obscure or hide totally any concentrations of surface artifacts).

Since settlement patterns are closely controlled by local variations in geology and soils, sample units should include a representative cross-section of local physical geography and also incorporate a mixture of land from different topographies, e.g. mountain, plateau, hill-land, plain, etc. Finally, adjacent political or administrative units may have divergent settlement histories, and this may include core-frontier effects in population dispersal. It is therefore desirable that sample units be taken from different political areas (if such exist within the overall project region).

In the identification of the first major sample region of the Boeotia Project, we selected the district centring on the village of Mavrommati (figs. 58 and 60), some 10 km. west of Thebes. The surrounding landscape for several kilometres comprised the requisite variation in geology (fig. 61), pedology and topography, and incorporated land considered to have belonged to three separate city-states in the Graeco-Roman era.

Method of fieldwalking and recording

Initially, in 1979, we began field-by-field inspection with walkers spaced at only 5-m. intervals. On the assumption that each walker could see surface finds up to about 2·5 m. either side, this meant that all ground was given total examination. However, the slow progress made because of this close formation, together with other extremely time-consuming rigorous practices on site (see below) forced us to review the necessity of absolute ground inspection. By the 1980 season the data on sites and intervening 'non-site' scatters indicated that detection of surface find concentrations down to the smallest 'foci' observable would not suffer greatly if intervals between walkers were increased to 15 m. (whereas land covered was increased by a factor of three). But a much more significant change occurred in 1980. In the original, 1979, season, we had attempted to map total surface finds across the landscape, excluding recognized 'sites', qualitatively (in verbal report and shading on field maps). This rather unsatisfactory recording system had been adopted in order to keep team movement as rapid as possible.

On the intelligent initiative of Paul Halstead, however, a rapid but efficient means of recording 'background' surface finds was found with the use of clicker tallies. These small devices, at the depression of a switch, notch up consecutive numbers on a visible display. They are very cheap and our team-members all carry one on a string around the neck. As each walker proceeds up his swathe of a transect, he clicks each visible sherd or flint within his actual swathe of perception (we estimate that 2·5 m. either side is seen in detail by the walker). The landscape is walked in contiguous transects, and for each one, a third has been 'seen' and produced a count of visible surface material, which can both be multiplied up to estimate total density for the surface area of that transect, and broken down to analyse variation across the transect from one walked swathe to the next. Since 1980 the total land area under survey (cf. fig. 62) has been walked in rectilinear transects laid end to end and side by side, easily plotted in the field onto maps of the field systems and tracks drawn off air photographs. Each transect is aligned by compass and along distant, spacing ranging poles. It is paced out by the team leader during the transect count, and can then be checked on the ground when mapped transects meet major boundaries. The system is very fast considering the amount of information being obtained, and a normal transect of some 60 m. width (a team of four walkers each 15 m. apart) and 100–150 m. long can be drawn in and counted in 10–15 minutes.

Obviously, such rapid progress in the field is the result of limiting non-site recording to mapping and quantification of all non-modern finds, *regardless of period*. It would not be possible if one were to try to separate out the contributions of each period to the non-site material. We have tended to assume, and qualitative impressions reinforce this, that material between sites is systematically related to the sites themselves. Indeed, we can already demonstrate quantitatively that non-site material (note that our *sites* can be very small) almost without exception forms a distinctive halo around sites. We hope, nonetheless, to carry out detailed sampling of non-site material in the near future, particularly as regards its chronological composition. At this stage we can, however, report that our study of these site 'haloes' suggests that they are a combination of

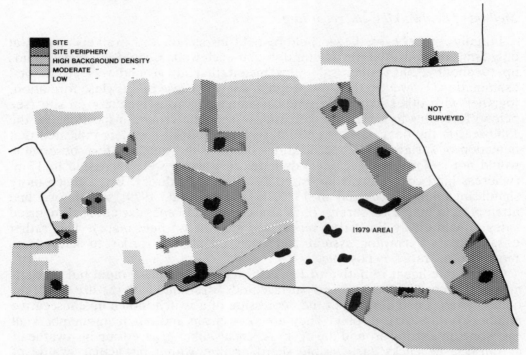

FIG. 62. South-eastern sector of the survey region showing surface pottery density for the total landscape and the effects observable around settlement sites. No background densities have yet been plotted for the 1979 sector

weathering smears radiating from sites and rubbish-disposal arcs. They could be the result of manuring practices from domestic settlements, but in localized 'infield' zones, since much excellent land in easy reach of major sites lacks this kind of evidence. Suspected tomb sites also significantly lack 'haloes', since their surface products tend to be far more limited in quantity and extent.

Sampling and recording surface sites

Wide reading led us in our first (1979) field season to put into operation a site sampling scheme of great ingenuity, incorporating numerous ideas from the literature on archaeological sampling. Over each site one or more modules were laid down, each a circle of 30-m. radius. Within this shape, some twenty to thirty small sample units (each *c*. 4 sq. m. in size) were located from a computer programme designed to scatter samples optimally over the 30-m. module. Some fudging had to be carried out to ensure that the small sample units included the central part of the site, and often major areas (up to half) of the site would have been unsampled without doctoring of the programme: to achieve better cover than a simple random scatter, the units were chosen from consecutive octants of the site and all site sampling cards lacking samples from the inner 12 per cent of the site and/or module were rejected. The result of this system was the collection of an average 200 sherds per module (*all* finds in the area defined by each sample

TABLE 1. Pottery laboratory statistics

	Diagnostic (and possibly so)	'Feature' sherds	'Rubbish'	Total number of sherds
1979				
Sample units:				
total collection	12% (+1%)	4%	83%	5,347
'Grab' samples for				
diagnostic sherds	38% (+7%)	24%	31%	807
1980				
Sample units:				
total collection	4·9% (+1%)	2·1%	92%	4,032
Sample units:				
diagnostic collection	34·1% (+4·5%)	22·1%	39·3%	539
'Grab' samples for				
diagnostic sherds	33·7% (+5·8%)	35·7%	24·8%	872

being brought back to base). As a precaution, the whole site was later walked in systematic traverses and rapidly 'grab sampled' for potentially diagnostic pottery. Only 3–8 per cent had been 'formally' sampled, however.

This cunning programme was inordinately time-consuming, and although we discovered and dual-sampled thirteen sites in 1979, we only fieldwalked 1·5 sq. km. of Boeotia! In 1980 we realized that we had to speed up site sampling in order that our larger aim—a meaningful sample of Boeotia—might be achieved in ten years. The 1980 site-sampling scheme was therefore simpler and faster. It consisted of a new sampling module, a 'Lego' shape, with a long central spine and six tentacles leading off at right-angles to it. Each element was a long, thin strip, and initially *all* finds were bagged from within this spider shape when it was laid down over each sector of the site. Easy subdivision across the limbs allowed separate data from thirty distinct units to be studied and located, and an average 8 per cent of the site was totally bagged in this fashion. Again, this formal sampling was followed by a swift collection or grab sample from *all* parts of the site.

Partly as a result of this faster sampling procedure, and the wider spacing of fieldwalkers on general survey (see above), we covered 4·5 sq. km. in 1980 and analysed seventeen new sites. Moreover, at this stage we had enough data to evaluate our performance from two years of sampling experiments on site. The statistics obtained from the pottery laboratory (table 1) were illuminating. The vast majority of sherds bagged as part of the total collection strategy from the formal samples were totally undiagnostic and mostly thrown away. Only a limited percentage of sherds were feature pieces (rims, bases, handles), and the number of clearly diagnostic pieces was very small indeed. But if one were to range alongside the 1979 and 1980 formal samples (total collection) the far smaller numbers of sherds collected in the parallel grab (selective) sampling activity from the total site area, then the mirror image emerges: high percentages of feature pot and diagnostic pot, despite the small overall numbers brought back. Indeed, during 1980 the wails from the pottery laboratory and the constant crashing of discards from that direction led us to shift in mid season to a collection strategy within the 'Lego' limbs that selected *only* feature pot or

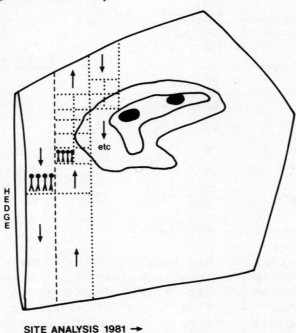

SITE ANALYSIS 1981 →

FIG. 63. Site analysis procedures since 1981. Fieldwalking of large transects
converts to mini-transects through a site. In the example above a large field is found
to contain a well-defined surface site, here represented by contours of increasing
pottery density

sherds with obvious ornament, paint, glaze or unusual fabrics. The statistics of
this later 1980 formal sample exactly match those from the 1980 and 1979 grab
samples. Not only was selective collection within the formal samples just as
efficient and far faster than total collection, but the grab samples—which derived
from 100 per cent of the site—were turning up periods not detected in the 3–8
per cent formal samples. Clearly an even more radical change of site sampling
approach was called for.

In 1981 we finally hit upon the solution to our difficulties, a site strategy that
met almost all the objections and obstacles hitherto encountered. This approach
has been so easy to use and so successful that it remains our operational system
as we approach the next, 1984, season. In essence (fig. 63), it is an extension of
our fieldwalking procedure, scaled down into 'mini-transects'. Let us imagine a
team of four walkers (with a non-transecting supervisor) proceeding up a typical
transect 60 m. wide by 100 m. long. As they move up the transect, their clicker
counts and parallel calls of '*sherd*' indicate a significant rise of surface-find
densities above local background. At the end of the planned transect the
supervisor confirms from the quantitative counts that a positive anomaly exists,
and from comparison of individual tallies can trace the lateral spread of the
'high'. The focus of activity and/or site is now studied on a more detailed level as
follows: the team retraces its path down the last transect to a measurable point
before the high counts began to appear; from here the significant sector of the
transect is rewalked by the team, but at *half* the interval between walkers, i.e. at

7·5 m. lateral spacing, and in 10-m. long spits at a time. In other words the transect is rewalked in two halves, and in short steps. This allows us to record finds in numerous contiguous and directly comparable units, each 30 m. wide and 10 m. 'long', at a time. If finds are very dense, each member of the team of four will bag his collection of finds and have his sherd count separately tallied for the 7·5 × 10 m. sub-unit he is personally responsible for studying. To avoid each walker counting or collecting in his neighbours' swathes, ropes are thrown down at paced 7·5 m. intervals across the mini-transect, and, being 10 m. long, effectively cordon off the individual sub-units. The walker now moves up his sub-unit, this time covering *all* the ground, clicking all surface finds numerically, then subsequently collecting feature pot and other diagnostic pieces, plus a range of fabric types.

The most important aspect of this system is the speed and ease of operation. The basic grid for the site analysis already exists in the system of field transects within which it is nested. No time is wasted setting up a new grid and fitting it to maps for each site. Secondly, 100 per cent of the site (in the medium to small categories, cf. below) is studied (fig. 64), yet without loss of detail (even the smallest sites will be spread over several sub-units within a single 30 × 10 m. unit, and average farm sites normally require a dozen or so units each with four sub-units). The regular, grid nature of the analysis, taken with both chronological and quantitative data for each unit, allow one to transform the site record with ease into a density contour plan. Currently we are using a computer programme (fig. 65) to produce print-outs of surface-find contours for each site at varying degrees of resolution. Concentrations of finds of particular periods allow one to trace the spatial variation of occupation across the site.

The combination of swifter fieldwalking and site processing, by 1981, pushed our season's coverage to a figure that was to be sustained in the following, 1982, season, of some 7–8 sq. km. of land totally surveyed per season. By the end of 1982 we had walked some 21 sq. km. and studied eighty-one sites. Applying the new norm, one may predict that at the end of the ten-year programme (1983 does not count, as it was only a study season) the Boeotia Project may expect to have operated a total, intensive survey of around 70 sq. km. or some 3 per cent of the surface of the county of Boeotia.

It remains to be pointed out that the present system of site analysis is excellent for almost all sites, but requires modification for the rarer large village and town sites. Our approach here must be conditioned by available time. The highly interesting minor town of Askra, for example, at some 25 ha., would eat up well over 800 study units of 30 × 10 m. and the whole of a field season without any time available for fieldwalking. That is not to say that such an exercise would not be immensely valuable and important (cf. Millon's (1973) work at Teotihuacan), merely that such a task is incompatible with a field study with a regional aim in mind and but a decade to work within. How then, are we to deal with the town sites, if at all? Clearly the rural settlement pattern is a limited sector of the total community if we ignore the fate of associated nucleations.

Our current solution is to opt for a speedy sampling strategy that ought to reveal the major trend of urban occupation phase by phase. Having isolated the built-up area of the population centre from fieldwalking around it on all sides, the site itself is tackled using the existing natural or artificial subdivisions visible

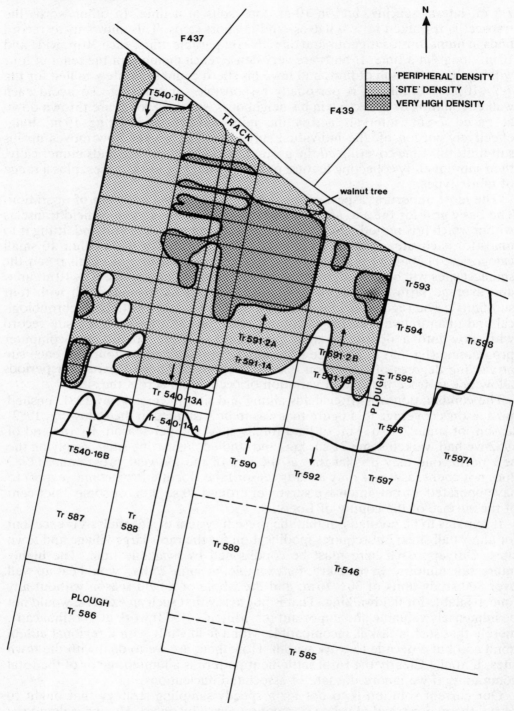

FIG. 64. The pattern of mini-transects as applied to a large Graeco-Roman villa site near the village of Palaiopanagia

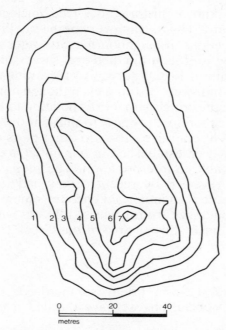

FIG. 65. Contours of sherd densities estimated from quasi-random sampling on a site in Boeotia. The densities are: contour 1, 0 sherds; contour 2, 5 sherds per sq. m. quadrat; contour 3, 10 sherds per sq. m. quadrat; ... contour 7, 30 sherds per sq. m. quadrat (computer analysis by J. Haigh and M. Kelly, Bradford University)

on its surface today, usually fields. A number of fields are chosen from the total complement covering the site, sufficient to include outer and inner sectors, and sectors from all points of the compass. Each field chosen is then studied using our standard intensive site procedure. This system can permit a later broadening of the sample units if time allows or research questions demand. A rapid grab sample from the intervening fields is desirable to preclude the failure to detect spatially limited occupations (such as could pre-date or post-date the main phases of extensive 'urban' occupation).

Regional logistics: future strategy

In the first four years of the Boeotia Project we have surveyed a continuous belt of land in all directions from our home base, the village of Mavrommati. We chose this initial procedure because we were suspicious of survey schemes which employ numerous small survey units scattered discretely across the landscape. Discovery of district settlement foci is quite likely to elude such a scatter-gun technique, and to our mind these sites are quite central to a true understanding of the overall, long-term pattern of settlement. Empirical field experience suggests that district foci in phases of settlement hierarchy should exist at reasonably regular intervals across those parts of the landscape that are densely populated. The area hitherto surveyed is already large enough for us to have passed the proposed territorial threshold for the existence of foci, at least in some directions from known historic foci (the ancient cities). Indeed our approach has been rewarded by the discovery of the satellite town of Askra lying intermediate to the locations of neighbouring city states of Thespiai, Haliartos and Thisbe (and nearby we found the medieval successor to Askra).

To confine our attention in the survey to a continuation of this intensive analysis of a sector of south-west Boeotia, even though it includes land of several city states, would invite the criticism that extrapolation to Boeotia as a whole was without foundation. We therefore propose to shift our operations to open up one or more additional foci of intensive survey in other parts of the province, in the hope that patterns now well established in our initial area will either recur, or vary in a fashion amenable to interpretation. The similarity to our preliminary results that has been revealed by recent survey activity in the Argolid and Arcadia regions of Greece is an important encouragement to our efforts to make the bold attempt to generalize from what is still, and will continue to be even after ten years, a statistically tiny sample of the Greek landscape.

Results

A number of topics may be briefly summarized, highlighting the more significant preliminary conclusions we have reached from the first four years' survey work.

Sites continue to be found. Our intensive survey has not reached the stage of diminishing returns. If one compares site density (figs. 66–71) to that recorded by older, extensive surveys, the results are predictable and on occasion spectacular. The University of Minnesota Survey of the province of Messenia, for example (McDonald and Rapp 1972), recorded a density of Classical Greek sites at 0·036 per sq. km. We find 3·3. The difference is a factor of 91! Despite contrasts in political arrangements, it is inconceivable that such variation is anything but the result of different survey techniques.

Pottery density on site. Although initially we felt that there was a neat correlation between site size and density per sq. m. of surface pottery, this was a reflection of our neglect of the time factor. Amongst the majority of sites, i.e. those in the small and medium site-size categories, surface pottery density varies only as a result of the length of use of the site. Apart from that, density does not vary significantly within that range of settlement sizes. However, there is a very great and clear distinction from our quantitative counts between the largest sites and all other sites, with considerably greater densities per sq. m., regardless of length of occupation.

Settlement patterns and the physical landscape. Site survey across the wide range of soils and topography within the area thus far covered confirms previous fieldwork as regards the strict determining influence on land use and settlement deriving from inherent variation in farming potential (cf. Bintliff 1977).

Site visibility. Revisits to previously recorded sites in subsequent seasons, or to areas believed to be devoid of sites, have demonstrated that sites 'come and go'. Since in some cases we know that a site disappearance gives way to a reappearance, it is not a simple case of a sherd reservoir 'running out' due to exposure and dispersal or destruction by weathering. We are currently trying to model the processes at work, but it is quite clear that no site survey could hope to

ARCHAIC - CLASSICAL - EARLY HELLENISTIC

500M

DEFINITE SITE ●
POSSIBLE SITE ○
UNCERTAIN ?

FIG. 67. Pattern of sites in the survey area of Archaic to (Early) Hellenistic date

PREHISTORIC

500M

DEFINITE SITE ●
POSSIBLE SITE ○
UNCERTAIN ?

FIG. 66. Pattern of prehistoric sites in the survey area

find all sites once inhabited in a landscape (reasons include: permanent burial under colluvium/alluvium; total erosion by weather and plough). Moreover, no survey could hope to *see* all sites that survive as 'sherd reservoirs', even if they can produce, on occasion, surface scatters (reasons include: varying veiling effects of surface vegetation, wild and cultivated, and present buildings; unclear sedimentary processes causing withholding or releasing of components of the 'sherd reservoir'). In order to obtain some information on the areas of the landscape likely to be particularly defective in revealing surface sites due to veiling by surface vegetation, every transect record contains an estimate from each fieldwalker of the average degree of visibility for the transect, on a scale of 0–10. The upper end is well-nigh perfect visibility, i.e. recently ploughed land with no impeding cover, versus a field totally obscured by a growing or only partially cleared crop (0–1).

Population. Population estimates based on site survey are fraught with apparently insoluble problems. If we are agreed that total recovery of the original complement of sites is inconceivable, can site numbers by phase be used in any other way than as a minimum demographic threshold? Can one, moreover, have confidence that the loss or veiling of sites strikes impartially at every settlement period, so that direct comparison of site numbers against time can be employed, if not for absolute population comparisons, at least for *relative* population comparisons?

In Boeotia we are remarkably fortunate in possessing more than one, indeed several, historical sources for the Classical Greek era, which allow us to suggest with confidence that the total population in the fourth century B.C., described by ancient writers as an era of very dense population, was in the range of 150,000–200,000 people (cf. table 2, and see Bintliff and Snodgrass 1985).

TABLE 2. Fifth–fourth-century B.C. Boeotia: population and land-use data

1. 11 regions, each contribute   1,000 hoplites (heavy-armed troops)
                                                1,000 light-armed troops
                                                100 cavalry
   plus a fleet of 50 triremes = 10,000 men
   Total forces = 33,100, × 5 for family and one slave = 165,500 population total
2. Ancient Boeotia—2,580 sq. km.
   in 1961 = ⅓ cultivable land. Anciently perhaps ½ in cultivation?
3. Hoplite landholding—5·4 ha.
   Either 50% or 33% fallow.
   Yields: 9–12 bushels per acre.
   Food needs, 1,000 kg. 'wheat equivalent' per family (+250 for slave) per year
4. 12,100 hoplite/cavalry × 5·4 ha. = 653 sq. km.
   ⅓ Boeotia = 860 sq. km.
   ½ Boeotia = 1,290 sq. km.

Given that we see little reason to doubt these separate sources, a number of very important conclusions can be drawn. Firstly, and using these figures on their own, it is an unavoidable fact that Classical Boeotia was staggeringly 'full'. In 1961 the cultivable area was put at around one-third of the county. Allowing for the slightly different boundaries of ancient Boeotia and the varying size of the giant Copais Lake, we can calculate that this would be equivalent to some 800 sq.

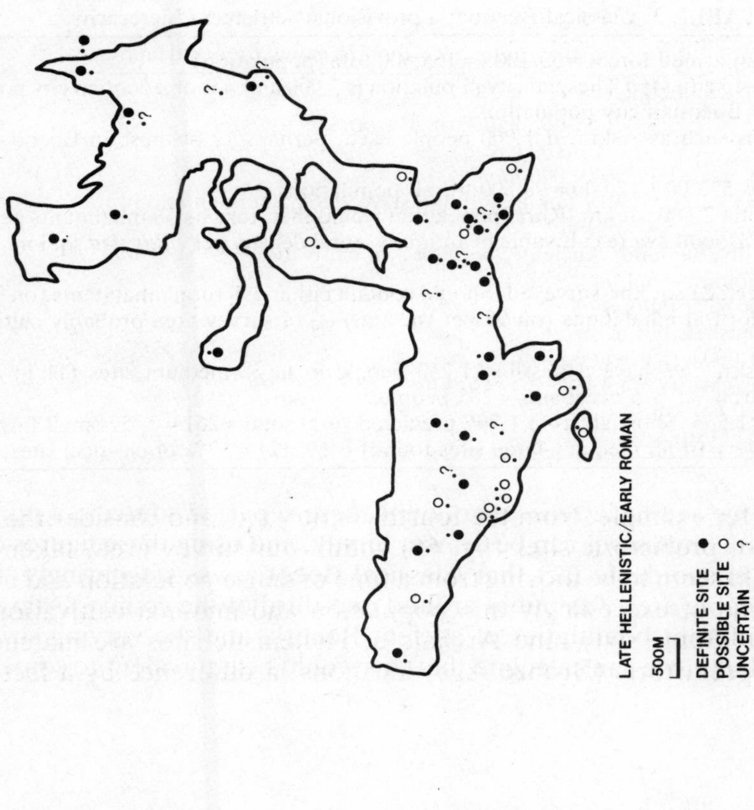

DEFINITE SITE ●
POSSIBLE SITE ○
UNCERTAIN ?

500M

LATE ROMAN

FIG. 69. Pattern of sites in the survey area of late Roman date

DEFINITE SITE ●
POSSIBLE SITE ○
UNCERTAIN ?

500M

LATE HELLENISTIC/EARLY ROMAN

FIG. 68. Pattern of sites in the survey area of (Late) Hellenistic and early Roman date

km. of cultivable land in antiquity, applying the same ratio. But our historic sources provide us with a social and economic breakdown of Classical Boeotian population, sufficient to suggest that around 650 sq. km. of arable land would have been required to maintain the yeoman farmer (hoplite) and aristocratic classes *alone*, leaving virtually no land for the equally numerous population of poorer peasant farmers. We must infer that anciently a far larger proportion of the landscape was under cultivation, or at least intensive herding, say 40 or even 50 per cent rather than one-third. Even so, this still leaves us with a population at a dangerously high level (90–100 per cent) of exploitation (anthropologists suggest 30 per cent as an appropriate level for long-term economic security, for actual population relative to maximum conceivable human carrying capacity). The continuous territorial wars, land expropriation and occasional localized genocide in ancient Greece take on a new perspective from these calculations. The social and political implications are also under investigation.

Secondly, it is quite in order to make a comparison of the historic density with that derivable purely from the site survey data (fig. 67). Admittedly working from but a limited sector of some 21 sq. km. (though nonetheless an area containing a wide range of site types and sizes), and knowing in advance the number of cities in Boeotia and their approximate extent—we can achieve an average 'archaeological' population density per sq. km. to compare with that inferable from the historical record (table 3). Direct comparison of these two sets of results suggests that site survey, however intensive, is picking up only 50–60 per cent of the settlement pattern for the period around 2,500 years ago (the Greek Classical era). This result is interesting in itself, but it may take us into even more intriguing speculations that affect other periods of the past.

TABLE 3. Classical Boeotia: a provisional settlement hiererachy

1. Total Boeotian armed forces = 33,100 (= 165,500 total population).
2. City total (14–15 cities); if Thespiai city population is 5,000 and = $\frac{1}{11}$ of Boeotian city population, 55,000 = total Boeotian city population.
3. Satellite towns such as Askra, if 1,000 people each, perhaps 12 of these in Boeotia = 12,000 people.
4. 165,500 minus 55,000 + 12,000 = 98,500 'rural' population.
5. Area of Boeotia 2,580 sq. km. Rural population would therefore be 38 inhabitants per sq. km. But if 40% of Boeotia were cultivable in antiquity, rural density per *cultivated* sq. km. would be 95 inhabitants.
6. Boeotia Project: 21 sq. km. surveyed. Should contain either 798 rural inhabitants (on 38 per sq. km.) or 1,796 rural inhabitants (on 95 per sq. km.) ($\frac{9}{10}$ of survey area probably cultivable in antiquity).
7. Excepting Askra, we have a possible 1,250 people in large–medium sites (11 in number), leaving 57 'farms' at *c.* 5 occupants = 285 people.
8. 1,250 + 285 = 1,535. Shortfall from 1,796 predicted rural total = 261 = *c.* 52 small farms.
9. Overall recovery (if all medium–large sites found) is 69 : 121 = 57% of classical sites.

If we turn, for example, from the fourth century B.C. and consider the density and number of prehistoric sites (fig. 66) within our survey area, taken at face value we would seem to be moving from a time of dense population and intensive land use to one of exceedingly thin population and minimal cultivation across the landscape. Some sixty-nine Archaic to Hellenistic sites are matched by a mere twelve prehistoric (Bronze Age) locations, a difference by a factor of 6.

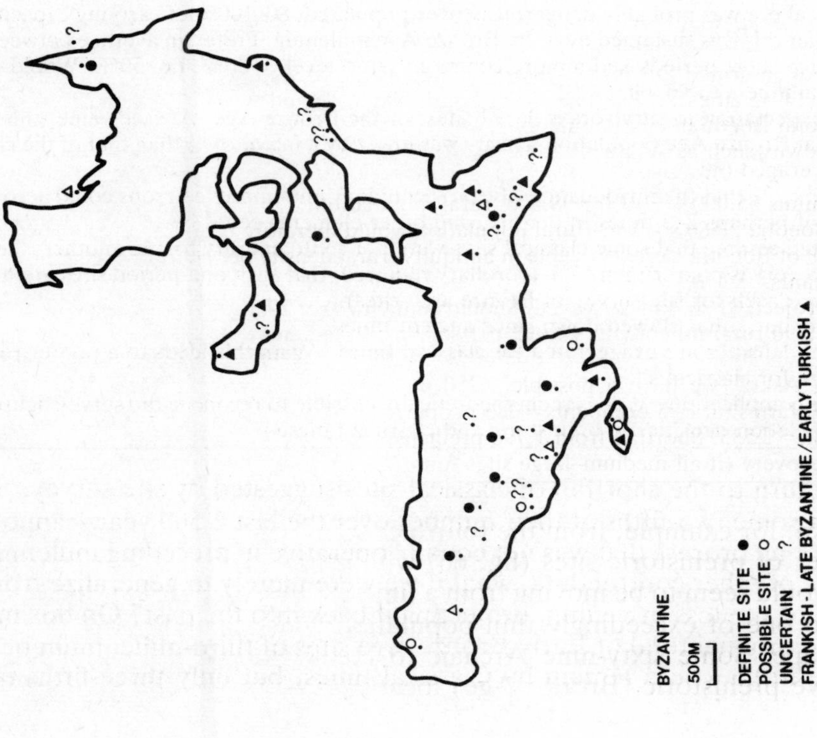

TURKISH - EARLY MODERN

500M

DEFINITE SITE ●
POSSIBLE SITE ○
UNCERTAIN ?
FRANKISH - LATE BYZANTINE / EARLY TURKISH ▲

FIG. 71. Pattern of sites in the survey area of
Turkish-Early Modern date.

BYZANTINE

500M

DEFINITE SITE ●
POSSIBLE SITE ○
UNCERTAIN ?
FRANKISH - LATE BYZANTINE / EARLY TURKISH ▲

FIG. 70. Pattern of sites in the survey area of
Byzantine-(Early) Turkish date

Moreover, the prehistoric era represented is many times the length (thousands of years) of the Greek classical era (hundreds of years), thus exaggerating the thinness of recorded prehistoric site densities even further (cf. table 4). Any attempt to suggest that Neolithic and Bronze Age populations ever approached 'florescence' by a full use of suitable land or from dense concentrations of manpower (cf. Renfrew 1972; Bintliff 1982), cannot be sustained from such data—and the Boeotia survey density is much greater than that available for the prehistory of the rest of Greece (our prehistoric sites are five to ten times more numerous than those recorded, for example, by the Minnesota survey of Messenia province). We are also faced with a remarkable paradox: that for the long era of some 6,000 years from the time of the first farming communities in Greece until climax classical times *c.* 500 B.C., mixed farming communities failed to achieve more than an insignificant fraction of the productivity and density of classical Greece, despite having a similar range of crops and livestock and concentrating on similar soil types.

TABLE 4. Bronze Age settlements: rarity problem

1. Boeotia Survey—12 Bronze Age to 69 classical (Archaic—Hellenistic) sites = 1 : 6. As the periods involved are 2,500 : 500 years, one might have expected a ratio of 5 : 1, i.e. 345 : 69 sites based on the classical figure.
2. If classical sources are reliable, we discover only about 57% of the original complement of classical sites in survey. If site erosion/burial is cumulative, a further 2,800 years could lose a further 43%, i.e. 12 Bronze Age sites were once 21 sites (compared to 69 classical survivors).
3. Frequent continuity exists between periods of the Bronze Age; this might lead us to use a factor of 2–3, not 5, for site numbers comparison between classical and Bronze Age (i.e. modifying the simple multiplier for variation in time period). This would produce an original Bronze Age : classical site total of 173 : 69.
4. The classical era was probably dangerously over-populated, 80–100% of carrying capacity; it is unlikely that this was sustained over the Bronze Age millennia. Prefer an average between such a density for short periods and a more common 'safer' level of 30%, i.e. 50%. Would reduce expected numbers to 96 : 69.
5. Ratio of expectation to survivors is 96 : 21 sites for the Bronze Age. At face value, this would suggest that Bronze Age population density was lower by a factor of $4\frac{1}{2}$ than that of the classical period, averaged out.
6. It is conceivable that the introduction of iron technology and improved crops could account for a growth of perhaps 2–3 times in density, and other elements could be:
   a. We could assume that some classical sites were not contemporary to one another, therefore our recovery is poorer than 57% (corollary required, that such one-period sites are unlikely to survive well for site survey of Bronze Age sites).
   b. Erosion/burial has slowed down since ancient times.
   c. 'Urban' densities are exaggerated for classical times. Again this leads to a poorer recovery estimate for classical sites.

Despite these complications, it does seem theoretically possible to reconcile the survey figures with plausible population densities in prehistoric and classical times.

Let us return to the shortfall of classical sites suggested by site survey. Surely the 'loss' of some two-fifths of their number over the last 2,500 years cannot be a once and for all process that was not equally operative in preceding millennia? In the absence of other control data, what if we were merely to generalize from the recent rate of site loss or veiling, projecting it back into the past? On this model, then, of the original total of Early Bronze Age sites of third-millennium bc date, some three-fifths would remain by Classical times, but only three-fifths *of that remnant* might be expected to survive or be visible by today. As for Early Neolithic sites of the sixth millennium bc, we might expect to see only some three-fifths of three-fifths of three-fifths of the original complement, at the present day.

This factor of cumulative disappearance of sites serves to reduce the tremendous disparity between observable prehistoric and historic site densities. We can suggest further factors contributing to the same effect. Firstly, it is unlikely that the climax classical population and site density was ever sustained for long in other periods of Boeotia's settlement history, given our belief that a dangerous saturation of the landscape existed by the fourth century B.C. The *subsequent* development of historic Boeotian settlement confirms this point, in eras where 'cumulative' site loss cannot be invoked to any greater extent than for the high classical period. It is most probable therefore, that in general in other periods the level of population relative to land potential was much reduced compared to the inferred fourth-century B.C. picture. Secondly, there is significant continuity of occupation at many prehistoric sites in Greece, which reduces the number of *separate* sites that should be predicted from a simple multiplication of the classical site total by the ratio of the timespan of classical Greece to the timespan of the Neolithic to Bronze Age era. Thirdly, the classical era is characterized by a highly dispersed settlement pattern of small farms; an alternation of more dispersed with more nucleated settlement patterns in prehistory (as is found in post-classical Greece) further reduces the total expected number of sites for later prehistoric times in Boeotia. Last but not least in our arguments is the essential recognition that there must indeed have been notable absolute transformations in population and productivity levels in Boeotia as the result of secular changes in technology and agricultural practice— but on a much smaller scale than might have served to reconcile our initial survey discrepancies. The effect of plough traction and olive cultivation may have raised population thresholds between the Neolithic and Bronze Age by a factor of 2–3. Improvements in the range and quality of crops, and the effects of iron technology, may in turn have raised population by an equivalent amount between the Bronze and Iron Ages (cf. Bintliff 1984).

Taken together, the sum of these arguments allows us to adjust our initial survey data in such a way that much more realistic population levels begin to emerge for the pre-classical era. Moreover, it helps us to understand why it is, for example, not totally incomprehensible that Crete, with a very early flourishing community of farmers at Knossos in 6100 bc, betrays virtually no other Neolithic sites for some thousands of years, until Late and Final Neolithic times. Nor need we marvel at the pitifully tiny number of Palaeolithic and Mesolithic sites in Greece, which represent a potential million years of human communities. And to take the other side of the coin, when the period from around 1000 to 800 B.C. or that from A.D. 650 to 850 (the two well-known 'Dark Ages' in Greece) reveal virtually no sites in the landscape, then we must surely accept a genuine catastrophic collapse of population in comparison to eras either side of these dates.

NOTE

[1] The Cambridge–Bradford Boeotia Project is jointly directed by the author and Professor Anthony Snodgrass, F.S.A., of Cambridge University. Its main funding stems from the British Academy, with secondary contributions from the British School of Archaeology at Athens and the two universities involved.

More detailed presentation of the results of the first four years of field seasons will be found in two forthcoming publications: *Actes du Colloque International du CNRS: La Béotie antique*, ed. P. Roesch and G. Argoud (contributions by Bintliff and Snodgrass), and a preliminary report to appear in the *J. Field Arch.*

BIBLIOGRAPHY

Bintliff, J. L. 1977. *Natural Environment and Human Settlement in Prehistoric Southern Greece*, BAR S28 (1–2), Oxford.
— 1982. 'Settlement patterns, land tenure and social structure', in Renfrew, C. and Shennan, S. (eds.), *Ranking, Resource and Exchange*, Cambridge, pp. 106–11.
— 1984. 'Neolithic social evolution', 'Iron Age social evolution', chs. 3 and 7 in Bintliff, J. (ed.), *European Social Evolution: Archaeological Perspectives*, Monographs, School of Archaeological Sciences, Bradford University.
Bintliff, J. L. and Snodgrass, A. 1985. 'The Cambridge–Bradford Expedition: the first four years', *J. Field Arch.* xii, 2, in press.
Doelle, W. H. 1977. 'A multiple survey strategy for cultural resource management studies', in Schiffer, M. and Gumerman, G. (eds.), *Conservation Archaeology*, New York, pp. 201–9.
McDonald, W. A. and Rapp, G. R. (eds.). 1972. *The Minnesota Messenia Expedition: Reconstructing a Bronze Age Regional Environment*, University of Minnesota Press, Minneapolis.
Millon, R. 1973. *The Teotihuacan Map. Urbanization at Teotihuacan, Mexico*, i, University of Texas Press, Austin.
Plog, S., Plog, F. and Wait, W. 1978. 'Decision making in modern surveys', in Schiffer, M. (ed.), *Advances in Archaeological Method and Theory*, i, New York, pp. 383–421.
Powell, S. and Klesert, A. L. 1980. 'Predicting the presence of structures on small sites', *Current Anthrop.* xxi, pp. 367–9.
Renfrew, C. 1972. *The Emergence of Civilisation*, London.
Renfrew, C. and Wagstaff, M. (eds.). 1982. *An Island Polity: the Archaeology of Exploitation in Melos*, Cambridge.

The Megalopolis Survey in Arcadia: Problems of Strategy and Tactics

J. A. Lloyd, F.S.A., E. J. Owens and J. Roy

Between 1981 and 1983 field survey in the *chora* of classical Megalopolis (in the Peloponnese) was conducted annually by a team from the Universities of Sheffield and Swansea, under the direction of the authors.[1] Like every other intensive archaeological survey the expedition discovered abundant ancient remains which had not been recorded hitherto. At the end of the third and final season in 1983, 294 findspots had been logged. The area of countryside examined amounted to *c*. 77 sq. km. and was made up of two transects of *c*. 30 sq. km., one of *c*. 12 sq. km. and an upland sample of *c*. 5 sq. km. Only a handful of sites had previously been reported (or their existence inferred) in the same locations.[2]

As a result of this work many additions and some alterations to the archaeological map of this part of Arcadia can now be proposed; and our findings will also affect the historical record. As an illustration, provisional chronological analysis indicates that findspots of Archaic to Hellenistic date far outnumber those of any other period up to the post-medieval era (there being four times as many as findspots of the medieval period, the nearest rival).[3] The survey evidence further suggests that in Archaic to Hellenistic times the pattern of occupation included both nucleated centres and numerous dispersed farmsteads. Neither development could have been predicted from the evidence provided by the literary and epigraphic sources.[4]

These results, however, are primarily of regional value. In the remainder of this paper emphasis is placed on two aspects of our work which are, perhaps, of wider interest. These are, first, the strategy chosen to achieve the aims of the project and, second, the tactics used to tackle the problem of site definition.

Survey strategy

The main objective of our work was to reconstruct settlement patterns in the *chora*, or territory, of the ancient city of Megalopolis. Above all our interest lay

FIG. 72. The Megalopolis Survey: general location map

in the Graeco-Roman period (as the choice of the target area indicates), although in the field we collected and recorded finds from all periods. The city was founded *c*. 368 B.C. by a synoecism which brought in settlers from a large number of pre-existing communities.[5] The newly formed city took over the land which had formerly belonged to these communities, thus becoming one of the largest city-states in mainland Greece. The total area involved amounted to *c*. 1,500 sq. km., much of it mountainous.[6]

The vast size of this territory presented us with a major strategic problem. With a three-year programme and a limited annual budget (on average £3,000) it would clearly be impossible to cover every inch of the Megalopolitan countryside. Some form of sampling was necessary and, since we hoped to achieve results which would allow general hypotheses of the development of settlement to be put forward, great care would have to be exercised in the choice of the fraction of the landscape that could be examined.

This appeared to be a problem which probability theory could do much to resolve. Professional advice was sought and was given freely and patiently.[7] After detailed discussion, however, we departed without a formula which met our particular needs and circumstances. If we have understood the arguments correctly, a sample programme could have been devised which would have allowed a statistically valid projection of the total number of sites in Megalopolitan territory. However, such a scheme could not guarantee that we would find many (or any) sites. This we hoped to avoid, for obvious reasons. 'The main purpose for conducting a survey is to find sites';[8] although negative evidence is very important, it does little for morale and is not helpful for raising funds. Furthermore, the procedure likely to have given the most reliable statistical information would have involved examining a great many small areas (of, say, 1 sq. km.) rather than a small number of much larger blocks of land. For several practical reasons this was not possible in our case. In setting up the survey we were advised by the British School at Athens that our application for a permit would stand a higher chance of success if we restricted annual fieldwork to the territory of no more than six modern villages. To follow this advice, as we have, entailed a considerable restraint on our freedom to manoeuvre. It is also not always easy to obtain large-scale maps and aerial photographic cover in Greece, a difficulty which would have been compounded by attempting to survey many widely scattered units. Difficulties of transport and of accurately locating randomly chosen sample areas in the undeveloped Arcadian terrain gave further weight to the counsel that such a strategy was operationally unworkable.

There were further practical limitations on the choice of survey territory. The excavation and redeposited spoil of the huge lignite mine situated in the Megalopolitan basin to the west of the ancient and modern cities meant that a sizeable chunk of our potential target area was inaccessible. There was also long-standing involvement in certain parts of the region by other national teams. French archaeologists, for example, had conducted an extensive programme of excavation and topographic research around the ancient city of Gortys in the north-western sector of the Megalopolitan *chora* in the 1940s and 1950s, and a Swedish team had investigated Asea and its surroundings in the late 1930s. Although there was no current activity at these places, or at other sites examined by different teams in the past, it seemed sensible to avoid, as far as possible, the danger of conflicting interests.

The parting advice from the statisticians was that in these circumstances the work we proposed was not susceptible of formal sampling procedures. We should therefore rely on our judgement in matching what was possible in the local situation to our goals, at the same time trying to ensure that we fairly tested the various factors which could be considered to have influenced the settlement pattern.

The strategy which was then devised took account of a wide number of variables. All the constraints listed above had to be incorporated. In addition it was necessary to ensure that a decent proportion of ploughed land was included within the survey transects. The pastoral image of Arcadia carries some truth in parts of the region around Megalopolis. Large tracts of the countryside are well wooded and agriculture is declining. As we observed on a reconnaissance visit in 1980, the visibility of surface remains in these conditions is poor.

At this stage we introduced a number of hypotheses about the development of settlement. The classical settlement pattern (the prime focus of our attention) was likely to have been influenced by a number of important factors, including environmental, economic, military, social, political and religious considerations. We tried to ensure, therefore, that from the parts of the *chora* which remained accessible to us, blocks of land were chosen where the traces of settlement might, in theory, reflect some of these influences, particularly the first five mentioned above. Thus the survey areas were positioned close to the city, at the border of its territory and in the distant mountains. Attested ancient roads ran through some sectors and not others. A wide variety of ecological zones was tested.

Figure 73 shows the area surveyed in the first season (1981). It consisted of a 10 × 3 km. transect close to the ancient city. Various elements of the local landscape could be tested in this strip, particularly the valley of the river Alpheus, the main Megalopolitan plain, the flanking terraces and the hillslopes above. In 1982 (fig. 74) we moved well beyond easy walking distance from Megalopolis. A transect of just under 30 sq. km. was examined close to the border with Messenia (ancient and modern). It included a greater proportion of hilly and mountainous country than the 1981 transect. In 1983 the mountainous terrain towards the northern fringe of the *chora* was sampled. The areas examined, situated close to the modern villages of Dhimitsana (ancient *Teuthis*) and Stemnitsa, about 25 km. north of Megalopolis, amounted to *c.* 5 sq. km. In addition we supplemented and tested our earlier findings with more work in the plain, exploring an area of *c.* 12 sq. km. a few kilometres to the north of the ancient city.

The technical term for the approach which we eventually adopted for the planning of our fieldwork is 'purposive or judgement sampling'.[9] This form of sampling, which does not incorporate a chance mechanism and relies on experience and/or prior knowledge, carries inherent dangers of bias. It does not allow the same quality of prediction as purer probabilistic methods, and this will have to be recognized when we formulate our conclusions about settlement in the final report. Had a more objective sampling strategy been possible in our circumstances it is likely that we would have pursued it (although all non-total sampling systems have their drawbacks, as has recently been pointed out).[10] However, for the reasons given above, this was not the case. Cherry has stated recently, in respect of survey design, that 'it is quite impossible to lay down golden rules or universally applicable procedures, cookbook style'.[11] The experience of the Megalopolis survey seems to illustrate this point very well.

Site definition

The simple question 'what is an archaeological site' has, when it has been tackled, produced a variety of answers. Most of them have come from American archaeologists and vary widely in their complexity.[12] We have found difficulty in trying to apply these definitions in our fieldwork and prefer, for the moment, to think of a site as 'the remains of significant human activity', which is simple and, so far, workable. The key word is 'significant'. We take this to exclude some of the ways by which archaeological material can be deposited. Manuring, for example, can create an illusion of settlement activity far from a habitation[13] and accidental deposition can happen in a variety of ways. In the Megalopolitan countryside heaps of broken tile, fallen from a donkey's back, are not uncommon finds. Presumably this could happen just as easily in antiquity. The debris of mobile groups, or of mobile elements in society (for example, hunter-gatherers or transhumant shepherds), is not excluded by this definition. Its identification, however, is an entirely different matter.

As far as survey is concerned, remains of monumental character, or consisting of a clear nucleus of artifacts, pose few problems (although even in the latter case it is not always easy to decide whether a small concentration of broken tile represents the tip of, say, a ploughed tile grave, or some much less deliberate action). Greater difficulties arise with what Cherry has called 'low grade scatters'. These, translated into sites in the published record, are often survey's major contribution to the data with which the archaeological and historical record is reappraised.[14] Yet in many instances it is far from easy to establish in

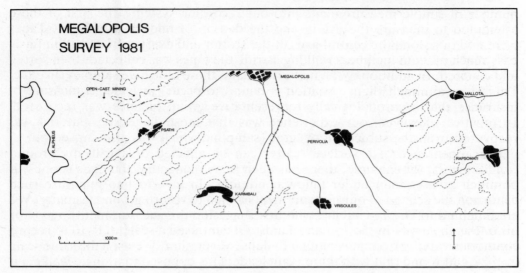

FIG. 73. The survey area in 1981

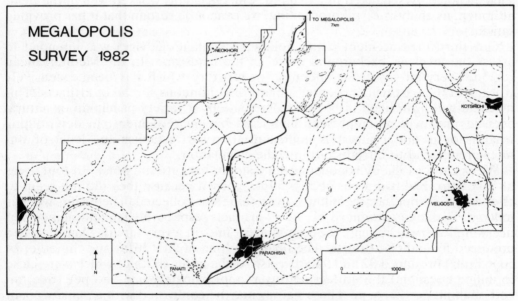

FIG. 74. The survey area in 1982

what ways such scatters differ from, for example, the debris brought out into the
fields with manure or (not wholly facetiously) the remains of a ploughman's
picnic.

For the moment, the Megalopolis survey is avoiding these difficulties by using
the term 'findspot' instead of site. This can only be a temporary measure,
however, and decisions will have to be made before final publication.

In order to help determine what was and what was not a site we introduced a number of simple measurements into our recording system. The first of these attempted to measure the extent and the density of finds at a findspot. Tapes were laid out along the central axes of the scatter and every artifact within fairly easy reach of team members walking astride the tapes was collected, then sorted and counted. In addition to the numerical data, these objective samples (in effect 1 m. wide, although slight variation is bound to occur) provided a measure of insurance that a chronologically representative group of finds was recovered. In practice, however, our experience was that most diagnostic material was recovered from the subjective or 'grab' sampling which was also carried out.

The appearance of a surface scatter can be affected drastically by ground conditions. If, for example, there has been fresh ploughing, the finds count will be much greater than under fallow conditions. In an effort to minimize such distortion the second of our measurements aimed to record ground visibility. We are indebted to Dr. T. Gallant, who first suggested this measurement to us. For his one-man survey in the Ionian islands, Gallant used a scale of 0–10 to record conditions varying from new plough to dense vegetation. We used the same scale in 1982, but found that with three team leaders (as opposed to a single walker) it offered too wide a choice, with consequent problems in ensuring uniform description. Since it was also evident that Arcadian conditions rarely justified such a choice, we changed to a 0–3 index in 1983. This worked well in the field, although, as analysis is still proceeding, we cannot be certain that it has provided satisfactory results.

Our third measurement (again following Gallant's advice) was intended to assess the level of 'background noise' in the landscape. In the Mediterranean region, every survey team operating in territory which has been extensively worked in the past will encounter a light, discontinuous spread of artifacts. This material will have been dispersed from a site by a variety of human or natural agencies and will not represent significant human settlement. In determining what is or is not a site it is important to try to establish the level of this interference and to introduce it into the calculation.

We began in 1982 by conducting six tests for background noise. In four areas of 50×50 m. and two areas of 50×30 m., chosen because they did not seem to offer a significant quantity of finds, everything was collected. The results were as follows. Two areas produced 11 and 14 artifacts respectively (small fragments of tile were overwhelmingly the commonest find in every area). Another two produced 57 and 68 artifacts. The final two (one of 50×30 m. and the other of 50×50 m.) produced 92 and 94 artifacts. At the latter (both of which were close to major findspots) the artifact density is approximately one find per 16 sq. m. and one find per 27 sq. m. These figures may be contrasted with a density count of three finds per square metre at a well-defined findspot (probably a classical farmstead) discovered in 1982. However, we had collected material from many places which had been much less prolific than this example. The surprisingly high counts in four of the sample areas were a cause of some concern. In 1983, therefore, we determined to carry out many more tests. As before, areas were sampled which appeared to have very little archaeological material on the surface. The sampling method, however, was different. In order to improve comparability we used the same system of density measurement used at findspots, that is, intersecting, 1-m. wide transects, instead of large area collections.[15] Fourteen tests were made. One produced 31 finds, another 14 and the rest less than 8 (four of these with no finds at all). In every case the sample consisted of two 50-m. long transects, with a total area of *c*. 100 sq. m. Scraps of tile were again by far the most frequent find. If an allowance is made for the different methods of collection, these results are broadly comparable to those obtained in 1982 (where the finds in each sample area were, spatially, fairly equally distributed). With the exception of the samples producing 31 and 14 artifacts, the 1983 findspots were very sharply distinguished against this background.

The lessons to be drawn from the various experiments we have made in objective recording during the three seasons of the survey are not yet clear in full detail. No doubt much will emerge during the final processing of the records. But we have learnt, through experience, that if the vital question of site definition is to be addressed systematically, some form of quantification in respect of size, visibility and density of finds is necessary from the outset. What methods are used will depend on advances in survey technique and what is feasible in the local circumstances.

This paper has given an account of one project carried out by one group of researchers in one part of Greece. The strategy and some of the tactics of our survey have been based to a large extent on pragmatic considerations. The criticism that they are rough-and-ready is therefore possible and perhaps justifiable. However, it should not be forgotten that field survey, by the very nature of surface remains, can never be the most precise branch of archaeology. This does not mean that methods cannot and should not improve. They can and we hope that they will.

Acknowledgements

The survey has been conducted by permission of the Greek Antiquities Service (our thanks go in particular to the local ephor, Dr. T. Spiropoulos) and with the support of the British School at Athens, the British Academy, the Craven Fund, the Society of Antiquaries, the Donald Atkinson Fund and the De Velling–Willis Fund of the University of Sheffield. We are grateful to the Director of the British School at Athens, Dr. H. Catling, F.S.A., for much assistance. Amongst many others to whom we are indebted are the students from Sheffield, Swansea and elsewhere who took part in the project and many friends in Megalopolis and adjacent villages.

NOTES

[1] Since 1982 we have been greatly assisted by Dr. A. J. N. W. Prag, F.S.A., who is responsible for the study of the survey finds, in particular those of the Archaic to Hellenistic periods. In 1983 Dr. J. W. Hayes, F.S.A., and Dr. C. Mee gave much helpful advice on finds of prehistoric, Roman and medieval date. Also in 1983 Dr. S. Gale undertook a study of the local sedimentology.

[2] The most up-to-date survey appears in *Α. Πετρονώτης Ἡ Μεγάλη Πόλις τῆς Ἀρκαδας* (Athens, 1973).

[3] We do not claim that all of our findspots (i.e. locations where we have collected material and/or completed recording sheets) are sites, using the definition of 'site' given above (p. 220). In the

final publication the number of sites may be much lower than the number of findspots presently recorded. Nonetheless, the net haul of genuine sites will remain several orders of magnitude greater than the total number of sites previously known or postulated.

[4] For full discussion of the literary and epigraphic record see J. Roy, 'Studies in the History of Arcadia in the Classical and Hellenistic Periods', unpublished Ph.D. dissertation, Cambridge University, 1968.

[5] Pausanias, VII.27.1–8; Diodorus Siculus, xv.72.4.

[6] This figure is approximate, since the boundaries of Megalopolitan territory varied slightly from time to time after the synoecism.

[7] We are indebted to Professor V. Barnett and in particular Dr. N. Fieller of the Department of Probability and Statistics, University of Sheffield, for their assistance. They cannot be held responsible, however, for our interpretation of their advice.

[8] T. Gallant, 'The Levkas-Pronnoi Survey', unpublished Ph.D. dissertation, Cambridge University, 1982, p. 102.

[9] J. F. Cherry, C. Gamble, and S. Shennan (eds.), *Sampling in Contemporary British Archaeology*, BAR 50 (Oxford, 1978), p. 409.

[10] See A. M. Snodgrass, 'The fruits of insularity', *Times Literary Supplement*, 4315 (2nd July 1982), p. 721, and the reply by J. F. Cherry in 'Frogs around the pond: perspectives on current archaeological survey projects in the Mediterranean region', in D. R. Keller and D. W. Rupp (eds.), *Archaeological Survey in the Mediterranean Area*, BAR S155 (Oxford, 1983), pp. 403–5.

[11] Cherry, *op. cit.* (n. 10), p. 390.

[12] A convenient review is given in Gallant, *op. cit.* (n. 8), pp. 102–5.

[13] See, for example, T. J. Wilkinson, 'The definition of ancient manured zones by means of extensive sherd-sampling techniques', *J. Field Arch.* ix (1982), pp. 323–33.

[14] J. F. Cherry, 'The Melos archaeological survey' in Keller and Rupp, *op. cit.* (n. 10), p. 280.

[15] We are indebted to Dr. S. Gale for this suggestion.

VII. NORTH AFRICA

Investigating Ancient Agriculture on the Saharan Fringe: the UNESCO Libyan Valleys Survey

Graeme Barker, F.S.A., and Barri Jones, F.S.A.

Introduction

'If archaeology is to be practised at all, then at least let it be relevant to the needs of the people today.' These words were spoken by Colonel Ghaddafi in his major budgetary review in 1978. He went on to suggest that the Libyan Department of Antiquities—hitherto primarily concerned with the excavation and consolidation of the major coastal cities of the Hellenistic and Roman periods, such as Sabratha and Lepcis Magna—should investigate instead the extensive remains of ancient agriculture which he himself had seen on the edge of the desert. His comments were the prelude to negotiations between the Department of Antiquities and UNESCO, which led to the initiation of the Libyan Valleys Survey in 1979. The Survey was originally intended to consist of a series of projects across the whole of Libya, with British, French and Italian archaeologists forming separate teams, but in each case working with Libyan archaeologists. The present writers, Dr. G. Barker of Sheffield University (now of the British School at Rome) and Professor G. D. B. Jones of Manchester University, were appointed co-directors of the British–Libyan team. The primary purpose of this paper is to describe some of our initial results and evaluate the methods we have employed to obtain them; but something will also be said of the social and political context, which has inevitably had a profound influence on the development of the project, including the sampling design and field techniques.

Our survey area in Tripolitania, the north-western province of Libya, was broadly defined as the Sofeggin and Zem Zem basins in the pre-desert, the region which separates the coastal zone from the rock desert and sand seas of the Sahara to the south: the towns of Mizda and Beni Ulid are on the northern boundary, and the Roman fort of Gheriat al-Garbia and the contemporary settlement of Ghirza on the southern boundary, on the margins of the Sahara

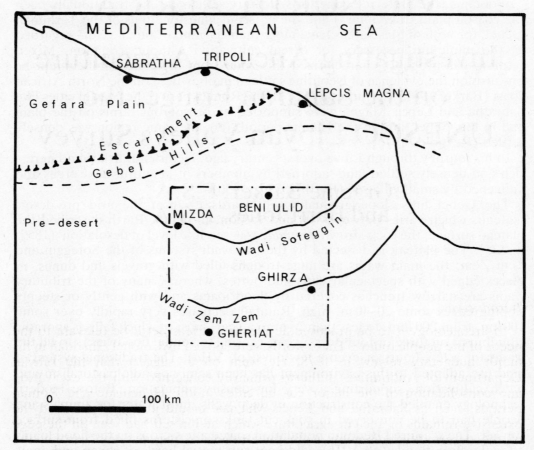

FIG. 75. Tripolitania, north-west Libya, showing the study area of the UNESCO Libyan Valleys Survey (the square enclosed with the dot-and-dash line). North is at the top of the map: the dashed line marks the 200 mm. isohyet

(fig. 75). We began work in 1979, as did a French–Libyan team in Sirtica to the east, based on the Roman fort of Bu Ngem, but for reasons discussed later only the British–Libyan team was allowed to continue fieldwork after 1980. Fieldwork continued for up to two months each year until 1981, with the British team consisting of staff from Manchester and Sheffield and postgraduates from Manchester, Sheffield, Newcastle and Cambridge universities; two further seasons of fieldwork are projected in 1984 and 1985 [see postscript].

The study area

Like much of North Africa, Libya consists of a populated, urbanized, and economically productive coastal zone, and a more or less empty interior. In Tripolitania, the preferred zone for sedentary settlement has traditionally been the coastal plain (the Gefara) and the adjacent limestone hills of the Tarhunan Gebel, for both of these areas have more than 200 mm. of rain a year—regarded as the minimum necessary for cereal cultivation without irrigation. Mixed farming has probably characterized this zone from the fourth millennium bc onwards on the evidence of Neolithic settlement elsewhere on the North African coast (Barker 1981; McBurney 1967). In the Roman period the coastal cities like Sabratha and Lepcis Magna were supported by prosperous farms on the plain and in the Gebel, and in the Islamic period, too, the same region was densely settled (Reynolds 1976).

In his journey through Libya over a century ago, Heinrich Barth found here a rich and densely settled land 'adorned by numbers of beautiful olive trees and enlivened by small villages' (Barth 1857, p. 450).

The Gebel hills slope gradually southwards to form the arid pre-desert plateau, which varies between 100 and 150 km. in depth. Barth described the plateau surface, the rock-strewn *hamada*, as a 'sea-like level of desolation' (1857, p. 125). The plateau is dissected by the two wadi systems of the Sofeggin and Zem Zem: the main wadis are huge troughs filled with gravels and dunes, in places edged with spectacular cliffs and buttes, whereas many of the tributary wadis are narrow trenches covered by flood loams and with gently or steeply sloping edges some 20–40 m. high. Rainfall decreases very rapidly over some 100 km. from 200 mm. to less than 25 mm. a year, most of which falls as sporadic cloudbursts on three or four days a year, causing torrential floodwaters to fill the wadis for a few hours or even a few days (pl. VIIa). The traditional system of land use adapted to this environment has been semi-nomadic pastoralism and patch cultivation, supporting a very low-density population. Before modern technology enabled the construction of deep wells, most water for animals and people had to be conserved in rock-cut tanks or cisterns filled from surface run-off. The scattered Bedouin population sowed a few crops on the flood loams after the flash floods (pl. VIIb), and kept substantial herds of sheep and goats and, to a lesser extent, camels. With rainfall so irregular, meagre and localized (one wadi may be drenched and an adjacent wadi left dry), cereal cultivation was extremely precarious and more or less total crop loss was normal every few years. Mobility was essential, and until recently most Bedouin spent the summer months in the northern pre-desert and the winter months on the desert margins to the south (Brehony 1960; Clarke 1960).

Late prehistoric and much Islamic land-use (the latter at least in the southern wadis) was probably much like this, but the archaeological record known before our survey suggested that there was a much denser pattern of settlement in the Roman period some 2,000 years ago, supported by a much more intensive system of land use.

The agricultural context

There are scores of stone 'castles' or fortified farms (in arabic, *gsur, gasr* in the singular) of the Roman period along the wadi edges, as well as hundreds of less substantial sites of the same period. Both are often associated with evidence for contemporary cultivation in the form of dry-stone walls built at frequent intervals across the wadis. The archaeology had first been described by Barth in the last century, and was then studied systematically by Goodchild and Brogan in the 1950s and 1960s (Reynolds 1976).

There was a group of particularly spectacular *gsur* and associated funerary structures visited by Barth at Ghirza south of the Zem Zem (pl. VIII*a*), in an area of minimal rainfall (Brogan and Smith 1957). Clearly the evidence suggested that the desolate plateau had once supported a very different pattern of agricultural settlement from that of recent times. What was the nature of the agricultural system, why did it begin, how and why had it eventually collapsed and been replaced by the subsistence agriculture that survives today? It is worthwhile pausing briefly to look at the agricultural needs of modern Libya, since our survey was initiated, and has only been allowed to continue, because its findings are expected to provide a critical archaeological perspective to present-day government plans to intensify pre-desert agriculture.

From 1911 until the last war, Libya was a satellite of Italy. Italian farmers were settled in very large numbers in coastal Tripolitania and Cyrenaica, on some 250,000 ha. of the prime arable land; the new commercial farms produced grain, olive oil, and other crops by irrigating the land from the renewable groundwater a few metres under the surface (Allan 1981; Moore 1940). Neither the Second World War nor the 'care and maintenance' policies of the ensuing British Military Administration did much to change the Italian pattern of agriculture. After independence in 1951, most Italian farmers left their holdings and Libyan farmers took over their land and their irrigation systems. After the 1969 Revolution, given the leadership's injunction that 'people who eat from overseas cannot claim to be independent', the new government initiated a colossal programme of agricultural investment with the aim of making Libya self-sufficient in food by 1980. Some 6,000 million dollars were spent in the intervening period (Wright 1981, p. 265), in two main areas of investment: the intensification of coastal farming, and the development of oasis farming in the south. Both projects have met with major problems. In the coastal zone, the rate of use of the underground water supplies had reached six times the rate of renewal in 1981, with the water level dropping by as much as a metre a year and, most seriously, with the sea water intruding in places and so threatening to render them useless for irrigation (Allan 1981, p. 99). In the south, the oasis projects have proved prohibitively expensive and inefficient (McLachlan 1982). Thus, today, Libyan agriculture provides only 14 per cent of the diet of the population, now three times more numerous than a century ago, and of course with greatly enhanced standards and expectations.

It is obvious that the proper management of agriculture is going to be critical to any strategy that hopes to sustain economic and social life at present levels after the exhaustion of existing supplies of oil early in the next century. Agricultural intensification in the pre-desert, the only other major agricultural

PLATE VII

a. The Wadi Mansur in the northern part of the survey area: a flash flood about 10 minutes after rain began to fall

b. Wadi Gobbeen, with flood-loam soaked after the rains and Bedouin sowing crops in the distance

PLATE VIII

a. Fortified Roman farm (*gasr*) at Ghirza, the major site in the study area

b. One of the slipways of the Wadi el Amud water-control system (cf. fig. 78)

resource available, must be a priority in such a strategy. Our archaeological research is just one of several projects investigating pre-desert farming, the largest and most encouraging of which is a series of experimental farms practising dry-farming techniques developed in western Australia.

Survey methodology

Our survey has been the first in this inhospitable region to use intensive searching on foot as well as traditional vehicle prospecting, and to integrate geomorphological and subsistence studies with the archaeological survey. The survey area allocated to us is colossal—about 15,000 sq. km.—and our resources in terms of time and manpower are very limited, whilst the logistical problems of working safely and accurately in this environment are obviously substantial. One guide to working conditions is the diet: virtually no fresh food is available, tinned meat contravenes Islamic law, and our daily protein therefore consists of either tinned fish or tinned cheese. Another guide is the vehicle attrition rate, which thus far includes two vehicles sunk in a flash flood, all the springs broken on a third in one season, and the chassis of the same vehicle fractured in the following season.

We have combined two approaches in our survey strategy. Original prospection by Goodchild and Brogan had already recorded the location and basic structural details of most of the major upstanding monuments of the Roman period (notably *gsur* and funerary obelisks). Our first approach has been to investigate overall trends in settlement by surveying individual wadis (or major lengths of wadis) using vehicle-based teams. First of all they have had to make base maps, as existing map coverage is rudimentary and often inaccurate; then visit and map all the major sites visible along the wadi edges (where virtually all of the major upstanding monuments are located), recording architectural details on standard forms (see fig. 76) and sherding them on a standard system using time units (eventually preferred to transects); and then return to a representative sample of the structures to make formal architectural plans. Secondly, we have conducted selected surveys on foot on a transect system both along the wadi edges and away from the wadis onto the *hamada*, to detail representative samples of the minor sites of all periods: small hut foundations, tent footings, burial cairns, small water-control systems (such as a section of dry-stone wall a few metres long and perhaps two or three courses high, built to guide floodwater into depressions on the plateaux), and lithic scatters. The research strategy for the agricultural investigation has been based primarily on detailed analyses of individual farming systems selected at different points on a north–south transect across the study area, described below.

Goodchild's original research suggested that most *gsur* were late Roman in date, and he linked their construction with historical references to Roman imperial frontier policy advocating the use of army veterans as soldier-farmers (*limitanei*) in sensitive frontier areas (Goodchild and Ward-Perkins 1949; see fig. 77 here). Our survey, however, has demonstrated that there was in fact a complex hierarchy of domestic and funerary sites, and that the phase of intensive settlement represented by them began earlier than expected—in the mid first century A.D. (Dore, in Barker and Jones 1983). The earliest major sites were

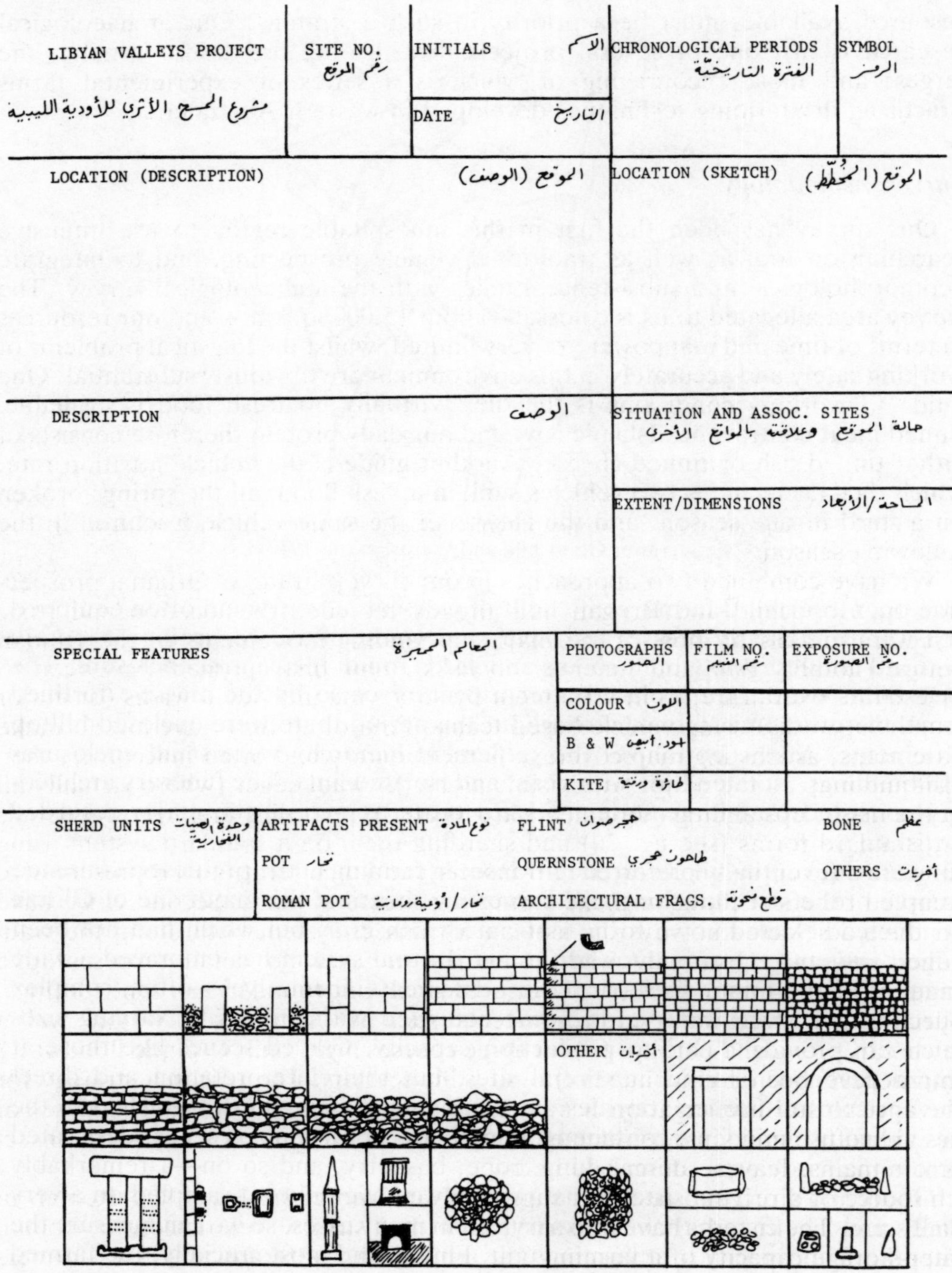

FIG. 76. The bilingual Libyan Valleys Survey form used in the field. Diagrams at the bottom are used to introduce precise descriptions of masonry features, particularly the quality of ashlar

FIG. 77. Funerary relief at Ghirza, interpreted as a *limitaneus* spearing a naked victim (after Goodchild and Ward-Perkins 1949)

large open courtyard farms, some built of well-cut masonry and often equipped with what are clearly presses for olives and vines, others consisting of loosely arranged and less finely built rooms and yards round the central enclosure. The open farms were then replaced after a century or so by the massive fortified farms, the *gsur*. In addition, throughout the period there were enclosed hilltop settlements. At the bottom of the settlement hierarchy were small enclosures with buildings, isolated huts with pens, and isolated huts. The funerary archaeology consisted of a large series of cairn types as well as the major recorded obelisks.

Before our survey, the evidence for Roman farming in the pre-desert consisted of carved reliefs of ploughing and harvesting scenes at the major site of Ghirza and the wadi walls known to be associated with *gsur*, but which had not been studied in detail. Our analysis of the agricultural system has embraced a wide range of data. First, there are the settlements themselves—often complex collections of rooms and yards, some equipped with presses of varying sizes which can provide a clue to production capacity. Carved scenes like those at Ghirza have been found at several sites, but their interpretation and direct relevance to subsistence activities are often rather ambiguous. Attached to the sites are refuse middens, containing animal bones, carbonized seeds, desiccated plant remains, leaves, animal dung, rope, basketry, and so on—a remarkably rich source of direct subsistence data which we have only yet sampled on a very small scale. The cisterns have also survived in many cases, so we can measure the water-storage capacity of a farming unit. Finally and most crucially, the farmed area in many wadis can be mapped from the distribution of walls. We have studied examples of these in great detail, and tried to develop criteria for identifying different wall functions—to control water, to trap soil, divide land, or combinations of all three (figs. 78–80).

Geomorphological studies have also been of paramount importance in the development of the project, for it has often been argued that intensive farming developed in the pre-desert in antiquity because the climate was wetter, or soil conditions were more favourable, or both. The investigations by D. D. Gilbertson and D. A. Jones (both of the Department of Prehistory and Archaeology, Sheffield University) have so far found little evidence to support the hypothesis of a wetter climate in the classical period, and evidence instead to suggest that the climate was probably essentially the same as today in its principal characteristics, although there was possibly a deeper soil on parts of the *hamada* at that time (Barker *et al*. 1983; Gilbertson and Jones 1982).

Principal results

The results of the project have been published in preliminary reports in *Libyan Studies* (Barker and Jones 1981, 1982, 1983; Barker *et al*. 1983; Jones and Barker 1980); the principal agricultural findings are described in Barker and Jones 1982 and 1984, and in Gilbertson *et al*. 1984.

The main components of the Roman agricultural system were cereals, olives, perhaps vines, sheep and goats. Everywhere the systems we have studied have demonstrated that the farmers had detailed local knowledge of run-off characteristics. Present rainfall is insufficient for many of the crops represented in the middens, and the elaborate systems of walls were clearly designed in most cases to concentrate the run-off from a large area of the plateau into a small area of cultivable soil on the wadi floor (figs. 78–80). We also think that the mix of crops and animals varied considerably. There was probably a broad trend to concentrate less on olives and more on animals further south, but we have also found differences within wadis corresponding not only to locational, but also to social, differences, and we are just beginning to detect chronological trends too.

Figure 78 illustrates one of the best-preserved wall systems, in the Wadi el Amud. A major farm complex had been built on the western side of the main wadi at the confluence with a major tributary. Traces of cross-wadi walls were found at the edge of the flood loam of the main wadi, but an impressive fan-shaped catchment system covering about 20 ha. had survived more or less intact in the tributary wadi. Where the main floodwaters entered the system, at the western 'neck' of the fan, the wall consisted of a series of sluices (gaps that could be left open or closed against the water, perhaps with wooden boards), formed by upright slabs about 1 m. apart. The outer walls of the system were also broken at regular intervals by similar sluices. On the northern side of the system, where the outer wall curved round the hillside separating the tributary from the main wadi, the wall had been massively strengthened (presumably to withstand a greater strength of water), but at several places it was interrupted by stone staircases or slipways about 3 or 4 m. wide, designed to direct water through the wall and out onto the main wadi without damaging the rest of the wall (pl. VIII*b*). Inside the catchment was a series of less substantial dividing walls and a large barrage extended across the mouth of the wadi (now gullied by floodwater channels). On the southern side the system ended in a small catchment area for two cisterns, and other cisterns were built in and around the main catchment zone. The water-control system of the tributary wadi was clearly designed to be able to divert water away from, as well as into, its fields. The buildings of the

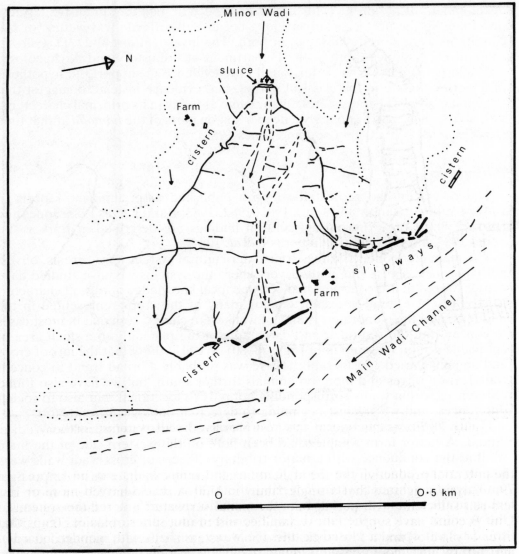

FIG. 78. Simplified plan of water-control system in the Wadi el Amud (designated by the alternative spelling 'Lamout' in our previous publications). The principal farm with the olive press is the one immediately south of the slipways (the gaps in the large barrage overlooking the main wadi channel); the arrows mark the direction of water-flow

main farm included a well-preserved olive press, and the system may well have been designed as a nursery area for young olive trees, which could be transplanted to the main wadi when they were strong enough to withstand the floodwaters there.

The complexity of the capacity data which can be obtained from the settlements, cisterns and fields, integrated with the preliminary study of the excavated subsistence data, has provided an unusual wealth of information about

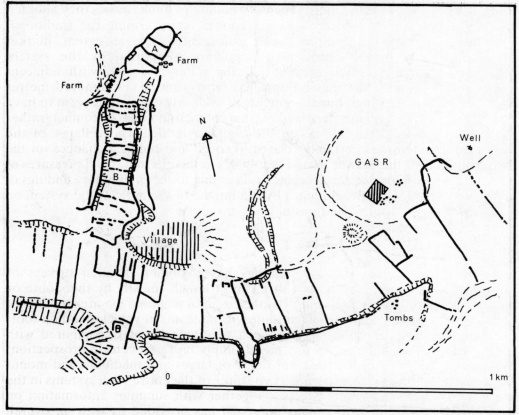

FIG. 79. Water-control system in the Wadi Mimoun. The direction of water-flow in
the principal wadi is from left to right

the potential productivity of the ancient farms. In the example illustrated as fig.
79, analysis suggested that a single family in Unit A would have been more or
less self-sufficient, with perhaps an occasional surplus of a few lambs or kids;
Unit B could have supported two families and produced a surplus of 500–1,500
litres of olive oil and a few stock; the whole system illustrated, managed as one
agricultural unit, could have sustained about fifty people, a flock of about 500
sheep or goats, and produced a substantial surplus of oil and lambs or kids (or
dairy products). (The detailed calculations are given in Barker and Jones 1982,
p. 20.) It is assumed that the surplus of foodstuffs was principally produced to
supply the urban markets of the coast; a preliminary statistical study of the
pottery from the farms has also indicated that the wadi communities were linked
to these markets in dendritic systems of exchange.

It is not clear whether the first major open farms with olive presses, of the mid
first century A.D., belonged to Romanized colonists, or to local people supported
by capital investment from the coast, or both. What is clear, however, is that in
the next few centuries the indigenous Libyan population of the pre-desert (for
inscriptions on the *gsur* are invariably of local Libyan names, and much of the
small-scale domestic and funerary architecture appears to be rooted in pre-

existing traditions) became more sedentary and more numerous as they adopted the new crops and techniques of water control, transforming the traditional subsistence economy into one that was, to a greater or lesser extent, market oriented. The increased densities of population supported by this system eventually led to increased competition for water and soil, with adjacent communities living in the massive fortified farms only a few hundred metres apart, farming increasingly small segments of wadi. Most *gsur* thus seem to have been symbols of indigenous prestige, internal competition and/or conflict, rather than the colonial defence works of the *limitanei* model. The collapse of the agricultural system was certainly related to social and political changes on the coast, but part of the answer also probably lies in the internal social pressures of a high population, perhaps exacerbated (according to the preliminary findings of the geormorphological programme) by the impact of the agricultural system on what was a very marginal and unstable environment.

Assessment

As described earlier, our methodology has combined detailed surveys of individual farming systems up to 1 or 2 km. in length (mostly by theodolite or plane-table planning), with a compromise system of mapping the archaeology of entire wadis (usually some 30–40 km. long) using teams in vehicles and on foot. Certainly the latter method has produced very valuable data compared with earlier knowledge of the pre-desert based simply on rapid vehicle prospection: we have probably recorded the total range of large- and medium-sized monuments in the selected wadis (perhaps two-thirds of the entire wadi systems in the study area which was allotted to us), together with summary information on associated agricultural works. This approach has provided us with an overall perspective on the distribution of major settlements and agricultural systems and on their chronology, both of which will be essential to our final interpretations. On the other hand, we are aware that our knowledge of small-scale archaeology, particularly that of the intervening plateaux, is still deficient.

The second approach, the detailed mapping of individual farms (and, of course, the study of their associated subsistence data, particularly the animal bones and plant remains from the middens), is giving us our primary data on the detailed functioning of the agricultural system. However, we are aware that in this kind of wadi-farming individual farms could not have functioned in isolation, and we need to develop methods of planning agricultural systems over several kilometres of wadi at the same level of detail as the individual farms illustrated if we hope to understand the social and economic relationships which must have linked them. In the Wadi Gobbeen, for example (fig. 80), we have mapped in full detail the wall system surrounding a cluster of farms; there are similar clusters of major farms and associated wall systems several kilometres away both above and below the illustrated example—yet there are also walls in the intervening lengths of wadi. Where there are regularly spaced farms, we need this scale of enquiry to investigate the extent to which they functioned in isolation, competition or co-operation. The whole exercise also rests on our ability to demonstrate a clear relationship between the wadi walls and the dated farms: a few can be dated by artifacts found within them, others can be dated

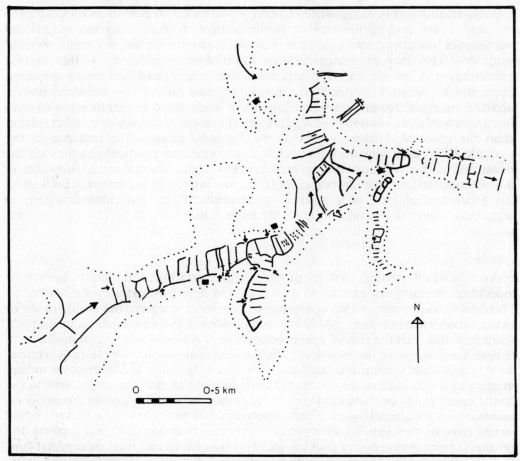

FIG. 80. Water-control system in the Wadi Gobbeen. The black squares mark the
fortified farms or *gsur*; the arrows mark the direction of water-flow

with reasonable assurance from structural and organizational details (as in the
examples illustrated), but many of the simpler and more isolated walls cannot be
dated, given the fact that much of the technology has survived to the present day
and may well have been used to a limited extent in pre-Roman times as well.
(Dating settlement on either side of the period when Roman pottery was used is
in any case extremely difficult, given the fact that the technology of most
pre-desert pastoralists before and after was flint-using and aceramic.) Finally, it
is clear that our two methods of survey are primarily suited to the narrow wadis
(less than 500 m. in width) which were selected by the *gsur* communities for
wadi-wall farming; but the massive wadis could not be used in the same way. The
enclosed hilltop settlements are mostly situated on the edge of the latter wadis
and are not associated with walls; the structural details of the sites and their
locations suggest that pastoralism was probably more important than crop
cultivation at these sites (as for the Bedouin using these wadis in recent times),
but to date we have not found an enclosed hilltop village with refuse deposits
preserved to test this hypothesis.

Undoubtedly a more rigorous sampling strategy could have been applied by our project, along the lines discussed by Mills in this volume and to some extent practised in the earlier survey directed by the first writer in the Biferno valley in southern Italy (Barker, in preparation). However, survey in Libya has to confront and adapt to logistical and administrative constraints rarely encountered in Europe: thus air photographs and/or modern maps would enormously facilitate both the formulation and execution of the field programme, whilst in the last instance the course of the fieldwork depends on the location of drinking water (and can the local population spare it?) and the amount of petrol that can be carried. False-colour satellite imagery is being used by the project to attempt to improve our assessment of how representative our data sample is likely to be. Despite the obvious problems in data collection and analysis, however, it seems clear that the project will be able to contribute important information in response to our brief to investigate the nature of the Roman agricultural system and the reasons for its inception, maintenance and demise.

Such a deliberate brief also differentiates our survey from the others described in this volume. We were asked to co-direct the project because of our previous interest in both survey and ancient agriculture, and there has never been any conflict between own research interests and the agricultural goals set by UNESCO. At the same time, however, we are very aware that we are working in an area that has never been the subject of detailed survey by archaeologists, but which is phenomenally rich in unrecorded ancient remains of every period, many of which are seriously threatened by massive construction programmes. Hence there is a strong feeling amongst the British and Libyan archaeologists of the team, which is certainly shared by the hard-pressed Department of Antiquities, that if at all possible the urgent needs of rescue archaeology should guide our activities, as well as the agricultural problem. Normally both goals have been served reasonably happily by the strategy described earlier, but a sharp reminder about our brief was given in 1979 by the Minister of Education when the Director of Antiquities began his report with the statement that the British–Libyan team in its first season had found 500 new archaeological sites: 'I don't care if they found 500 or 5,000—what *use* is this for me to tell the Libyan people?' As a result, the agricultural goals, and the techniques of palaeoeconomy and environmental archaeology necessary to investigate them, have remained central to our strategy throughout. The French–Libyan project in Sirtica was based on an existing excavation at the major Roman fort of Bu Ngem; when it emerged after two years of fieldwork that the excavation had remained a central part of the programme, that survey had been restricted to its environs, and that few agricultural or geomorphological data had been collected, the project was summarily cancelled.

For many Libyans the spectacular archaeology of the Roman period represents the epitome of the colonial heritage they have left behind. Mussolini declared in 1934 that 'civilization, in fact, is what Italy is creating on the fourth shore of our sea; western civilization in general and Fascist civilization in particular' (Wright 1981, p. 38), but Libya in the 1930s was primarily a settlement colony for Italians, the country run largely for their benefit, with the Arab population regarded as a resource of menial manpower for the colony's development schemes. From being one of the world's poorest nations in 1945, with the principal export consisting of battlefield scrap-metal, the Libyan population of three million people now has the highest per capita income in Africa. The Department of Antiquities works under considerable difficulties to preserve the great classical monuments and to persuade the government that the cultural heritage in its entirety has shaped the present, and that the people of the emergent nation should be made conscious of their responsibility to preserve all the heritage for future generations, because of its contribution to their identity.

One helpful trend in recent years has been the evidence from archaeology that Libya in the Roman period—like Britain—consisted principally of indigenous peoples, to a greater or lesser extent affected by the social and economic transformations of the Roman empire with, in the cities, Romanized locals side by side with the same range of immigrant peoples as was the norm in other great cities of the Roman world. In the case of the pre-desert, as outlined earlier, our survey has indicated that there was probably a broad similarity between domestic and funerary building traditions in late prehistoric, Romano–Libyan and Islamic times, with an underlying continuity in pre-desert culture over thousands of years; *gsur* settlement and the system of farming associated with it have also been interpreted primarily in terms of an indigenous response to external market and political forces. Clearly such arguments are culturally or ideologically preferable to colonization by *limitanei* for modern Libyans, but they also mirror the findings of contemporary archaeological research in many other parts of the world where invasion or colonial archaeology formerly held sway. In our case, moreover, we are endeavouring to develop criteria for recognizing in the archaeological record the social and political complexities of the settlement system we are studying, where there may well have been industrial farms with local client or slave labour, household farms more or less dependent on *gsur* communities, and formal military establishments, side by side in the same wadi. Whilst obviously not being in the best position to judge the project objectively, we believe that the survey would not have produced significantly different results if we had a less clearly defined research brief or less emphatic political context. 'For Libyan history is a record both of the repeated rejection and dissolution of alien, largely urban civilizations and of the largely unremarked, perennial survival of the immemorial figure of the Berber or Arab desert nomad. Ghaddafi himself epitomizes the Libyan nomad, once again emerged from the desert to claim and dominate a land where so many alien civilizations have foundered' (Wright 1981, p. 280).

Postscript

Since this paper was written, a further season of fieldwork has taken place in March and April 1984, which concentrated on the excavation of the el Amud farm and the re-analysis of its field system; the preliminary results are described in Barker and Jones 1984. Another season is projected in 1985.

BIBLIOGRAPHY

Allan, J. A. 1981. *Libya: the Experience of Oil*, London.
Barker, G. W. W. 1981. 'Early agriculture and economic change in North Africa', in Allan, J. A. (ed.), *Sahara: Ecological Change and Early Economic History*, London, pp. 131–45.
— in preparation (ed.). *Archaeology and History in a Mediterranean Valley*, Cambridge.
Barker, G. W. W. and Jones, G. D. B. 1981. 'The Unesco Libyan Valleys Survey, 1980', *Libyan Studies*, xii, pp. 9–48.
— 1982. 'The Unesco Libyan Valleys Survey 1979–81: palaeoeconomy and environmental archaeology in the pre-desert', *Libyan Studies*, xiii, pp. 1–34.
— 1983. 'The Unesco Libyan Valleys Survey IV: further contributions to the archaeology of the Tripolitanian pre-desert', *Libyan Studies*, xiv, pp. 39–68 (with contributions by D. Buck, R. Burns, J. Dore, D. Mattingly and D. Welsby).
— 1984. 'The Unesco Libyan Valleys Survey VI: investigations of a Romano-Libyan farm in the Tripolitanian pre-desert, Part One', *Libyan Studies*, xv, pp. 1–44.
Barker, G. W. W., Gilbertson, D. D., Griffin, C. M., Hayes, P. P. and Jones, D. A. 1983. 'The Unesco Libyan Valleys Survey V: sedimentological properties of Holocene wadi floor and plateau deposits in Tripolitania, northwest Libya', *Libyan Studies*, xiv, pp. 69–85.
Barth, H. 1857. *Travels and Discoveries in North and Central Africa*, London.
Brehony, J. A. N. 1960. 'Semi-nomadism in the Jebel Tarhuna', in Willimott, S. G. and Clarke, J. I. (eds.), *Field Studies in Libya*, Durham, Dept. of Geography Research Papers Ser. 4, pp. 60–9.
Brogan, O. and Smith, D. E. 1957. 'The Roman frontier settlement at Ghirza: an interim report', *JRS* xlvii, pp. 173–84.
Clarke, J. I. 1960. 'The Siaan: pastoralists of the Jefara', in Willimott, S. G. and Clarke, J. I. (eds.), *Field Studies in Libya*, Durham, Dept. of Geography Research Papers Ser. 4, pp. 52–9.
Gilbertson, D. D., Hayes, P. P., Barker, G. W. W. and Hunt, C. O. 1984. 'The UNESCO Libyan Valleys Survey VII: an interim classification and functional analysis of ancient wall technology and land use', *Libyan Studies*, xv, pp. 45–70.
Gilbertson, D. D. and Jones, D. A. 1982. 'Ancient environments and the impact of man', pp. 21–31 in Barker and Jones 1982.
Goodchild, R. G. and Ward-Perkins, J. B. 1949. 'The *Limes Tripolitanus* in the light of recent discoveries', *JRS* xxxix, pp. 81–95.
Jones. G. D. B. and Barker, G. W. W. 1980. 'The Libyan Valleys Survey 1979', *Libyan Studies*, xi, pp. 11–36.
McBurney, C. B. M. 1967. *The Haua Fteah in Cyrenaica*, Cambridge.
McLachlan, K. S. 1982. 'Strategies for agricultural development in Libya', in Allan, J. A. (ed.), *Libya since Independence: Economic and Political Development*, London, pp. 9–24.
Moore, M. 1940. *Fourth Shore. Italy's Mass Colonisation of Libya*, London.
Reynolds, J. M. (ed.). 1976. *Libyan Studies: Select Papers of the Late R. G. Goodchild*, London.
Wright, J. 1981. *Libya: a Modern History*, London.

Concluding Remarks

Barri Jones, F.S.A.

The foregoing articles effectively offer a broad conspectus of field archaeology *sensu stricto* originating in or from this country. In my introductory remarks I touched upon air photography as an important element in the overall picture. I may perhaps reuse it as an example here because the application of aerial archaeology still tends to be seen as a centripetal activity, a desirable if not essential prerequisite of what is perceived as 'real' archaeology, i.e. excavation. Part of the same approach has also tended to rub off on topographical fieldwork, partly because, as Mercer stresses, it is often the pursuit of a gifted individual, and partly because of its failure to attract a methodologically orientated literature in British publications. This is why I believe that the present volume, so rich in the diversity of its contents, may ultimately have a greater methodological value. One can hope that it marks the moment when fieldwork promoted in or from this country corporately came of age by setting out to establish appropriate academic and practical criteria that have been relatively lacking in the literature of landscape archaeology so far, at least in this country. As such it surely must be seen as a corporate attempt to establish field archaeology not as a centripetal activity but as an independent objective amid several other core activities, of which set-piece excavation is but one. Such is the aim implicit in many of these papers, alongside, of course, that of simply informing of work completed or in progress. In this way we can perhaps appreciate more fully that archaeological field survey is not only an act of record, but in its higher levels a generator of concepts and questions that can influence the overall design of research into the development of the landscape. In this conceptual setting field survey becomes 'an act of reassessment in the unending procedure of the enhanced understanding of the processes that have created our present landscape'.

Index

Compiled by PHOEBE M. PROCTER

Wood, Peter, Dorset Ridgeway project directed by, 70

Yorkshire: investigation in, 25, 26; Wolds, prehistoric land-use of, 33

Zadar, plain of (Ravni Kotari) (Dalmatia): study region, 161, 162, 163; artifact densities, 184, 189; 1973 survey of archipelago, 158, 159, 163; deforestation, 158, 161, 174, 188; ecological climax, 161–2; erosion, 160, 161, 162; excavation, 159; geology, 165, 174, 181, 182, 188; pollen analysis, 160, 168; population density, 189; Palaeolithic, 159, 172, 174, 181, 182, 190; Neolithic: 158, 159, 172, 186, 190; pottery, 172, (clay analysis) 160, (Impressed Ware) 186; Bronze Age: 159, 172, 174, 181, 189; Mataci-Jazvinački Brig excavation, 187–8; Pridraga cairnfield, 185–6; Iron Age: 159, 172, 174, 181, 182, 189; Nadin hillfort, 186; Venac-Rtina hillfort, tumuli near, 181; Roman, 182, 186; Byzantine, 186; Arheološki Muzej: collections of, 166, (*Spondylus* bracelets) 174; Iron Age survey by, 181

Zem Zem basin, *see* Sofeggin